STRATEGY IN CRISIS

Strategy in Crisis

Why business urgently needs a completely new approach

Michael de Kare-Silver

First published 1997 by
MACMILLAN PRESS LTD
Houndmills, Basingstoke, Hampshire RG21 6XS
and London
Companies and representatives
throughout the world

ISBN 0–333–68090–1

A catalogue record for this book is available
from the British Library.

This book is printed on paper suitable for recycling and
made from fully managed and sustained forest sources.

10   9   8   7   6   5   4   3   2
05   04   03   02   01   00   99   98   97

Copy-edited and typeset by Povey–Edmondson
Tavistock and Rochdale, England

Printed and bound in Great Britain by
Creative Print and Design (Wales), Ebbw Vale

93451

Contents

v

Preface

This book is about strategy, about beating the competition. It's an attempt to retrieve and rejuvenate the lost art of successful strategy development. It provides a model, a way forward, a practical solution that's easy to use. It urges companies and management to re-examine the way they develop strategy, what their strategy is, how well it's working. It emphasises some basic principles which many organisations pay lip service to but do not apply. It provides a way of identifying sources of lasting growth. It signposts how to identify those growth opportunities, how to predict and measure their impact on the business and how to capture them.

It's a practical approach based on empirical research and experience. It's drawn from many case studies and actual examples. It is not a teach-in manual, but it can be used as a step-by-step guide. It's not a placebo. It might be a panacea. The key is the **rigorous** pursuit of what is outlined. Half-hearted efforts that do not engage and excite the total organisation will fail. When we start talking about 'commitment to winning' in the marketplace we are talking a total application, focus and prioritisation on that goal. It requires every available $ of investment and every resource to pursue it.

The marketplace has now become saturated with competition. New products and new competitors are emerging with increasing frequency in every industry. Mapping the way through this market maze is an enormous challenge. The winning companies we will describe are ones who are seizing that challenge firmly in both hands and with every effort. It's a zero-sum game. Companies of often equal strength are arrayed on all sides. What will distinguish the winner? What advantages are available? What steps will enable one company to take advantage of the opportunities ahead of another?

The path suggested here must be taken by the leaders of the company. Lasting success is so fragile that the challenge of effective strategy development cannot be left to others alone to initiate and pursue. The generals must marshal their troops.

My search for a model or framework that will guide and assist the development of strategy began a number of years ago. It was triggered by collapses at once-dominant companies like IBM and GM. It has been inspired by continuous success at companies like Procter & Gamble, WalMart and British Airways. Many of the case studies and examples are drawn from personal consulting experience with numerous European and American companies. Occasionally leaders emerge with the guts and determination to drive through change, who have become convinced and committed to a strategy and way forward and who are prepared to break down walls to get there.

Many people have played a part in the development of this book; a number are clients but a policy of respecting confidential client relationships prevents identifying a number of contributors. However I would like to thank Stephen Rutt of Macmillan for sharing my vision about the crisis and opportunities in strategy, Robert Heller who has been a constant source of both encouragement and inspiration and who has provided a number of case examples, my partners in the Kalchas Consulting Group, especially Julian Vyner, who have helped create the opportunity and experiences to write this book, Deborah Maher, my partner in life, whose commercial acumen has been invaluable and who has provided a key test of what is practical and realistic, the Rt Hon Lord Peter Walker, who has provided energy, enthusiasm, a number of introductions and set an example in professionalism, ethics and behaviour which I admire, and Walter Goldsmith for all his ideas, encouragement and support.

Michael de Kare-Silver

1   The Lost Art of Strategy

I despair when I come across these sort of headlines:

- 'Robert Eaton (on his appointment as Chairman of Chrysler) thinks "vision" is overrated and he is not alone.'[1]   (*Wall Street Journal*)

- 'Welcome to the 1990s, vision and business strategy may not exactly be dead in corporate America, but a surprising number of chief executives are casting aside their crystal balls.' [The article goes on to refer to Apple, IBM, and General Motors – all icons of once-dominant multinationals and now of course struggling to recover lost glories.][2]   (*Wall Street Journal*)

- Only 20% of CEOs surveyed put strategy as their starting point in building their company.'[3]   (*Maximum Leadership*, 1995)

- 'I have spent three years waiting for a clear strategy to emerge from the company, it's frustrating that it's still not clear what their vision is or how they plan to implement it.'[4]
  (Institutional Stockholder of c. £50m in Pearson shares)

- As few as 6% of business people in USA would rate their company excellent at planning for the long term future.'[5]
  (*Business Week*, survey, 1996)

- 'We don't have a long term strategy, what's the point when the world is so uncertain.'
  (Senior VP of a global Information Services Provider)

- 'You shouldn't be talking to me about strategy, that's up to others, like my business unit managers.'
  (CEO of a $5bn Specialty Chemicals Company)

Drawing on many years of consulting experience with multinational companies my firm conclusion is that most have lost the art of strategic thinking and development. Effective competitive strategy has ceased to be the driving force in many organisations. Strategy has been relegated down the executive agenda. It's typically a staff function that comes out of its back office once a year to facilitate the annual budget review. It's often seen as theory rather than practice. It's sometimes regarded as a waste of time, out of touch with the immediate needs of line managers.

1

Where there is a statement about strategy it's often lost in some vague mission about 'global growth', or it comes out as a summary of the next two to three-year plans of the individual businesses or a communication of financial targets. If you speak to employees it is rare to find any universal awareness or appreciation of precisely what is the strategy of their company. There will be different views and opinions, different understanding of priorities, targets, timeframes and competitiveness. There is rarely a shared vision and purpose.

Indeed as the marketplace has got tougher so companies have turned inward, re-engineering, downsizing, improving processes and efficiencies, reducing costs and time, marvelling at information technology (IT), worrying about internal change. Many have retreated from confronting the marketplace challenges head-on with aggression, investment, commitment and focused resources. They are typically more comfortable with the internal, that is under their direct control, than the external which they perceive is outside that control. They face the external environment unarmed, with no clear guidelines and with limited understanding of what is required to succeed.

The building blocks of effective strategy development lie worn and in ruins in many companies. Few can tell what their key sources of competitive advantage are and whether each customer sees and values that advantage, few understand what their competitors' future plans and strategies are, few have the capabilities to monitor and measure the competitive strengths and weaknesses of their products. Few understand where they truly make money on which product lines and with which customers, most have no idea where they will be in five years time nor what they should be striving for.

In this environment, strategy is in crisis. It's a perspective as true in Europe as it is in North America.

Where are the bold strategies that put stakes in the ground for the future, that look ahead five or ten years, contain insight and under-standing into how customer needs and markets will evolve, that declare a set of goals that are stretching, almost infeasible, but exciting to investors and to the workforce in the company? Where are those management teams of conviction and commitment who so understand their markets, their products, the technology, their customers, their competitors that they can set and implement an agenda that can transform the competitive strength of their companies?

There are a few today, encouragingly, and we will be examining them later, but they are the exceptions rather than the norm.

In writing this book my experience with many western multinationals is that there is a need to provoke, to 'rattle the cage', to shake up complacency, to stimulate different thinking and action. If you read these words and feel these statements do not apply to your organisation then I am delighted and relieved to find more exceptions, but I would urge you to challenge and check your perceptions one more time.

Let's get to some evidence and examples. I'm going to consider

- what priority does strategy typically have on a CEO's agenda today;
- the demise of corporate planning;
- the effects of the re-engineering obsession; and
- how poor strategy leads to failure.

The importance of strategy on the CEO's agenda

To provide a context for some of the headlines and quotations, we can describe some compelling research. In a recent survey[6] of 100 chief executives of the top 100 companies based in the UK and the USA, and carried out by my colleagues and I at Kalchas:

- only 14 put 'strategy' at the top of their list; and
- on average 'strategy' was ranked sixth in importance of ten key agenda items, shown in Table 1.1.

Table 1.1 Where would strategy typically rank on your agenda

Suggested priority agenda items	Average ranking
• Future strategy	6
• Technology	8
• Re-engingeering	5
• People management	1
• Financial performance	2
• Stockholders	3
• Customers	4
• New products	7
• Regulatory environment	10
• Information management	9

- 'There is no way we spend enough time thinking about things like "competitive advantage" or the long term.'

- 'There's too many other pressures.'

- 'You talk to me about the importance of strategy, next week someone's in here talking about how important something else is.'

- 'It's a struggle to get people thinking more than one year ahead.'

- 'I would agree, if we did give more attention to long term strategy, there's more value to shareholders.'

This low ranking for strategy is confirmed by other surveys. For example, another piece of research reviewed in the book *Maximum Leadership*[7] concluded that only about 20 per cent of CEOs described strategy formulation as their defining role. While most acknowledged its importance, at the same time they put other items such as people, change management and core competencies ahead on their list of priorities: 'In reality, many of the CEOs we interviewed felt entirely comfortable saying they believed the days of top-down strategy formulation are past.'

Yet this poor response is at odds with all the research we shall see later. This research demonstrates unequivocally the value and power of effective strategy. It shows how it can be the driving force for an organisation, how it can be the 'holy grail' that energises and inspires. Some of the evidence is anecdotal, a lot of it empirical. It's clear that companies without this central driving force have a disturbing vacuum. They will wallow, as if rudderless, uncertain where to go in the storm-tossed seas of competition.

In today's environment if a company does not have an *effective* strategy as we shall define it, if it doesn't know where it's going, it's as if dead in the water.

We shall describe the evidence in support of effective strategy-making as we move through the book. In the meantime a few quotations from different sources will capture the spirit of what is being advocated here.

- 'Because nowadays we're making ever bigger bets of investments in technology, we can't afford to spend a whole lot of money in one direction and then find out five years later that it was the wrong direction . . . strategy is the most important management issue.'[8]

  (Chairman: United Parcel Service)

- 'Would you tell me, please, which way I ought to go from here?' asked Alice.
  'That depends a good deal on where you want to get to.'

  (Lewis Carroll, *Alice's Adventures in Wonderland*)

- 'Objectives are not fate; they are direction. They are not commands; they are commitments. They do not determine the future, they are the means to mobilise the resources and energies of the business for the *making* of the future.'[9]   (Peter Drucker)

- 'Know the enemy and know yourself; in a hundred battles you will not be in peril.'[10]   (Sun Tzu)

- 'It is planning, not gambling that produces profits and security.'[11]
                                                                         (Marcus Aurelius)

The demise of corporate planning

The corporate planning function – the department usually specifically responsible for strategy development – is in disarray.

The head of the department has lost voice and clout. He/she is rarely on the board or executive committee of the company. At my last count in the UK looking at FTSE 100 companies, little more than 15 per cent gave the head of planning or strategy development such senior status. Among Standard-and-Poor (S&P) top 200 companies, I could find only 18 per cent with a senior VP for strategy on the main executive committee.[12]

As a result strategy development and long-term planning are commonly seen as a staff function, off-line. Their principal task is relegated to facilitating the annual budget review process and to nag at individual business unit managers to fill out the business plan forms and fill in the numbers for the next couple of years.

What is extraordinary is how planning department managers have allowed this decline in their importance. They have abdicated responsibility. It leaves the function isolated rather than integrated into the main thrust of the business. In the 1980s, putting it centre-stage to the business's development was the vogue. In the 1990s, the planning department has become a prime candidate for downsizing or outsourcing or even elimination.

The typical absence of any central drive from planning is both a symptom and a cause of the crisis strategy faces. Its weak position reinforces the attitude that strategy plays a back office role instead of one next to the CEO. The function has been displaced by more 'fashionable' interests and has failed to fight back.

In recent conversations with senior offices of companies I have heard these sort of comments:

- 'What's the point in looking into the future, it's so uncertain.'
- 'Here's a copy of our 1996 to 2002 strategy, actually it's pretty meaningless.'
- 'Looking anything more than 3 years out is a complete waste of time.'
- 'Our strategy plan basically takes historic trends and extrapolates them.'
- 'I leave all that strategy stuff to my planning group, they've got the MBAs.'

Disappointingly there seems little interest either from the planning function itself or from most CEOs to do much about it.

Without some informed expertise to act as catalyst, it's not surprising that strategy falls down the agenda. It's also not surprising in these circumstances that the understanding of what strategy is and how to build and develop it is missing. The managers who dominate companies come from other disciplines and interests, especially finance, operations and sometimes marketing. For them, a three-month strategy course on an MBA programme or as part of some management development course will have only scratched the surface and cannot have inculcated or embedded any deep-rooted understanding of strategy.

As a result, the whole strategy development process in many companies is a shambles. How many executives quite readily admit that the once-a-year exercise is no more than a filling-out of budget numbers, a bottom-up exercise where the main task is to 'get through the process', 'get through the budgets agreed for next year', so they can get back to the day-to-day running of the business.

It's perceived as 'a chore, a waste of time, it takes too long, it's painful, it's a constant round of playing with numbers', till you finally find a set that the bosses agree with. 'It's formulaic, it's filling in standard proformas first developed fifteen years ago, it's keeping things bland so as not to rock the boat.'

Does that sound like your organisation? In many years of consulting with numerous European and American multinationals, I would say that this is the typical situation.

And of course resulting strategies are weak, lacking in hard competitiveness and direction and offering generic statements of good intent rather than stretching ambition and excitement. We'll review more of this later but to briefly illustrate we can compare two statements of strategy – one from General Motors and the other from Toyota (guess which belongs to which company).

'Although we are the world's leader we must do more in meeting and exceeding the expectations of customers. As we go through the 1990s our strategy must be to improve our care for the customer, improve our productivity, raise our quality and reduce our costs'.

'Our strength is with the consumer. Our domestic market share is 30%. Our goal is to achieve that same leading position in at least 3 markets of our choice beyond our shores. Our principle strength is as a manufacturer of product excellence. Through organising our intelligence we will target 100% product reliability without fault. We will deliver this at affordable prices to our customers'.

Problems with the re-engineering obsession

We can look no further than the current re-engineering obsession to find more evidence for the lost art of strategy and why it's in crisis.

We have created armies of re-engineers over the past few years, expert at looking at internal processes and efficiencies. As Hamel and Prahalad have put it – 'An entire generation of denominator managers has been established who can downsize, declutter, delayer and divest'.[13]

But what about the top line, understanding how to grow and build for the future? Indeed in a 1995 Kalchas survey,[14] over 38 per cent of senior executives interviewed saw the main source of profit growth in their organisations over the next three years coming from re-engineering. And this expectation and perspective was also confirmed in an American Management Association survey of 700 US corporations carried out at about the same time.[15]

Not only does this internal focus displace external market development as a priority, but in the majority of cases it doesn't even deliver results!

A Watson Wyatt survey[16] reported in 1995 is but one example of a number of pieces of research on the effectiveness of re-engineering and the results that typically get achieved. In this particular report only 22 per cent of managers said they had been able to hit their targets; less than half the companies surveyed managed an increase in operating profits and only 2 per cent saw an increase in employee morale.

With these sort of results the underlying value of a company's stock is unlikely to meet the increased expectations created when re-engineering initiatives are announced. In fact the firm Mitchell & Co. found that the value of stock in companies that downsized was 26 per cent lower than the share value in similar organisations that had not![17]

Clearly re-engineering, if effectively carried out and implemented wholeheartedly, can be advantageous and indeed necessary, but the issues of change it creates have become a major burden and distraction on management time and energies. And the focus on cutting, reducing and improving internal processes as the main source of profit growth has led to a wariness and discomfort with the challenge of planning the future. So it's not surprising to see research which laments the weakness of management skills and capabilities in areas other than re-engineering, emphasising poverty in long-term planning and highlighting the more typical shorter term perspectives that are taken.

We have already briefly quoted from the 1996 *Business Week* survey.[18] In that, a tiny percentage of people interviewed rated companies highly for their long-term planning skills. This was reinforced by a further excellent *Wall Street Journal* article a few months after the *Business Week* survey.[19] This described research showing how a large number of organisations are now struggling to redevelop the skills and know-how that relate to growth as opposed to cost control, and to develop new external revenue-based opportunities as opposed to working on continuing internal effectiveness:

- 'Boosting profits through downsizing was easier . . . the questions now are whether executives skilled at cost-cutting are also skilled at revenue raising.'

- 'Wall Street won't pay anymore for raising profit margins on a stagnant sales base.'

In fact years of 'denominator management' has resulted in a significant number of major companies nowadays struggling to achieve any meaningful sales growth organically.

A review of the top 100 UK companies carried out by Kalchas in 1996[20] (and reinforced in a *Sunday Times* survey for 1997)[21] showed that 29 per cent had failed to achieve organic real sales growth above inflation over the previous five-year period (stripping out for example any significant acquisitions or disposals over the time). In fact average revenue growth rates were only 2.6 per cent in real terms. A number of well-known British companies such as ICI, Grand Metropolitan and GEC had in fact suffered real revenue declines (again taking out any effects from disposals). In similar vein, research by Mercer of 800 US companies found that only 23 per cent of companies had managed to effectively switch to above-average revenue growth as the catalyst for above-average profit growth in 1995.[22]

So we are looking at a situation where not only are the skills for future planning and strategy lost, but there is no functional expertise of any potency in-house to revive it. Strategy thinking and development would appear to be in crisis. And it is far from clear that companies have the desire or capabilities to address the problem – it's become a lost art.

This state of affairs is an important backcloth for the writing of this book. Further exhortations about the need for more effective strategy development may be useless if we do not at the same time provide some new thinking and a new framework that can stimulate and encourage discussion and debate in this area and point a way forward for better strategy development.

Poor strategy leads to failure

Let us review some examples:

1. One European company after another has failed in the personal computer business. In the first six months in 1996, France's Groupe Bull announced it was quitting the market, Britain's ICL turned over its PC operations to its Japanese owners, Escom has filed for bankruptcy, Olivetti is reported as trying to sell its PC business, and Siemens Nixdorf is still struggling with six years of losses.

    Just looking at Siemens Nixdorf, Wall Street analysts reckon the worldwide business outside of Germany and its immediate neighbours is close to dying.[23]

    Siemens Nixdorf appears to have no clear strategy. Away from Germany and Siemens' domestic network, it is a number-5 player looking to compete in the tough domestic PC market with less up-to-date products, while facing among others Compaq and Hewlett Packard who have twice the market share and resources. Its products' performance have been unreliable though improving, and rated lower than competitors for overall quality. It made efforts to compete on price but it had high cost problems. It had developed stronger market positions in other sectors such as touch-screen ATMs but it has not prioritised those nor channelled resources into them. It is only because of the deep pockets of parent Siemens that it has survived this far. But this has simply enabled the company to continue to compete, though outclassed and outmanoeuvred and suffering mounting losses! What is Siemens Nixdorf trying to do, where was it going, how does it hope to win?

2. By way of another example we can look at car rental. Two of the
   biggest US car-rental firms, Budget Rent-a-Car and Alamo, are ailing
   badly, reporting losses in 1995. In fact, these major rental companies
   have been their own worst enemy and one of their key failings has
   been a lack of any clear-sighted, forward-looking strategy. Through
   the 1980s and early 1990s there was relatively easy money from tax
   credits and cashbacks and the companies could afford to keep their
   prices aggressively low. They didn't install new computer technology,
   they didn't focus on customer service. Where they did spend money it
   was on high-profile advertising and price promotion campaigns.
   Revenues and any profit came from collision insurance not from
   renting cars.[24]

   'The truth was they didn't really know what it takes to make
   money in their core business', one industry observer has pointed out.

These two examples are emblematic. How many once-great companies
are now struggling? Companies like Whirlpool, Daimler Benz, General
Motors, Apple, IBM, or DEC who rose to no. 27 in the Fortune 500 list
in 1990 and subsequently collapsed. In the insurance industry the list of
strugglers or casualties is long and given the pressures building is likely to
get longer (see Table 1.2).

Table 1.2   Once dominant insurance companies

Continental	Home
Travellers	Provident Mutual
Hartford	Confederation Life
Cigna	London Life
Aetna	Prudential (US)?

Further evidence of the failures caused by poor strategy come from
work by Collins and Porras, that I shall also return to later.[25] They
looked at companies that they defined as lacking clear-sighted strategies,
and compared them to their more forward-thinking rivals. So Chase
Manhattan was compared to Citicorp, Westinghouse with General
Electric, Colgate with Procter & Gamble, Nabisco with Philip Morris.
The stock market performance of these two sets of companies was then
examined and compared over a long period of time.

Those companies without clear strategy and vision were subsequently
outperformed on the stock market by their rivals by over six-fold! They

were increasingly being outmanoeuvred in their market sectors by their more adroit competitors. They had become followers instead of leaders.

Such 'followers' might have pointed out in their defence that until recently companies could 'get away with' a bland or weak strategy and instead focus on other levers of the business. The pace of change through the 1970s and early 1980s was slower and the nature of change more predictable.

In those relatively calmer times, customers' buying patterns were more entrenched. They would buy from a Sears catalogue or from IBM or go to Schroders for advice or to a local Forte hotel because that was the established pattern and way of doing things, and the level of aggressive new competitor activity was relatively limited or contained within defined industry and geographic boundaries.

But the tide of technological, demographic, political and regulatory change emerging in the late 1980s and thereafter has swept away the traditional barriers. The sleepy giants have either been shocked or forced into a rude awakening and regeneration. Trying to 'get away with' a poor strategy is becoming a recipe for failure. Some companies like Xerox, Dell Computer, Du Pont or British Airways were ones to respond. Others have been swept aside like Pan Am, like Britain's once-independent banking houses Midland and Warburgs, and like once-dominant broadcasters like ABC and CBS.

There are numerous other examples of how a poor strategy has been the major cause of failure or decline. In many instances the company's problems seemed obvious. For example how could Apple go on hoping to compete effectively when its equipment was incompatible with the increasingly dominant software in the marketplace? The challenge was obvious to many industry commentators some time before Apple's collapse in early 1996. In other instances the sleepy giants like Sears sat back while their market territory gradually became eroded by more focused and dedicated players who had a clearer strategy of what they wanted to achieve and how they were going to get there, like The Limited.

What is extraordinary is how, despite the case studies and the examples, companies turn their attention away from strategy as a priority, put it down the agenda, delegate – or is it abdicate – responsibility to others elsewhere in the organisation, turn inward to re-engineering, focus on the immediate short term and relegate the longer-term issues and opportunities.

In the context of a tougher, ever more competitive environment, the **requirement** to give strategy priority attention, to map a way through the market maze, must be ever more pressing and urgent.

It is vital to get a grip on the markets and customers that the organisation is dealing with, to be so close to them that the changes can be seen and anticipated at the earliest point and certainly not a moment later than a rival. It is crucial to develop a strategy that is built on a highly-developed forward-looking understanding of market opportunities and for an organisation to take a proactive market-driving role.

We are going to talk later about getting a grip on markets and customers. We shall consider ideas such as 'immersion' in the market and a total 'commitment' and 'focus' on staying ahead of the competition. We shall encourage the choosing of markets where there is an opportunity to achieve competitive advantage. We shall urge the bringing of **all** the resources that are required together in a concentrated effort to achieve the strategy and its target results.

Future success is going to demand that organisations confront this crisis of inadequate strategy and better understand the power of making it the effective driving force for the company.

Summary

Our starting premise is that 'most companies have lost the art of strategic thinking'; the question for the reader is 'has yours?' To what extent do the ideas in this book potentially need to be absorbed within your own organisation?

In my work with different companies, I have developed a simple set of questions to test out how meaningfully effective a company's strategy is and at the same time to begin to stretch the thinking as to the power and scope that should be contained within it.

A very strong yes to the following questions would score 10, a very strong no 0, and an average rating would score 5. Best-practice organisations are typically scoring 80-plus, most companies are around 50 or below.

1. Is future strategy planning given sufficient time and priority by the senior executives of the company?   _____

2. Is there a rigorous 5-year view developed of where the company needs to be in the marketplace?   _____

3. Is that future position defined **credibly** and **believably** in terms of market position, share, margins and timeframe and is the required investment fully thought through and feasible?   _____

4. Is there a deep-rooted understanding of what is the company's prime source of competitive advantage for each of its major product groups and how that specific advantage is going to be maintained?   _____

5. Is there a mechanism for measuring and monitoring the size of that competitive advantage in the market with individual customers?   _____

6. Does the organisation have a clear understanding of its competitors' future plans and strategies?   _____

7. Does the organisation have a clear understanding of its customers' future plans and strategies?   _____

8. Do the senior executives of the company spend sufficient time out in the marketplace talking and listening to customers?   _____

9. Does the strategy represent a top-down CEO-driving view of the future rather than simply a bottom-up collection of the individual businesses' plans?   _____

10. Is the strategy something that excites and motivates the workforce into a collective effort to win?   _____

Many organisations I have worked with actually find these questions difficult to score realistically. This is because the art of understanding what is a truly effective strategy, and so the knowledge of how to develop it more powerfully, is lost. Some organisations in fact find it difficult to realise they have a problem.

There is sometimes a complacency effect to have to deal with. Some company leaders when challenged will give righteous replies to the vigour and effect of their strategy. It's often lower down in the ranks where the real challenge is taking place and where the absence of effective strategy direction is most acutely felt.

The remedy is to ensure the '10 questions' and others are answered by a full cross-section of the company from senior to junior, from centre to subsidiary, from function to business unit, from established operation to new start-up.

In all these situations, those motivated to make strategy more effective must recognise the vicious circle they have to deal with. I include it here as it summarises the impoverished position strategy-making finds itself in and the enormous challenge those intent on addressing the problem face.

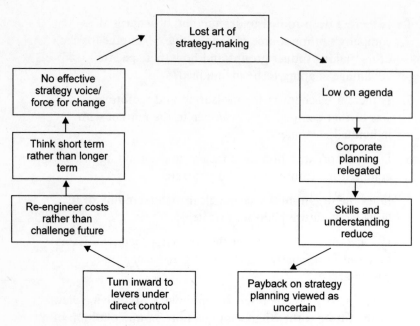

Figure 1.1   Losing the art of strategy-making: a vicious circle

Circulating the 10 questions among colleagues may be a way of opening minds in the company to the possible need for change in this area. Certainly if an organisation gets a low score it may provide the rude awakening and the start on the road to self-improvement.

*   *   *

As we set off down this road, rediscovering the power and potential of strategy, I'd like to set out a brief guide to the structure of the book and some of the milestones we'll come upon.

In overview the book contains a diagnostic of both the crisis and the opportunity, provides insight and a new approach to strategy thinking and lays out the key success factors for translating the new learning and understanding about strategy into results.

This chapter and the next three are diagnostic. They set out why strategy is in crisis and demonstrate that in this rapidly changing world and with ever more competitive markets there is now an even greater need for a company to map out a path for its future if it is to survive and succeed. We will see how critical it is to define clear goals and targets and to determine **in a calculated manner** how to beat the competition.

Chapter 4 specifically shows how companies that do search to develop strategy more powerfully are currently let down and misled by existing strategy tools and frameworks. These can be shown to be out-of-date and out-of-touch with contemporary market dynamics and so incapable of meeting the needs of strategy makers in the late 1990s.

Chapter 5 introduces the new approach to strategy thinking and decision-making – the Market Commitment Model – and describes in overview how it works and how it can be used to easily engage busy management teams to think more widely and challengingly about their competitive position and future sources of competitive advantage and opportunity.

Chapters 6 to 8 describe the first dimension of the model – that is Commitment – and lay out the critical elements of determination, horizon-setting and market immersion required to succeed. Microsoft provides the best illustration of this commitment, of this long-term planning, focus and determination that courses through the whole organisation and underpins its march to success.

Chapters 9 to 12 provide case studies, research and illustration of each of the four prime forms of strategy defined in the new model. In turn Performance, Service Hustle, Price and our new discovery! – 'Emotion' – are described.

Emotion, or 'E' as we shall shorthand it in Chapter 12, deserves early mention. How can it be that all other strategy models have overlooked and ignored this extraordinary and compelling source of fundamental competitive advantage? Why choose Coca-Cola or Shell Oil or Chanel or Rubbermaid housewares or Intel or Citibank? In these ever more competitive times, when many products are becoming increasingly commodity-like in performance, Emotion or the E factor may be the only true distinguishing feature. And it's being increasingly recognised that for a number of companies this is the force that can most drive customer decision-making and provide competitive advantage.

Each of the prime strategy options are shown to represent a fundamental decision about how to compete, how to operate in the market, how to structure the company, what to invest in. Effectively developed, they provide the platform for future success.

Chapter 13 is a toolkit, setting out a ten-step guide for applying the model and using it to structure the strategy-development process and engage business management teams.

Chapters 14 and 15 are about making it happen, institutionalising more rigorous strategic planning, mobilising the workforce, measuring progress and translating ambition into action and impact in the marketplace.

Throughout the book the intent is to keep things practical and straightforward, overcoming typical organisation roadblocks and developing something that can be readily understood and easily applied, so that it can be taken forward by busy line managers juggling other priorities and generally coping with the constant and enormous pressure to keep changing and responding to the competitive environment around them.

The aim is to end the crisis strategy finds itself in. Strategy thinking and decision making need to be revitalised, put back centre-stage, their power and potential recognised, their importance institutionalised. Those responsible for future strategy, the leaders of the business, must be persuaded of its pivotal role in driving the organisation forward, defining the priorities and determining which advantages to pursue and how best to compete.

If this approach and the new Market Commitment Model succeed in stimulating wider and deeper strategy discussion and debate then it will have achieved at least part of its goal. If it can go on and convince management teams to reappraise and redefine the power of strategy and the role that effective strategy development can play then we'll be nearly there in putting strategy back centre-stage. If finally the companies that do this at the same time transform their process in this area from being burdensome and perfunctory into something rewarding and motivating then a framework for lasting success will have been created. It will be those companies that seize this message and totally revitalise strategy in their organisations who will have the best chance of mapping their way successfully through the future and becoming one of the winners we all talk about.

2 What is Strategy?

At this point, it is worth clearing up some undoubted confusion as to what the word strategy means. A recent Kalchas survey showed a wide variety of definitions among chief executives and also among corporate planning VPs:[1]

- 28% defined strategy as being an 'overarching philosophy' for the company. An example might be 'our goal is to build market leading products';
- 39% defined it as being a 'mission statement' e.g.: 'we are committed to building our business across the globe and having a significant presence in every major market'
- 13% defined it as a 'more precise statement of competitive advantage' for the company in its chosen markets; for example, 'we will carry more passengers than any other airline in North America and Europe and achieve market leadership in those regions by providing the best service at fair prices';
- some 20% felt it was a mix of all three.

Given this confusion and uncertainty as to what strategy is, then it is less surprising that few chief executives put strategy as their defining role and responsibility and their starting point in driving the success of the business. If they are not sure what it means or feel it is simply some vague and potentially superficial philosophy or broad mission statement they may well struggle to see what value can be derived from spending time thinking and developing it.

What does strategy mean? It comes from a Greek word and literally means 'Generalship'. Its original connotation was in war, and based on the OED definition strategy means 'the management of an army in a campaign, moving troops or ships so as to impose upon the enemy the place and time and conditions for fighting **preferred by oneself**, the detail of which are the tactics or the realisation of the strategy'.

Quite naturally, then, the chief executive – as leader or general of the company – should be given the formal responsibility for the development of strategy and for overseeing its realisation. And it's a proactive, forcing role and responsibility. The CEO having been elected leader must take

17

responsibility and be the best placed to orchestrate the battle, balance the resources and lead the campaign to find the winning set of conditions. As leader, the CEO may be out-front sharing the fighting with the troops or may direct from base camp but the army, the organisation, needs both a figurehead and also direction, it requires management as well as orchestration. Inspiring words alone are not enough.

If we translate this classical and traditional definition into business competition in the 1990s, we can say that strategy is about setting the direction for the management of the resources in the business, and about identifying the conditions that will give the best advantage to help win in the marketplace. In other words the guts of strategy in my definition is about 'future intentions' and 'competitive advantage'.

So in the Gulf War, Colin Powell not only clearly established his future intent 'to prevent the Iraqi dictator from ever again threatening the West', but critically went on to identify the key source of competitive advantage which was to be 'airborne supremacy'. So also did Sam Walton set a firm future target, 'we will double the number of stores and increase the sales volume per square foot by 60 per cent by the year 2000 [set in 1990]'. But he also went on to reconfirm the principle sources of competitive advantage that would underpin that drive for growth: 'we exist to provide value to our customers through lower prices and better service – all else is secondary'.

While many commentators on business and management differ in their own definitions of strategy, all do acknowledge it is the essence of what the organisation is about:

- 'It is a combination of the ends for which the firm is striving and the means by which it is seeking to get there.'[2]   (Michael Porter)

- 'It deals with the most fundamental and basic questions that involve the very existence of the whole organisation and guide the whole company's future.'[3]   (Kerry Napuk)

- 'Envisioning the future and mapping out how to get there.'[4]

  (*Maximum Leadership*)

The elements of strategy

In this book we will define and refer to strategy as having two essential elements, and treat it as the essence that binds and drives the company (see Figure 2.1).

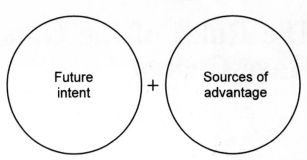

Figure 2.1 The two elements of strategy

We will describe 'future intent' as the development of a long-term, far-reaching view and the establishment of a commitment to achieving it, choosing particular markets, as the focus of the company's energies.

We will describe advantage as a so highly developed understanding of the company's chosen marketplaces and its customers that it enables and leads to an identification of **how** best to compete. It's about how best to leverage the company's forces to achieve maximum effect in those markets with those customers to the disadvantage of competitors

'Future intent' and 'advantage' must go hand-in-hand. Future intentions **should only be established where advantage can be achieved**. Advantage once defined must be captured in a framework of future intent and ambition. What emerges must be feasible and believable and, while stretching, still achievable.

Where these two elements have been rigorously thought-through and developed we will find the guts of compelling strategy. While strategy remains in the realms of vague mission statements it will lack the drive and energy and inspiration that the company desperately needs. When it does touch the life force of the whole organisation and points out how to win, it can become the framework for success.

3 The Rules of the Game Have Changed

The evidence so far: the art of strategy making has been lost, what is truly effective strategy is widely misunderstood, its true power and role in driving the company is frequently overlooked. Strategy making as a result finds itself caught in a 'vicious circle', relegated down the agenda, treated with scepticism and displaced by alternatives such as inward-looking process improvement.

To survive and to succeed, companies have to break out of the vicious circle. The art of effective strategy making has to be rediscovered. Strategy makers need to find a way to put strategy back to the top of the agenda. The key is to find a means to re-educate management teams as to its power and potential.

Years of strategy consulting has shown unequivocally that the root of the problem lies in the inadequacy of existing strategy development tools and frameworks. As we shall go on to describe, they are just no longer relevant enough to modern business. When companies turn to them for help in strategy making they are disappointed. They do not provide the guidance that is required. They describe out-of-date concepts. They are typically found to be 'too vague and theoretical' and can sometimes be actually misleading.

If I am right and this is the main problem, then what business urgently now require is a new approach. We need a new strategy making framework that does clearly and positively set the art of effective strategy making in current times. We need a new construct that reflects the dynamics of a marketplace coming up to the millennium. We need something that is practical and easy to apply that can quickly engage and explain itself to sceptical management teams.

To determine what the new strategy framework should look like we must first understand the problems and the situation it needs to address. Critically, life has moved on since the first strategy frameworks of Michael Porter, Boston Consulting and PIMS (profit impact of market strategy) were introduced as much as 20 years ago. And yet despite the enormous changes in the business environment these early frameworks

20

have not been updated. They are still the tools management teams are most aware of and the ones they turn to generally for assistance in strategy making in the absence of anything better.

What this chapter does is explain the differences between the business realities of the late 1990s and the time when Michael Porter *et al.* established their approaches to strategy. We need to see clearly and precisely what has changed and in precisely what ways market conditions are different. We do not need to rehearse all the now well-worn observations about recent market place trends in globalisation, disintermediation, deregulation, commoditisation and so forth. But we do need to understand their specific impact on strategy development and the new rules that they create. With this understanding we can better establish the new parameters for strategy making and for any new strategy framework that is introduced.

We can capture some of the spirit of these changed market conditions by examining some recent headlines that show by just how much the rules of the game have changed.

- 'Within 15 years, there will be no more than 20 front rank component suppliers in the world. There will be major consolidation as winning companies seek strategically to align or merge to meet the challenges of the global vehicle industry. Although many UK companies have reasonable organic growth prospects this is not going to be enough. Some great company names may well lose out – British Steel, GKN, Lucas itself, Pilkington, TI, T&N, BBA, Laird are all current significant UK players. Yet none of these is wholly focused on the motor industry and they face the same sort of pressures in their other sectors.'[1]   (George Simpson, then CEO of Lucas)

- The OECD reported in 1996 that 4 Asian 'tigers' – South Korea, Taiwan, Hong Kong and Singapore – had doubled their share of world manufacturing exports from 6 to 12% since the early 1980s.

- 'Europe's age of consolidation' seems finally at hand. Even its ablest companies have run out of growth domestically. Mergers previously have been an option but have now become a stark necessity. Global pressures for industrial efficiency are becoming too strong to withstand. If a company is out of line with these changes it will be swallowed up. Four of Britain's leading Banking houses, S. G. Warburg, Morgan Grenfell, Kleinwort Benson and Smith New Court have all fallen into foreign hands for these reasons.[3]
                    (Salamon Brothers report 1996)

- 'No industry can guarantee safe shelter from the seismic movements that are reshaping the economy. Some like Banking (disintermediation), Retailing (saturation), Telecommunications and Utilities (deregulation) are so vulnerable it will feel like working on top of the San Andreas fault.'[4]   (*Fortune*)

- Intel, which produced the first computer-on-a-chip in 1971 from a couple of thousand transistors, now has chips with millions of transistors. Today's chips crunch numbers faster than a Cray supercomputer could in the late 1980s and at lower cost. Within a dozen years, Intel expects a version that will beat a dozen of today's fastest supercomputers.

Things are not as they were! Today's market conditions are very different from the early strategy framework days 20 years ago. The new parameters for effective and successful strategy development must reflect these changes. The major ones can be summarised in this way:

- Power, in nearly every industry, has firmly shifted to the customer.
- Scale is not necessarily an advantage.
- Borders and boundaries have collapsed – both geographically and business.
- Technology is ever more quickly copied.
- There is a constant stream of new, low-cost competitors.
- Information technology has revolutionised what can be done and what can be accessed.
- The global spread has now made it even more difficult for a corporate centre to manage the company.

What's the impact of these changed conditions for strategy? We shall examine the more important of these changes for strategy makers in the rest of this chapter.

Power has shifted to the customer

This is perhaps the most remarkable phenomenon of the past 20 years. It is the biggest change, the most important new rule in the game and one with the biggest impact for strategy making.

In most every industry the 'customer is now king'. Long gone are the days when manufacturers' products were supreme and when distributors were merely intermediaries in the supply chain. Companies are now constantly urged to court the customer. Indeed many commentators advocate that mere courtship is insufficient but that at minimum engagement, even marriage, may be required for success!

Effective customer management and 'customer service' specifically appear to be prime routes for competitive success, and we see this in all industries. For example in consumer service, retailers such as Nordstrom and Marks & Spencer lead the way in creating service cultures among their workforce that make them stand out for the consumer. In business services, Xerox is an excellent example of a company that has gone through a service revolution in the past decade, putting customer-satisfaction as the number-one driving goal in the business. Even traditionally product-led manufacturers such as the pharmaceutical companies have begun to recognise the importance of the customer; that selling their drug alone may be insufficient as competition intensifies and that they need to find new ways to court and serve their customers by providing a total treatment care package which they are calling 'disease management'.

In this new environment it is not just that the customer is king. The customer also sets the agenda. It is the customer's needs now and in the future that determine what the supplier or manufacturer must do to be successful. The winners are those who **best** understand what their customers want. In fact to stay as a winner, the supplier manufacturer must not only understand these existing customer needs but additionally be able to go on and **anticipate** what the customer will also want in the future.

As we approach the next millennium there is increasing understanding and awareness of this customer dynamic. In the financial services field, for example, there is growing sophistication in customer management. Companies such as USAA in Insurance, American Express, Fidelity, and MBNA America Bank are all developing comprehensive customer databases, training their staff to degrees of customer excellence and seeing their continued earnings success based on so understanding the customer that they develop near symbiotic relationships. So USAA has such detailed databases of their customers' history and preferences that each written and verbal communication becomes highly personalised and tailored. Each customer feels they are being treated as an important individual in their own right. It is not just a database with a list of names and addresses. The company is looking to establish a lifetime relationship.

What is the implication of this powershift for future strategy makers? It means, put simply, that all strategy discussion must start in the marketplace with what the customer wants.

It means being market-driven, not asset-driven. It's no use starting with 'what are we good at', or 'what are our core competencies'; they can only become relevant once we've understood what the marketplace requires. It means that strategy development templates based on such concepts as 'core competencies' or 'parenting' are all very interesting but potentially misleading. What the company is good at may be of no interest to the customer or may be inadequate in shifting customer purchasing behaviour. The first question has to be 'what does the customer need and **then** how can we provide that better than anyone else?'

For success, a strategy must be rooted in a detailed understanding of these customer and market conditions. Winning strategy makers must understand their markets better than anyone else. Only through such understanding – what we shall describe as a deep-rooted 'immersion' – will competitive advantages emerge.

We can illustrate this with an analogy from the world of stock market investment. Jim Slater, a leading UK authority on stock market portfolio investment has identified an approach that he calls the 'Zulu principle'. Slater quite simply describes the roots of success for any would-be investor:[6]

> 'My wife read a four page article on Zulus in *Reader's Digest*. From that moment on she knew more than me about Zulus. If she had then borrowed all the available books on the subject from the local library and read them carefully she would have known more about Zulus than most people. If she had decided subsequently to visit South Africa, live for six months in a Zulu Kraal and study all the available literature she would have become one of the leading authorities in Britain and possibly the world.'

Through investigative, rigorous and comprehensive research it's possible to become an expert. By adopting this 'Zulu principle' and immersing oneself totally in a chosen marketplace, the strategy makers of the future can hope to so understand their customers that they can find new opportunities for success. If they are the ones who go furthest in this 'immersion' process, they are the most likely to find more competitive leverage and opportunties and win out.

No commentator or industry observer disputes that power nowadays is generally and firmly with the customer, and success must be built upon recognising that premise. But, nevertheless, many companies still pay only lip-service to this. Only a few have truly grasped the nettle and turned this dynamic round to their advantage. Companies like Xerox,

Nordstrom, British Airways and Procter & Gamble stand out and remain the exception rather than the norm.

So why the delay? What are the roadblocks that appear to be preventing more companies becoming excellent at managing their customers? After all, understanding and meeting customer needs ought not to be some mysterious and elusive thing, it should be relatively straightforward. It's a paradox that still so few organisations do this truly effectively. If we can better understand what the roadblocks might be we can provide some further guidance for strategy makers struggling to educate and stimulate and put strategy back on top of the agenda.

Before considering the other forces of change in today's market, let's consider three main roadblocks that inhibit better and more effective market and customer management.

There is a misconception that customers don't always know what they want

Just as some managers will deny the value of strategy, arguing there's no point in looking to the future when it's so uncertain, so others will deny the value of consumer research or 'getting close to customers' suggesting customers don't always know what they want.

But in my experience and observation customers ultimately **do** know what they want and companies should be restless in getting so close to their customers that they can pick out exactly what are the underlying and latent needs and wants. The problem is that most companies don't do this. A *Wall Street Journal* survey of 2000 American consumers reported that only 5 per cent felt they were being listened to![7]

Fortunately, some companies do listen and do get deeply in-tune with their customers. A classic example of this is the Sony Walkman. Commentators describing the development of this innovative new product often do so pointing out how the standard written process of consumer research and customer questionnaires showed consumers had little interest in walking around with a tape recorder strapped to their waists. However when Akio Morita, Sony's Chairman, was interviewed on the subject of the development of this famous idea he did not support comments that he had had to make some great leap of innovative faith, that it was some unique vision and that the customers did not know what they wanted.

In his book *Made in Japan*, and in other interviews, he pointed out that Sony had in fact developed an extraordinary commitment to the development of consumer micro-electronics and products that were 'pocketable'. They had put considerable effort in deeply immersing themselves with their target consumers. They knew from all their investigation that consumers were frustrated that they could only listen to their favourite music in the house or in the car and wanted the opportunity to listen whenever they wanted to, in the park, in the street and so on. 'I can't sit by the stereo all day, I'd like to take the music with me but it's too heavy.' They also knew people 'like to listen to music but don't want to disturb others'. As the Sony team got closer and closer to truly understanding their customers' frustrations and needs, so they came to see how convenient, private, 'pocketable' mobile listening would be attractive and they came to develop the product concept of the Walkman. It was a far more rational and logical process than is typically described.[8]

Another example comes with Marks & Spencer's recent entry into Germany establishing their first store in Cologne. All the basic market research suggested there would be little interest amongst consumers for M&S style sandwiches which come wrapped in plastic packaging. German consumers were too used to their existing lunch-time eating habits. But in fact it turned out consumers did value both the convenience – being able to quickly obtain their lunch without waiting for the sandwich to be prepared – and the price which was set to be affordable. This, combined with forceful reassurances on freshness and quality, has been enough to make the sandwich a winner. M&S introduced the product – **despite** the standard consumer research – because it got so close in talking with its customers that it understood there was a latent need in the marketplace and any consumer uncertainty could be overcome.

What comes through is the high degree of 'immersion' in the way customers think that went on and still goes on at companies like Sony and Marks & Spencer. These companies go beyond the basic research to develop an in-depth almost intuitive feel for their markets. They so understand, are so close to their customers that they can find out what their customers really need. They break through the inadequacies of standard pieces of consumer research which are generally just too superficial.

The database of understanding may be inadequate

Another roadblock preventing more effective customer management is that the customer database in many companies is just too weak and limited. Even if the right data is available it's often not distilled in some user-friendly simple report that highlights the key insights for management. If there is no regular, rigorous and insightful measuring and monitoring of customer trends and needs, there will obviously be a vacuum in understanding and awareness of new opportunities.

British Airways is one of the exceptions. It believes that the customer database that it is continuously building and refining is one of its most valuable assets. Its former IT Director, John Watson, commented:

'We create our competitive advantage by knowing and serving our customers better than anyone else. This requires excellent information management. The analysis of data on customer preferences is fundamental to our decision-making. Our customer database is becoming ever more important. The more intelligence we can get out of the database the more we can feed the selling machine of BA. It needs to be so detailed, so thoughtful that it both informs and challenges our view of what our customers want. Building this database is a sophisticated art. We need to collect data at every point of customer contact.'

Despite British Airways example, we can still count on one hand the number of leading customer-oriented organisations with this sort of investment and expertise in customer information management. How come UPS for example has got itself so far ahead of DHL and TNT in this area? We still look at large parts of traditional industrial manufacturing such as in chemicals or steel and wonder when they will actually acknowledge their general customer information inadequacy and start developing the necessary leading-edge research, monitoring and recording of their customers that could begin to influence how they behave and advantageously shape their future strategy and direction.

Multinationals are slow to respond to local customer situations

The third roadblock is in organisation structure. As markets and customers globalise and the spread of business grows in scope and also in complexity, so multinationals struggle to easily marry being global with having to respond to local customers. There's a built-in tension in developing a worldwide pan-regional operation yet at the same time having to acknowledge and confront the fact that customer needs can, and often do, vary enormously between one country and another. Having to treat customers differently can mean a denial or reduction in the very synergies that drive globalisation in the first place. Hence operations managers may push to take a more homogeneous view of the world, while sales and marketing teams will likely be more acutely conscious of required local variations.

In practice these sort of tensions can delay and compromise the extent to which a company immerses itself successfully in fully understanding the needs of all its different customers. And as the world gets more competitive this differential understanding will become all the more critical to be successful.

Asea Brown Boveri is one of the few multinationals who do seem to have discovered an appropriate balance, and they have created both a structural form and culture that both understands the global versus local tension but also deals positively with it. ABB's credo has becomes well-known – 'act local think global' – and has become a template and possible solution for other multinationals struggling to find an effective global versus local matrix. In effect, ABB encourages local market immersion and decision-making while retaining certain pre-defined global synergies. It has a form of 'back:front' organisation structure where the 'Front' remains separated and distinct around identified customer segments and groups, while the 'back' is the area where the company seeks its global economies and synergies. It's not as black and white as that but it provides a general recognition of the need to balance local and global needs and opportunities. (Other possible solutions are considered further in Chapter 15.)

Scale is not necessarily an advantage

Returning to the main forces of change in the market, we should review what advantage scale now brings. Many of us grew up in an era where scale did provide advantage, it was a critical barrier to entry and a means of competing. As Michael Porter commented in 1980 in his seminal work on strategy, *Competitive Strategy*: 'economies of scale deter entry by forcing the entrant to come in at large scale and risk strong reaction from existing firms or come in at small scale and accept a cost disadvantage'.[9]

Indeed many of the strategy frameworks that are still in use today were developed in the era where scale did generally provide a source of advantage. Not just in Porter's work, but in PIMS and with the Boston Matrix, there is a built-in assumption as to the power and competitiveness of scale.

Yet as Michael Porter has since acknowledged and has been recorded as saying by Mike Johnston in *Managing in the Next Millennium*:[10]

'Scale is being defeated by the pace of change. Today we find you can be very efficient in doing what was done in the past – but that doesn't get you very much. The big company of today is not being defeated by another big company, but by small companies. As information flows very rapidly, as companies compete globally, inputs and scale are no longer a competitive advantage.'

The implications for strategy makers of this turnaround in the importance of scale are far-reaching. It is no wonder that companies find the current set of strategy development tools inadequate. They are in fact out-of-date! They just do not reflect the realities of the late twentieth century. What's worse, they actually mislead and misdirect. They still suggest that scale and size by themselves can be the basis of effective strategy while in fact market conditions have moved right along.

The marketplace has now changed that fundamentally. Until even quite recently the trend in business has been for size – the big just got bigger, aiming through scale to dominate their markets. But the new global arena is more demanding. Right now being biggest doesn't necessarily mean a company can dominate. British Airways may be the world's largest airline but it is still struggling to access the vast American market where it remains a weaker player and is often out-competed by, for example, smaller regionally-dedicated airlines. ICI Paints may be the world's largest paint company but equally in large parts of the world – until recently in all South America and still in Continental Europe – it remains a small player with limited local market leverage. IBM, General Motors and others are all huge global players but their strength will still vary in different markets. Their greater global scale counts for little when a local customer in one country, for example, is evaluating whether to buy from them or from another player who may be smaller but has a more competitive local customer franchise.

Most dramatically, smaller companies have proven they can now at least put themselves on the same footing as their larger global rivals. One method is through networking and strategic alliances. So Canon starting from a much smaller base was not disadvantaged in competing with Xerox because it had linked with Kodak; Corning (c. $5bn in turnover) in similar fashion could stand up to AT&T in optical fibre; and Samsung got a head-start in the US by making microwaves for GE.

Alternatively, smaller companies can compete with their larger rivals on price and can do so profitably on the back of a lower cost base. Many Asian producers for example, though much smaller in scale terms, can easily overcome that apparent disadvantage, leverage their low cost base, push quickly into new markets, offer low prices and still be profitable.

In this new era entering the twenty-first century, competitors around the world are no longer respecters of established scale. It no longer always requires some breakthrough technology or product differentiation or massive investment to break down previous scale barriers. The deregulated global economy provides easy cross-border access into different markets and there are now many tactics proven and developed for competing effectively and successfully against what were previously entrenched bigger competitors.

All this poses a further challenge for strategy makers. One of the principal old rules of the game no longer applies. Even more reason for the strategy maker then to ensure the organisation recognises the new threat and has a complete and comprehensive understanding of the market, knowing who all the possible competitors might be – from the largest to the smallest – and identifying all things that can be done – apart from scale – to keep these competitors at bay. The strategy maker must be totally clear what the new rules are before being able to go on and develop any effective strategy.

Put another way, a scale-based strategy was a symptom of the 1970s' and 1980s' more 'asset-led' approach. It reflected a Porter view of the market where big was still a barrier. Today scale by itself is irrelevant, it is not enough. Success is now about finding a form of advantage that the customer wants, needs and recognises. If a company has scale then its challenge is to translate that into something the customer wants and values.

We are moving to a world where doing something well matters more than doing a lot of it.

Borders and boundaries have collapsed

Globalisation and its impact on strategy making has already been described, its general effects well-known. But less attention is typically given to the nevertheless equally dramatic collapse of more traditional business boundaries – those within an organisation and those between its previously separate and discrete suppliers and customers. This erosion of former boundaries is giving rise to new sources of advantage and competitive opportunity:

- By replacing its traditional functional processes with fully accountable cross-functional teams composed of engineers, marketers, manufacturing experts, etc., Motorola has taken years out of its new product development cycle. Now what took three to five years to plan can in some cases be executed in three to five months especially in its leading cellular phones business.

- Procter & Gamble, together with WalMart its leading customer, have reinvented the supply chain – P&G is now doing things unheard of ten years ago, such as managing the stock of its products in WalMart warehouses and managing the frequency and size of WalMart reordering at store level. The two companies have so integrated their operation for the benefits of efficiency that there is now one seamless supply chain where only a few years ago there were firm corporate boundaries and two very separate operations.

Not surprisingly given the years of focus on re-engineering, process change is now happening ever more quickly and historic boundaries are crumbling. One benefit has typically been the reduced time to get things done and where an internal improvement is also translated into some form of noticeable customer advantage, then it can provide new opportunities for competing more effectively.

With all the high-profile best-practice re-engineering and process innovation going on, leading organisations are putting considerable efforts into exploring ways to break down these functions and other business boundaries. They are looking for ways to leverage their **total** company skills and capabilities to give themselves a better chance of competing successfully. The search is on both internally within the organisation, but it's also starting externally – challenging structures with suppliers and with customers to find new opportunities for competing that will be more profitable to all involved in the supply chain. As a result new benchmarks for organisational effectiveness are emerging that are all about providing product more quickly and better meeting new customers' needs, and much less about basic functional expertise or specialisations.

For the strategy maker, the impact of change in this area is exciting. It can open up new possibilities in finding and developing competitive advantage. This is especially true in the areas of providing things 'more quickly' for customers, or otherwise saving customers time as a result of process re-engineering and innovation. It also creates opportunities in the arena of improved or even new forms of customer service effectiveness.

Taking these sort of developments a stage further we now have talk of the 'virtual company'. This is a company without boundaries. It so organises itself that it can focus on the one or two areas of value-added that the customer most wants and which most drive its advantage, while outsourcing everything else in a network of supply and subcontracted functional support.

In this regard British Airways announced in early 1996 that is was intent on doing just that: transforming itself into a 'virtual airline' before the year 2000. It has in mind to potentially contract out all operations except the key front-line functions that interface with the customer, such as pilots, crew, reservations staff and sales and marketing personnel. Even these 'core customer competencies' may be subcontracted to regional third-party carriers.

The collapse of business boundaries must be taken by strategy makers as an opportunity rather than a threat. For Procter & Gamble, for example, it has opened up new customer service opportunities in the supply chain that had previously been denied it by now doing things its customers used to do and doing them better. For Motorola, it has provided the opportunity to break down internal functional barriers and get things done for customers more quickly. For British Airways, the plan will be to focus down ever closer on the one or two key areas driving its customer advantage that it can invest in and get even better at, to the exclusion of all other distractions.

Technology is ever more quickly copied

New technology that establishes a customer-noticeable differentiated product is of enormous value. It provides in many ways the most tangible form of advantage. In theory, if not always in practice, it can be effectively patented and provide – even in today's highly competitive environment – the most robust 'barrier to entry'.

But things are changing in this area too. Research has shown that:[11]

- 60% of all patented innovations are now imitated on average within four years.
- The ratio of imitation time to innovation time is on average 70%.
- The ratio of imitation cost to innovation cost is on average 60%.

And these ratios are constantly improving in favour of the imitator. In fact recent research goes on to show that imitations succeed as often as innovations and being 'first-in' a market is no guarantee whatsoever of future success. (This has been further evidenced in detailed research by Steve Schnaars, Professor of Marketing at New York's City University, who has demonstrated the many instances where later entrants seized markets from pioneers.)

Worse still for the innovator and the technology leader, the apparent strength of patent protection is often undermined helping the imitator at the expense of the innovator. Companies are becoming increasingly adept at finding a way around patent protection, for example, by using slightly different materials or design configurations. One famous example is Johnson & Johnson's litigation with Fonar in the early 1980s.

Fonar had patented the MRI scanner technology but that did not stop both J&J and GE developing and selling this diagnostic equipment. Fonar sued and lost. The judge recognised that Fonar had discovered the technology but was persuaded that the patent covered only the 'imaging of bodily tissue, not the imaging of internal organs'!

Another weapon in fighting patent protection, in undermining the value and advantage of new technology and being able to copy the innovator is through delaying litigation tactics. An example is Kodak's fight with Polaroid over instant film. In 1976 Kodak launched its own line of instant cameras competing directly with Polaroid. Polaroid sued claiming Kodak had infringed ten of its key patents. The litigation went on for 13 years. In the meantime Kodak was able to continue to sell its instant cameras, (though it gradually lost interest as the total instant market shrank). Only in 1990 did Kodak finally respond to a court order paying out $900m in settlement. That was a lot less than the $12bn Polaroid had claimed!

In fact, there has been a falling-off generally in the last decade of the number of true ground-breaking technologies that have been able to drive and sustain lasting market advantage for companies and be resistant to being imitated and copied. Ways around patent protection is only a partial reason for this. One other key reason is cost pressure reducing significantly the amount of 'blue sky', breakthrough research that a company will do, focusing expenditure instead on the future development and application of existing technology in the hope that that will be more immediately productive. Pharmaceutical companies for example are increasingly recognising that they cannot rely for their future solely on breakthrough new drugs where they will be able to sustain a meaningful and long-lasting technical differentiation from competition. If they do come up with these breakthroughs, chances are imitators will be just around the corner.

For many organisations where there has been a history of success built on product research and technical differentiation, this change in the lasting value of technology is creating a culture shock which they are still coming to terms with. Often so technically oriented is the company's traditional skill base that it is struggling to recognise it might need new skills in successfully selling and marketing less differentiated, often near commodity products. Many companies are unable to make the skill and culture transformation quickly or easily and so press on with an ad hoc mix of continued search for technical superiority, but allied with weak efforts in other areas which might provide additional advantage.

Old-established chemical companies such as Germany's Hoechst and BASF and Britain's ICI and Zeneca are such examples. Their success has been built on technology and research. Despite recent initiatives paying lip-service to the changing environment, such as internal market-effectiveness awards, few in either organisation would credibly claim market or customer management are core competencies. Their search for additional forms of advantage is lacklustre. In fact many in the workforce would still actively deny that such broader market capabilities are truly required and that if R&D would just get more funding it would be able to deliver the next major new product that customers would just have to buy!

As they struggle to compensate for a lack of long-lasting technical differentiation, many companies now face markets where to them price appears to be the only determinant of customer purchasing behaviour. As we shall see in later chapters, this is often nonsense. Many products in fact have enormous potential to be lifted out of the commodity price bracket – even without any technical distinction – through a better understanding of the alternative sources of advantage available in the market. As Professor Levitt has said, almost anything can be 'differentiated or augmented'.

But to realise these sort of possibilities, companies like ICI and Zeneca will require an organisation-wide change in their thinking, capabilities and their understanding of their markets and what is required for success. For strategy makers the major implication here is that competitive strategies based on technically differentiated product performance are still of great value, but their life and sustainability is now significantly less reliable.

Other changing market circumstances

- A stream of new low cost competitors.
- The information technology revolution.
- A global spread that makes it more difficult to manage

We need not dwell on these items except to draw conclusions for future strategy making. The rush of low-cost low-priced competition from Asia, Eastern Europe, Latin America and elsewhere has been well-documented.

What this has done is put Price firmly on the agenda and reconfirmed views that simply having scale is now irrelevant in the modern day. It's the price that gets charged that counts, and there are many ways to profitably price even at a low price level.

Equally, the IT revolution has been well-documented and continues to occupy much of modern management literature and speculation. What is clear for strategy makers is that IT has created an environment where customers perceive almost anything is possible. Indeed it has encouraged the view that there can be continuous improvement in doing things faster, or making tasks easier or services more convenient, and generally that it will all get cheaper.

So companies such as Cisco, 3Com, Bay Networks, or Sun Microsystems, while leaders in among other things designing and manufacturing the hubs, routers and switching gear that link computers to networks, are also ultimately searching for advantage with products that make it easier or quicker for their customers to do things – and if they can help customers save money at the same time then it's a near-perfect product proposition for customers increasingly demanding immediate results and improvements.

Finally a few further words on the new challenge of global management. Management was never easy. Now there are often diverse operating companies headquartered in different countries, speaking different languages, with different cultures and spread across often 50 or more countries around the world. For the strategy maker sitting in one office it has become just physically impossible to visit, let alone get to know, each site or operation during a normal career lifetime in one corporation. There are therefore large parts of the company's operation that the strategy maker will never fully understand and certainly not be able to appreciate the market or customer dynamics to the deep-rooted level we have been encouraging.

The consequences of this global spread are that the strategy maker must rely on insight and understanding developed by others, and to do that there must be in place the most effective strategy development process that reliably gets to grips with the various market opportunities and synthesises them into something the strategy maker can deal with.

This requires resources and a process the organisation buys into and is ready to carry out wholeheartedly. It means a common understanding as to what is strategy and how it is best developed. It requires a process that is deliberate in its own right and not tacked on to a set of budget numbers. It requires again the breaking of the 'vicious circle' and an effective process and exercise in strategy development.

Given the strategically myopic position most companies are coming from today, moving to such a successful development process is a considerable challenge. We shall spend more time discussing this in later chapters, but suffice it to say the globalisation of business has put new requirements on the whole process of strategy development.

Summary

We can now describe some of the new rules for strategy makers:

- Recognise the influence and power of the customer. Be so immersed in chosen markets with customers that you do not just understand better than anyone else (the Zulu principle) what opportunities there are, but you can actually anticipate future market competitive conditions and customer needs.
- Size and scale are no longer sources of advantage *per se*.
- Product differentiation based on new technology does not always provide any sustainable advantage.
- The collapse in borders and boundaries geographically and within and without the organisation opens up a vast new opportunity to look across the total supply chain and examine the more complete set of functional capabilities for new opportunities with customers.
- The IT revolution has increased expectations for companies to provide things faster, easier (and cheaper) and these are becoming more accessible forms of advantage for companies now to pursue.
- Price is increasingly prominent as low-cost competitors employ it as a major competitive weapon to enter new markets.
- And, to repeat, successful strategy development is not just about working with these new rules. It is also about breaking down the strategy myopia and the 'vicious circle' afflicting organisations which manifests itself not just in weak strategy development but also in poor realisation and execution. Success will require bringing the whole company on board with a revitalised understanding of the power of strategy and leveraging its full resources and capabilities in pursuit of a winning competitive position.

4 The Inadequacies of Existing Strategy Models

It is clear that the competitive environment has changed – fundamentally and forever. What we now need to understand in more detail is what impact this has on existing strategy tools and frameworks. In that way we can see more precisely why they are inadequate and are failing today's management. We need to identify what the specific lessons are so that any new model that is put forward builds on them and guides future strategic thinking in the most relevant and contemporary way.

A recent Kalchas study examined attitudes and satisfaction with existing strategy tools and frameworks and asked CEOs and Corporate Planning VPs what they thought about them:[1]

- More then 60% found them 'too theoretical, superficial and confusing'.
- 38% said they found them 'inapplicable' to their business situation.
- More than a quarter of interviewees agreed that existing tools were not helpful enough in today's competitive environment.
- A significant majority felt that 'some **new** model was required', that was also practical and helped identify potential sources of competitive advantage.
- A majority also agreed that any such framework must start by being customer and market-driven (as opposed to being driven by the corporation's own strengths).

A clear conclusion from this study with over 100 senior management respondents from UK and US corporations is that existing strategy tools are generally not helpful.

Many of the interviewees went on to comment that developing strategy felt like 'crystal ball gazing' or like 'trying to find a needle in a haystack'. A number commented how strategy debates in their companies often felt unreal, divorced from day-to-day realities:

- 'what we do is form filling, we *should* be having great big arguments about where the market's going';

- 'we don't seem to have a process or something that really deals with strategy and that people around here accept';

- 'everyone's got a different view about what strategy is and so we don't ever seem to get to grips with it'.

For these sort of reasons many Corporate Planning VPs especially talked about how difficult they found it to engage operating line managers and get them to stand back from the business and think about the future.

Against this background, there was a lot of consensus around the idea of developing a new strategy tool that would be easy and practical to apply – 'it must be immediately obvious to any busy line manager and require only the minimum of explanation'. There was also a general demand for making that new strategy tool specific rather than theoretical – 'we need to deal with practical ways of competing', 'it's no use talking about "differentiation" if there's no examples about what that means'.

The findings of this research are stark. They cry out for a new approach to strategy and a new model or framework that works. And this new approach must start by addressing the problems we've uncovered so far. It must deal with what CEOs and Planning VPs are saying. There's a great need for something that's practical and specific and easy to use rather than theoretical or superficial, something that defines what strategy is and shows people how to think about it.

And in building this new strategy model we also need to address the demands of these times and these late 1990s market conditions to deal with the new rules of the game, to move on from anachronistic concepts such as scale, to leave behind the asset-led approach of 'what are we good at, what are our strengths', and replace that with a model rooted in the business realities of the marketplace, of what customers will value and pay for now and in the future.

Taking this and other research into account we can identify seven criteria which should be used to govern the development of any new framework. And we can also use these same criteria to more precisely evaluate existing strategy tools. We can see more clearly where they succeed but also where they fail to meet the new demands of the marketplace, and learn what contribution, if any, they can make to strategy planning and thinking in the future.

The seven criteria are:

- reflecting the business realities of the late 1990s;
- starting with customers;
- rooted and immersed in market understanding;
- practical (not theoretical);
- specific (not superficial);
- encouraging a longer-term view;
- measurable.

In today's increasingly competitive environment it is ever more critical that an organisation does rediscover strategy and the art of most effective strategy development according to these criteria. It is vital that a direction and course is set which will help map a way through. Giving up or being stuck with 'crystal ball gazing' or any other poor strategy process cannot be the answer.

There is a choice. Either be buffeted continually by the storm winds of change, or build on the right sort of understanding and set the destination and establish the intent to get there. For sure, that course will need to be refined and adjusted to take account of the uncertainties and unpredictable events. But knowing where you want to get to get to has to be better. The ship **can** ride the storm if effectively navigated!

What tools can we use to set the best course? Let us examine some of the major strategy tools in use today, learning about their weaknesses as well as their strengths, and see how we can use the seven criteria we've identified to start shaping the new strategy model for the future.

There are a number of strategy tools and frameworks, but there are six in particular that are most in use or referred to and which should therefore be evaluated:

- The Boston matrix.
- PIMS (Profit Impact of Market Strategy).
- Porter's '5 forces' and '3 generic strategies'.
- Core competencies.
- Parenting.
- The 3 Value Disciplines.

Let us use our new-found criteria to determine where they succeed and fail us today, and what can we learn from them.

The Boston matrix

We are all familiar with 'Dogs', 'Stars' and 'Cash cows'. The Boston matrix[2] was first introduced by The Boston Consulting Group as long ago as the early 1970s! It has not been revised since.

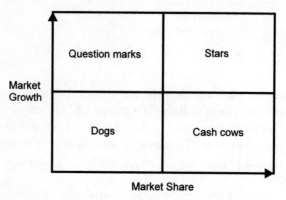

Figure 4.1   The Boston matrix

The matrix classifies products and businesses according to two variables: share of total market and the rate of the market's growth. The best products or businesses are obviously those with high shares of buoyant markets. The matrix directs the company to promote its 'stars' and use the 'cash cows' for funding; divest the dogs and treat 'question marks' with caution selecting only some for investment.

Strengths

• It does provide a practical easy-to-use guide to help a company think about the different investment needs of its portfolio of businesses.
• It is especially appropriate to diversified organisations, helping them put some prioritisation and direction into their spread of business activities.

Weaknesses

• It is not a guide to strategy, it's a guide to investment!
• It tries to influence business planning on the basis of just two factors – growth rate and market share. All of the many other factors affecting

profitability such as competitive intensity, competitive advantage or customer needs are ignored.

- It suggests cash flow is largely dependent on market growth and market share; that is, businesses with dominant shares of reasonably stable or mature or declining markets should be cash generators. While there is simplicity here the problem is that it is often wrong.

  For example if we were to map ICI's different businesses onto this Boston matrix we would probably draw some very misleading conclusions. Looking at one of the divisions, ICI Paints, it operates in Europe and North America with often strong market shares in relatively mature low-growth markets. Yet the business is far from being a cash cow. It requires significant levels of expenditure in advertising and selling support, as well as in research to develop new product technologies and applications and in maintenance of high-capital-intensive manufacturing plant. Any suggestion that it was appropriate to milk or treat this business as a cash cow would probably have led to a rapid erosion of competitiveness and future cash potential.

- There is an assumption, which we will also see with PIMS, that market share is definable and that market sector boundaries are stable. But as we have discussed in the last chapter, the new competitive environment shows a situation which is far from stable, where geographic boundaries especially are blurring. It's hard to define what the market share is and develop long-term plans when the market boundaries keep changing!

  For example let's consider L'Oreal's market share in hair shampoo. The same product under the brand name, Kérastase, is sold in a number of different countries across Europe, either direct by local selling operations or through export. For the purpose of using the Boston matrix, what is the market share we should use? Is it share in one of the countries or is it share of the total European shampoo market? Depending on the share definition we would draw very different planning conclusions. While L'Oreal's Kérastase market share is strong in some European countries such as in Italy, Spain and France, it is weak in others such as in the UK. Overall, its share in its market segment across Europe is high. Should we take the high overall share as our measure? After all there are some pan-European cross-border customers who see Europe as one market. If we do, then according to the Boston matrix in this relatively flat market we are looking at cash-cow planning. If on the other hand we take the weaker share areas we are looking at a completely different set of market imperatives and planning actions. As market boundaries blur, this sort of uncertainty can only lead to confusion if we try to use market share specifically as our chief indicator for future investment planning.

- There is nothing in this tool, for example, which aids decision-making on what form of competitive advantage might lead to success. It assumes a market share position – it gives no indication on what strategy will get us there or sustain that position! If anything, it's more about investment priorities once we have got there instead of about how to build and establish a successful competitive position.

Summing up (see Figure 4.2), the Boston matrix makes little useful contribution to today's debate about strategy development. It's just too simplistic and does not deal with the fundamental elements of what competitive strategy is all about.

Criteria	Score ● high ○ low
• Rooted and immersed in market understanding	◑
• Starting with customers	○
• Reflecting 1990s business realities	○
• Practical	◐
• Specific	○
• Encourages a longer-term view	○
• Measurable	◐

Figure 4.2 Effectiveness of the Boston matrix

PIMS[3]

PIMS (Profit Impact of Market Strategy) was another strategy tool that was initiated some time ago – in this instance as long ago as 1972. Over the following few years a substantial database was built containing financial and market data for over 3000 business units. From this empirical research the PIMS team identified relationships between market and competitive conditions, compared with financial performance.

The key conclusions were that: 'market share is a major driver of profitability', and that 'relative quality is the single factor affecting a business unit's performance and market share'.

Strengths

- Identifying relative quality of products and services as the key underlying driver of performance was an important step. It high-lighted 'relative competitiveness' of products and services as the key factor for success (how much better are they than their rivals), and in doing so laid some of the empirical groundwork and thinking for Michael Porter who went on to conceptualise this 'relative quality' as 'Competitive Advantage' (see Figure 4.3).

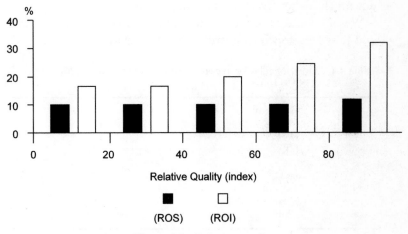

Figure 4.3   Relative quality

- Acknowledging that any assessment of relative quality must start with the customer – it is the 'perceived' quality that is the important measure, not the company's own view of the quality of its products.

Weaknesses

- The empirical database from which PIMS initial conclusions are drawn is more than 20 years old and, even though it has been subsequently added to, that original framework cannot adequately reflect all the changed market and competitive conditions.

- The conclusions about the profit impact of market share and its direct, near-linear relationship to ROS/ROI must now be challenged:

  - as we have discussed, market share definitions are much more uncertain in a global marketplace and can be misleading;
  - a key premise for the market share conclusion rests on the value of economies of scale. Again, as we have shown, such value is today far more questionable, for example in the face of small, nimble but low-cost competitors;
  - there are increasing examples of companies with low shares which are actually more profitable than companies with high shares in the same industry. For example low-cost Asian suppliers – more than capable now of competing cross-border in the global economy – are often getting higher returns than their larger more cumbersome western rivals who may have higher market shares but much higher overhead and wage bills.

  We only need review comparative labour costs between western and Less Developed Countries (LDC) for evidence (see Table 4.1).

Table 4.1 Index of relative average cost per hour of production workers (USA = 100)[4]

Germany	152
France	112
US	100
UK	81
Korea	39
Taiwan	32
Mexico	17
China	4

- A 1997 study by Bain & Company (reported in the *Harvard Business Review*) confirms market share alone can no longer be counted on to drive profitability.

- Guidance as to more **specific** sources of competitive advantage is absent. There are only general statements such as relative quality leading to success. Such statements are a little like Michael Porter's broad 'differentiation' being put forward as a principal form of strategy. OK, it highlights the need to be competitive but then what, what are the options, what specific types of competitiveness are there, what does relative quality really mean? It's at this sort of point that strategy makers yearn for greater specificity and guidance.

- The whole approach of PIMS is insular and incremental. It's all about working with predetermined market drivers in existing markets that have been defined in the database. It encourages an organisation to pick markets which have been shown by its empirical analysis to be already profitable or attractive, and then improve within that area. It does not encourage an organisation to find a fresh approach, a new way of competing that might overturn the existing industry dynamics and drivers as PIMS has defined them. It offers no encouragement to evaluate future market opportunities where a company can forge new types of competitive advantage, write its own script and perhaps achieve new levels of profitability and success.

In summary we must acknowledge that PIMS has put some important stakes in the ground, especially in terms of its empirically-based findings on relative quality. But, ultimately, it fails management by placing too much emphasis on gaining market share for the sake of it, and like the Boston matrix it does not provide any specific or practical guidance as to how to develop competitive advantage and what particular form that advantage might take (see Figure 4.4).

Criteria	Score ● high ○ low
• Rooted and immersed in market understanding	●
• Starting with customers	●
• Reflecting 1990s business realities	○
• Practical	◑
• Specific	◑
• Encourages a longer-term view	○
• Measurable	●

Figure 4.4 Effectiveness of PIMS

Porter's five forces and three generic strategies[5]

Michael Porter of course has made an invaluable contribution to the development of strategic thinking. Though originated more than 15 years ago his frameworks are still the most commonly used and the best known.

Strengths

- His writings have institutionalised the concept of competitive advantage as the basis for strategic success. While some commentators and business figures may still argue the merits of having a strategy at all, few deny competitive advantage as the prime building block.
- His 'five-forces' model is an easy-to-use synthesis of market forces and is still widely employed by companies trying to distil what are the key trends and dynamics in their industry (see Figure 4.5).

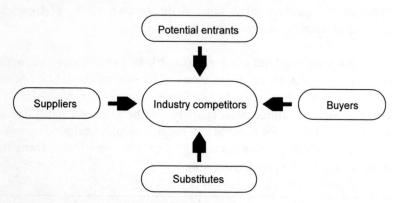

Figure 4.5   Porter's five-forces model

While today's more complex competitive environment suggest there are often more than five forces to consider, this original distillation remains powerful.

- His 'three generic strategies' – lowest cost, differentiation and focus (or niche) demonstrated for the first time that ultimately there are, despite all the different variables and industry situations, only a few meaningful strategic options. By describing what these options are he began to point out, albeit at a still quite superficial level, what directions an organisation might pursue.
- He has also pioneered the understanding of the 'value chain', encouraging the examination of each aspect of what a company does to discover where it can add value more competitively than its rivals.

Weaknesses

- Porter himself has already acknowledged that the key basis for one of his generic strategies – lowest cost – no longer applies. Lowest cost as a strategic route was based principally on achieving economies of scale, but as we described earlier Porter has acknowledged that 'scale is being defeated by the pace of change . . . the big company of today is not being defeated by another big company, but by the small companies'. What's more, the customer just cares less about a manufacturer/supplier's relative cost position. So what? It's the price that the customer is interested in.

Discussing cost leadership as a strategic option can be particularly misleading then in today's global, more aggressively competitive economy. Scale can't provide any sustainable competitive advantage and the low-cost LDC-based competitors – as mavericks often playing to their own pricing rules – are ready to undermine any achieved cost position of their rivals.

Many suppliers are just not respecters of others' scale. If they benefit from a LDC's lower cost base they'll exploit it and be ready to use it to price aggressively and win business. But even if they don't have that cost advantage, nowadays there are many suppliers still ready to compete aggressively on price. Even without making much, if any, profit they may still become significant long-term low-price competitors. And it's not all small businesses doing this. Samsung is a classic example. Its aim in entering the European consumer electricals market was to build volume and market share. It had no scale in Europe and its relative cost position wasn't that much of an advantage. Nevertheless it took a market-based view determining what price would be required to achieve its volume targets and set a long-term low-pricing strategy. Eventually Samsung may decide to stop subsidising its activities in this area from profits in other divisions but it has maintained such a strategy for more than six years. Price is its competitive weapon, cost is irrelevant, scale of others is no barrier. Daewoo is another large company operating with a similar pricing philosophy.

- In later writings Porter began to blur the distinction between focus and differentiation, often talking about 'the two basic forms of competitive advantage: cost leadership and differentiation' and implying that 'focus' is no more than differentiation in one segment rather than across a whole industry. Are there two generic strategies then or three? In today's highly competitive environment most companies are compelled to focus anyway on particular buying segments and look for 'focused differentiation', rather than aiming to compete with advantage across a whole industry. Industry-wide differentiation is unlikely to be realistic or achievable in today's competitive market conditions. So Porter's example of IBM having advantage because of its industry-wide differentiation in 'computers' looks untenable today. In fact, that sort of industry-wide, unsegmented, unfocused thinking no doubt contributed to IBM's downfall as it of course failed to fully realise the different segmentation and buying needs that were emerging.

- Much of Porter's work and thinking is written in a time when power had not yet shifted to the customer, and so his suggested generic strategies are largely manufacturer-asset-driven, rather than rooted in market understanding and starting with customers. Somewhat tendentiously in this regard we could point to Porter's old-fashioned notion of 'buyers' rather than talking about 'customers', reflecting a 1970s view that it was all about selling and purchasing rather than dealing with someone who is largely setting the agenda.

By way of another example, Porter talks about cost-leadership. Even were that a viable strategy in today's customer-led marketplaces, the customer – as we now understand that entitiy in the late 1990s – ultimately cares less about the supplier's relative cost position. What the customer cares about and what is now demonstrably more relevant is the price that the product or service is supplied at.

- Porter's principally asset-led thinking, based on market conditions prevalent in the late 1970s early 1980s, was also the common background for the Boston matrix and PIMS. In each case the thinking behind the strategic framework assumed that manufacturers and suppliers largely held the balance of power in most industries. The starting point was, 'what does the manufacturer/supplier have to offer?' The challenge was directed to outwitting other competitor manufacturers/suppliers. It was more readily assumed the buyer would purchase the best on offer. The challenge was not directed with anything like the same force to the distributor/user end of the supply chain, and certainly not to the point of treating the customer as setting the agenda. It was an era where, for example, manufacturer brands dominated and where distributors and intermediaries were almost compelled to take the products on the terms the manufacturer dictated.

Of course since that time, industries have seen their key customers grow in size and sophistication and begin to leverage their power and position. Responding to that and being market and customer-based has now become a prequisite, not an option. And as we shall continually highlight in this book, manufacturers and suppliers must recognise that and go on to truly embrace the driving influence of their customer base; though this recognition must not be treated as a surrender. Quite the contrary, it must be the stepping-stone to determine how to work with the new market conditions and turn them to the manufacturer/supplier's own ultimate advantage.

The surprise is that this asset-led, rather than market and customer-led approach, continues to characterise some of the more recent strategy tools that have been developed and publicised, and it's a pitfall that strategy makers must look out for and obviously avoid. Porter's work is an enormous contribution and stimulus to strategic thinking, but it has in a number of significant respects been overtaken by the new set of business realities of the late 1990s.

- Finally, Porter's 'three generic strategies' are by definition superficial. Like PIMS and the Boston matrix they provide little practical or specific guidance, other than cost-leadership (which should be disregarded), for finding the specific forms of competitive advantage that might drive the business performance. While it might be argued that the lack of specificity is a good thing encouraging blue-sky thinking and brainstorming, nevertheless all our CEO and Planning VP research finds this too-generic approach unhelpful.

Most executives find new strategy development tough. It's hard to get a handle on future market dynamics, it's difficult to know what to look for in terms of possible competitive advantage options. Whilst not constraining that debate, the general feeling is that there is a need to guide it with some greater degree of specificity to provide a more practical, easier-to-use tool to stimulate more effective strategic development.

The effectiveness of Porter's model is summarised in Figure 4.6.

Criteria	Score ● high ○ low
• Rooted and immersed in market understanding	◐
• Starting with customers	○
• Reflecting 1990s business realities	○
• Practical	◐
• Specific	◐
• Encourages a longer-term view	◕
• Measurable	◑

Figure 4.6 Effectiveness of Porter's framework

Core competencies[6]

The authors of 'core competency' thinking – Prahalad and Hamel – define it as, 'the collective learning in the organisation, especially how to co-ordinate diverse production skills and integrate multiple streams of technologies'. Introduced in 1990, this approach argued that organisations should move on from portfolio planning and assessment of individual businesses and begin to examine the collective strengths that the total organisation had. The intent is to encourage a company to find and develop those cross-company skills or competencies which will open up new avenues of opportunity and success in the market.

Strengths

- It is a helpful reinforcement and reminder to a company to play to its strengths in an ever more competitive world.
- It was timely in that it coincided with a recession in the West where organisations were looking to cut costs. Core competency thinking provided the rationale to stop doing things which were not 'core competencies'. One result is that it has fuelled the outsourcing industry. It also facilitated the development of re-engineering as a means to help companies reorganise around what they defined as their core processes.
- It establishes the need to think across boundaries within an organisation and so leverage common processes rather than individual function activities
- Its greatest contribution comes less from the concept itself and more from the book it led to, *Competing for the Future*. This is an outstanding contribution to strategy thinking being the first major writing of the 1990s to urge companies to plan proactively for the future. Building from core competency thinking, it takes a 'boundary-less' view of competition without geographic borders or functional barriers.

  It urges companies to think widely about their opportunities and explore ways of collecting and orchestrating their strengths, skills and experience to find new approaches and product/service propositions.

  The authors also suggest that doing this and succeeding in it requires a long-term and persistent plan that involves continued investment to translate the combined competencies into specific product leadership.

Weaknesses

- Despite Prahalad and Hamel urging companies to think about how to compete in the future, their core competency framework is principally company asset-driven. It starts more from within the company on what **it** is good at rather than with the customer and what the customer needs.

    One excuse that the authors offer for this is that customers don't always know what they need. But as we've the discussed, experiences of Sony, Marks & Spencer and many others has shown that while customers may not be able to describe the precise product requirement and specification, they nevertheless **do** know, extremely well, the generality of what they have not got and what they want. It is all about listening, understanding and, as we shall describe later, being totally immersed in customer thinking. So while it is true that customers may not have specified cellular telephones or fax machines or cars with on-board navigation systems specifically, any in-depth understanding of what customers underlying needs are would quickly have revealed requirements for easier more-mobile communications (paging devices were an obvious forerunner), or problems with inadequate road signage and reading maps while driving. The roadblocks are less with the customer not knowing and more with the manufacturer/supplier converting a need into an acceptable product or service form at an appropriate price.

- There is no framework on how to actually define what an organisation's core competencies are. Look through their writings. There are plenty of case studies but how does a company go about selecting its core competencies, how many core competencies are realistic, what should the company do with what's not core?

- The definitions and illustrations that we are given of what are successful core competency developments are generally very broad to the point of superficiality. So the authors discuss, for example, Sharp and Toshiba's leadership in 'flat screen display', Merck's 'drug discovery' skills, 3M's core competencies in 'adhesives, substitutes and advanced materials', and AT&T's work on 'video compression'. These ideas are so broad that we might argue there is something missing. Where is the specific translation of these skills into something that the customer values – into what will drive competitive advantage in the market?

- So we are given somewhat superficial and internal-looking definitions of core competencies, and little guidance on how to identify the more specific skills and experiences required to actually make a particular product or service successful in the marketplace. As Goold, Campbell and Alexander[8] in their own research work point out, a company like Texas Instruments may have had an effective core competence in semi-conductor technology but it had no developed skill in consumer-oriented businesses. So it failed when it tried to translate its semi-conductor competence into consumer watches, calculators and home computers. Its core competence did not give it any understanding of particular market sectors it wanted to enter. Equally, Procter & Gamble may have excellence in certain areas such as product innovation and consumer marketing, but it failed with its soft drinks business Crush because among other things it had no developed expertise in managing the local bottlers who controlled the distribution. Its internal core competencies didn't capture the necessary market insights.

Summing up, Prahalad and Hamel have made a more valuable contribution to strategy thinking and development with their broader debate in their book about competing for the future than they have with their specific core competency framework. Disappointingly, their core competency thinking has become a basis and rationale for outsourcing, downsizing and re-engineering instead of the, no doubt, intended goal of encouraging a different view about how to compete. Perhaps our disappointment comes most through the absence of any specific and practical guidelines on how to identify these core competencies and how to translate them into specific advantages in the marketplace with customers. The effectiveness of their framework is summarised in Figure 4.7.

Criteria	Score ● high ○ low
● Rooted and immersed in market understanding	◑
● Starting with customers	○
● Reflecting 1990s business realities	◑
● Practical	◑
● Specific	○
● Encourages a longer-term view	●
● Measurable	○

Figure 4.7 Effectiveness of Core Competencies

Parenting[9]

The 'Parenting' concept was introduced in 1994 by Goold, Campbell and Alexander as a tool for 'multibusiness companies' to choose the most appropriate portfolio of different businesses to which the parent can best add value. At one level it's another view on portfolio management of a diverse group of businesses 20 years after the Boston matrix. As the authors intend it, it is a means for defining the core skills (or competencies) that the parent centre must develop and apply to assist each business unit in the pursuit of its own goals (see Figure 4.8).

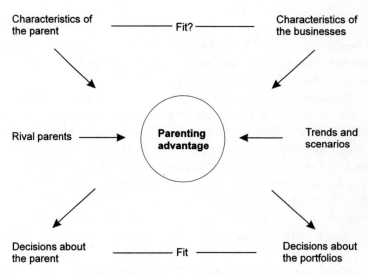

Figure 4.8   The 'parenting' concept

Strengths

- The 'parenting' concept does highlight the role of the centre in adding value and suggests that corporate strategy need not be just a summary of the strategies of the individual businesses. Instead the parent can define a corporate role which does influence and shape what each business sets out to achieve and how effectively it achieves it.
- The thinking does encourage a corporation to focus, to find those areas or markets or businesses – its 'heartland' – where it can add value, so there is accumulated learning and skill in the parent in certain chosen areas.

- The research for the parenting work also demonstrates how few companies had any meaningful insight into the corporate centre's role and responsibility in formulating strategy. Many had in effect delegated or abdicated their role as parent and their responsibility for strategy to each business unit manager, leaving them at the centre with few and principally financial responsibilities. In spotlighting this problem, their research does reinforce the conviction that companies have lost their way in strategy, that the centre is uncertain of its role in that area and that as a result it's mostly left to others.

Weaknesses

- At least two of the 15 'champion' companies used by the authors to illustrate their concept have recently acknowledged that 'parenting' as they had defined it is not working for them. So, for example, Hanson is physically breaking up into four, more focused, industry-specific organisations. BTR is actively disposing of a number of businesses, acknowledging that its parenting 'financial control skills' are not enough in the ever more competitive 1990s, and that it needs to do more at the centre to strengthen strategies and find synergies.
- In a world where conglomerates are increasingly unfashionable and where focused, dedicated commitment to individual markets appears to show more reward, frameworks such as this one for helping companies manage diverse or multibusiness portfolios are likely to be less and less useful. As we shall illustrate later on, there is compelling empirical evidence that the fewer different businesses a company is involved in, typically the higher its earnings growth and more impressive its shareholder value creation are.
- Like 'core competencies', this is principally an asset-driven framework. It's about the relationship between the centre and its individual business. It's inward-looking rather than market-based. Customers don't even appear in the parenting framework. Success with customers, in this model, would be a by-product of effective parenting. They are not the starting point.
- Not surprisingly, given this approach, there is no thinking about marketplace-based competitive advantage nor any specific guidance on what forms such advantage might take.

The effectiveness of the parenting framework is summarised in Figure 4.9.

Criteria	Score ● high ○ low
• Rooted and immersed in market understanding	○
• Starting with customers	○
• Reflecting 1990s business realities	◐
• Practical	◕
• Specific	○
• Encourages a longer-term view	◐
• Measurable	◕

Figure 4.9   Effectiveness of parenting

The three value disciplines

The most recent of the frameworks to be discussed was introduced in 1995. Its authors Michael Treacy and Fred Wiersema identify three alternative types of value-added that organisations can choose to pursue and they demonstrate that market leaders typically focus relentlessly on one of these three 'value disciplines' to excel at. The value alternatives are Operational Excellence, Product Leadership or Customer Intimacy. The authors urge companies to focus on one of these disciplines and 'stake their reputation on it', and not try to succeed in all three and try to be all things to all customers.

Overview

• At last we do come across a strategy framework that is contemporary. The thinking behind these value disciplines is firmly rooted in the business realities of the 1990s. It is a compelling advocate of being immersed in markets and with customers to develop that fundamental understanding of future trends and dynamics. It firmly acknowledges the influence and drive of customers in determining what will succeed. It also has moved beyond old-fashioned simplistic ideas about scale or unit cost, and instead talks for example about a total operational excellence which combines cost efficiency and service excellence into a more complete market proposition.

- It encourages companies to focus. It suggests picking on one form of value-added, finding one particular source of competitive advantage in the market that will be the long-term driver of its success. And it urges this focus while acknowledging that a company must still achieve threshold levels of performance in the other value areas too.
- It emphasises that success is more than just the pursuit of these value-added disciplines. It is rather the relentless, continuous investment in operating excellence or in transforming the culture of the company so that it adopts 'the cult of the customer'. It's the going to extraordinary lengths that separates the winners from the losers.
- But even in the few years since value disciplines were first written up, there is increasing recognition that power in the market place has now firmly shifted to the customer. In that light, 'customer intimacy' may become less a choice value discipline and even more a requirement for market success.

The effectiveness of the three value disciplines is summarised in Figure 4.10.

Criteria	Score ● high ○ low
• Rooted and immersed in market understanding • Starting with customers • Reflecting 1990s business realities • Practical • Specific • Encourages a longer-term view • Measurable	● ◐ ◐ ◐ ◐ ◐ ◐

Figure 4.10 Effectiveness of value disciplines

*   *   *

We have now looked at each of the major strategy tools and aids that are in use by corporations today in developing their strategy. In summary, it should now be clear why existing strategy tools and frameworks are inadequate. Against the seven criteria we have identified, these tools in the round fail to provide management with effective guidance in the development of strategies that could be effective and winning.

The older tools such as the Boston matrix and PIMS fail especially because they reflect a set of market and competitive conditions more from the 1970s as opposed to the 1990s. The more recent tools such as core competencies, parenting and especially value disciplines are much more up-to-date in their analysis and presentation, but ultimately still suffer from being too generic and superficial and not providing specific guidance on competitive advantage options.

Surprisingly, despite the shift to customer power acknowledged by most if not all commentators today, even the more recent tools are more manufacturer/supplier asset-led than market-driven. This is especially true of core competencies and parenting where the basic idea is related more internally to the company than externally to the market.

Only Porter's work, principally because of its pioneering impact when it was first introduced, retains an inherent attractiveness. His 'five forces', even if there may sometimes be more than five today, provide a basic framework for analysis that has become institutionalised and accepted as a simple way to analyse market trends. His concept of 'competitive advantage' has certainly stood the test of time and remains the cornerstone of all subsequent strategic thinking. And his value-chain analysis opens up the idea of looking for value-added in different parts of the organisation, for example in operations, in products and with customers.

My intention in searching for and developing a new framework is certainly to build on the positive contributions made especially by Porter but also found in certain aspects of each of the other tools and frameworks discussed. Most importantly, though, the goal is to match and meet the demands of the seven criteria head-on.

It is going to be critical if strategy making is ever to recover its rightful place and priority in corporate development that a new strategy making tool **is** found that is regarded as practical, specific, easy to explain, and which encourages long-term thinking and reflects and addresses a set of business conditions that all strategy makers have to deal with.

The rest of the book goes on to describe and illustrate the new Market Commitment Model. We shall regularly refer to the seven criteria or themes that underpin them. The aim by the end of this book is to have stimulated a total reappraisal of how to think about strategy and how to establish it so that it does become a driving force in the organisation.

5   Introduction to the Market Commitment Model

The Market Commitment Model provides a new framework for strategy making. It is built upon a deep-rooted understanding of markets and customers. Through that understanding and immersion in how markets are developing and customer needs are changing come the insights, initiatives and ideas – the strategy – that can lead to business success. The model provides a framework to search out and develop a customer value-based strategy that is more competitive and effective than those of rival companies. It embodies the notion of competitive advantage and the requirement to find and develop those long-term sustainable sources of advantage in the market place that will drive a company's future performance and earnings.

Its starting point is not 'what is the company good at'. It is rather 'what do different customers want now and in the future and how can a supplier company meet those evolving needs better than all possible rivals?'

The market commitment model does not take an asset-led approach. In other words it crucially does **not** depend upon a company's core competencies or its scale. Instead it goes right beyond that and asks: 'what are those worth to customers?' 'What strengths and skills do **customers** value, and do they value them enough to switch their purchasing permanently from company A to company B? Is there a clear **customer**-perceived and recognised difference in what B is offering? Do we, as customers, see that B is totally committed to providing long term the most competitive offering to us?'

By starting with markets and customers the Model is not suggesting a reactive response to customer needs. On the contrary; the intention is that a company must be proactive, must be so in-tune with its markets and customers, so much better informed than its rivals that it can **anticipate**. It can see and develop nascent opportunities. Instead of being strategically myopic, the company develops strategic foresight. It can become 'market-driving'. It can act like Sony with the Walkman development. The company must so understand its market that it can be in a position to develop desirable new products and services – ahead of the game.

The market commitment model is not about short-term tactical advantage. It's not about squeezing price or putting pressure on distributors or offering promotional incentives or increasing sales people's commissions. Those may be effective short-term marketing tactics but they are not the underpinnings of long-term competitive success.

The model is about creating lasting wealth and employment, about building successful and profitable corporations. It's the stuff that Microsoft, Coca-Cola, Procter & Gamble and Du Pont and the like are made of. It's about putting stakes in the ground for the future, identifying the best form of strategic advantage and setting clear targets and goals to drive the company forward.

As we describe the model and how to use and exploit it, we shall look at many successful corporations by way of example, but there is one key learning and message to highlight right up front. The model is not the answer by itself. Success is also dependent upon how it is used and how the ideas emerging are implemented. The watchwords are about rigour, discipline, objectivity and determination. Exhaustively understanding customers, rigorously monitoring and measuring changing market and customer needs, constantly evaluating the competitiveness of your offering versus those of your rivals, proactively dealing with any changes rather than just discussing them, committing the whole organisation to the development and realisation of the strategy – these are some of the executional elements which will ultimately distinguish the long-term successes and which we shall return to.

I have found in working with the model in practice that it can apply effectively no matter what the industry, no matter the size or diversity of the organisation. I find it can provide a comprehensive tool for an organisation to challenge and develop its strategic position. I would not claim, however, to have discovered the universal laws of strategy. There may be some unique industry situation where the model does not provide every single one of the options. Of course this is possible but I would expect it to be an exception. (And even in such a case, the model does provide the basic framework and necessary steps that effective strategy making should **still** go through.) Also, like all contributions to strategic thinking, it must be seen as contemporary, reflecting the challenges and market conditions as we enter into the twenty-first century. It cannot be a model forever into the future, and will inevitably and eventually require its own remodelling.

In the rest of this chapter I shall describe in outline the market commitment model and briefly explore how to use it most effectively. Once this is established subsequent chapters will deal in more detail and with greater illustration of how each element of the model should be applied and how it can lead to building most effective and profitable strategies.

The market commitment model has three levels or dimensions:

1 Commitment
2 The four prime axes or forms of competitive advantage
3 The underlying sources of that competitive advantage

The model must be seen as holistic. Each of the three dimensions must be worked through and evaluated. Together they represent the essential stepping-stones to finding and developing lasting competitive advantage and market place success. The basic model, built on the two dimensions of commitment and four prime axes of competitive advantage, is shown in Figure 5.1.

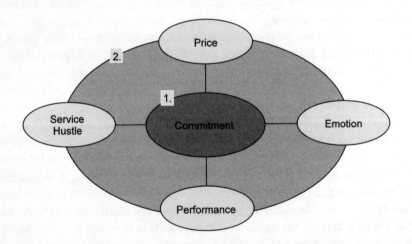

Figure 5.1   The market commitment model – overview

The full market commitment model, with its threee dimensions including the more specific underlying sources of advantage at the third level, is set out in Figure 5.2.

The first dimension: commitment

This is about long-term commitment to the market place in which the company competes. This is the bedrock for any lasting success.

Commitment includes two key elements: (1) developing an understanding and immersion in the market with customers, and (2) establishing a long-term horizon and determination to win out, overcoming the inevitable uncertainties and unpredictable nature of any late 1990s market place. These two elements go hand-in-hand; identifying future goals and opportunities must be born out of totally rigorous, deep-rooted market immersion.

As we analyse the key factors for success driving any admired organisation, we will find commitment as defined here as the major foundation stone.

Our current champion and immediate example is Microsoft.[1] As reported in *Micronews*, Microsoft's in-house newsletter, one of the company's employees developed this 'battle hymn':

'Oh our eyes have seen the glory of the coming of the Net
We are ramping up our market share, objectives will be met
Soon our browser will be everywhere, you ain't seen nothin' yet
We embrace and we extend!'

1996 saw an extraordinary commitment from Microsoft to be the leader and win in its chosen markets. It is racing to catch up with the Internet revolution and its rivals like Netscape, Sun Microsystems, Yahoo! and others who got a head-start in that area. It has switched an enormous part of its resources into a 'catching-up' operation with the aim of emerging as the dominant player.

The story is now familiar. Leading in computer software, the company was so obsessed with Windows and beating back government regulators worried about alleged anti-competitive practices that the company missed out on early Net developments. By 1995, others had taken control.

Would Microsoft suffer like IBM, General Motors, Apple or Olivetti? Corporations once with market dominance only to lose it when technology and markets change before them. That was potentially Microsoft's fate – an amazing 20-year success, domination in its field, highly-profitable – but blindsided?

However, in early 1995, Bill Gates the CEO announced a U-turn, recognising that the Internet was going to become a key driver in the development of PCs and software. Critically, Gates acknowledged the

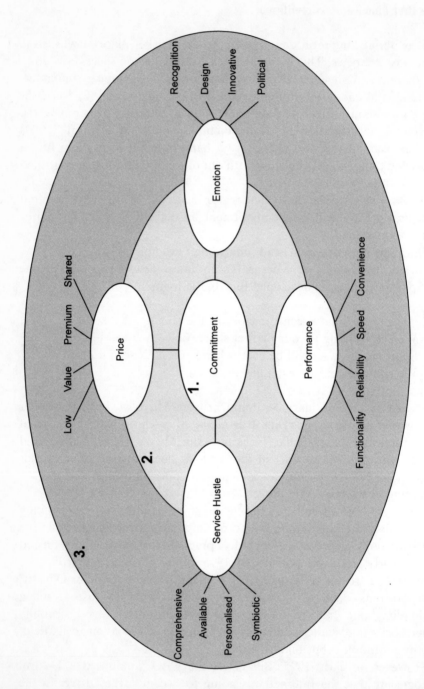

Figure 5.2 The market commitment model – in detail

need to play by the market's rules, not the PC rules Microsoft had written with Windows. The goal was to turn and become 'web-centric', leaving behind what didn't fit and reshaping everything else in an effort to stay on top.

In less than six months Microsoft had announced among other things:

- An increase in R&D spending by nearly 50 per cent to $1.5bn, to 'mainly meet the challenges posed by the Internet'.[2]
- Alliances with MCI, Hughes Electronics, Intel and UUNet Technologies.[3]
- Acquisitions of a number of promising web start-ups to help it move more quickly onto the Net,[4] including
  - Vermeer Technologies who have tools for creating and managing web documents,
  - Colusa Software, makers of object-oriented programming,
  - eShop Inc., a leader in Internet commerce software, and
  - Electric Gravity makers of multiplayer games.
- A plan to broaden the use of the Internet for home banking and challenge rival Intuit's transaction processing business by developing technical specifications for handling data securely. Microsoft has already signed up Visa International to act as its transaction processing arm.[5]
- Tie-ins with nearly all the commercial on-line services and Internet access providers to make its browser the standard tool to surf the net.

As I write, the impact of Microsoft's huge web investment and development programme has not fully come to fruition but the signs are positive.

'People aren't asking anymore if Microsoft will be killed by the Internet but whether and when Microsoft will dominate the Internet.'

(Gartner Group Inc. research)

'I can't think of one corporation that has had this kind of success and after 20 years just stopped and decided to reinvent itself from the ground up.' (Dreamworks)

'Our competitors were laughing, said our network was a fake
Saw the Internet economy as simply theirs to take
They'll regret the fateful day
The sleeping giant did awake
We embrace and we extend!' (Verse II of Microsoft battle hymn)

Only with this commitment, this extraordinary determination, can any organisation expect to achieve any enduring success. Only in this way will it either anticipate the market changes and be first in, the pioneer of new products and services, or will it be able to effectively catch up and come from behind and still emerge a winner.

As the commentators on this Microsoft story point out, this sort of commitment is surprisingly unusual. But there is no reason in principle why any organisation large or small cannot put its best resources and dedicated energies together to build its chosen path in the best way to stay ahead in the market.

Indeed the simple demonstration of this total commitment can by itself be a competitive weapon. As Brian Arthur, Professor of Economics at Stanford, has recently pointed out:[6]

'Rivals will back off in a market not only if it is locked in but if they *believe* it will be locked in by someone else. Hence we see psychological jockeying in the form of . . . threatened alliances, technological preening . . . this posturing . . . discourages competitors from taking on a potentially dominant rival.'

Future chapters explore and illustrate more precisely what the model means by commitment, and what is actually required for an organisation to become effectively and competitively committed.

The four prime axes of competitive advantage – the second dimension

Turning now to the second dimension of the market commitment model, this contains the four prime axes or forms of competitive advantage. Together they provide a comprehensive set of strategic options for a company looking to translate its commitment into an enduring and effective strategy in the market place. See Figure 5.1 repeated here. All four forms of advantage are mutually compatible and reinforcing, combining superior performance of the product or service, sold at the most leveraged price, with extraordinary levels of service hustle and compelling emotional values.

In some industry situations it will be possible to achieve effective advantage along one axis only; in other situations an organisation may need to work along more than one axis simultaneously and sometimes along all four axes to provide a sufficiently differentiated competitive

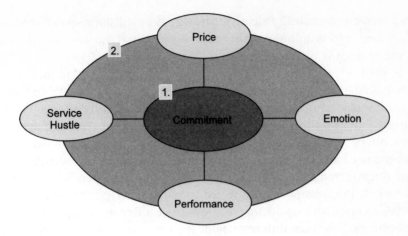

Figure 5.1

offering to its customers. The principle is that all four must be considered and evaluated and opportunities developed and pursued wherever it may add to competitiveness and significantly influence customer purchasing.

Let us briefly define more clearly what advantage each of these axes represents. Subsequent chapters more fully describe how to best apply these opportunities to deliver the most competitive strategy in the market place. (The market commitment model applies equally to products and services. The term 'product' will frequently, however, be used in the broader sense to refer to both products and services.)

Price

Price, not cost. Be market-driven, not asset-driven. The customer cares less about relative cost positions, so we're not going to talk about cost-leadership or operational excellence. We will avoid the old asset-led approaches. Instead we will be customer-oriented and market-based.

The customer cares about the price of the product. Sometimes pricing will be the critical driver of a customer's decision-making. At other times the price will be a component part of a broader customer value-based proposition.

Pricing does not have to be the lowest price; it could be any differentiated or validated pricing proposition, including deliberate premium pricing. But it's a long-term proposition, not something short-term and tactical. Pricing as strategy is establishing something on a consistent and continuous basis that signals how the customer should perceive what is offered.

Fujitsu, Daewoo and Aldi, for example, deliberately plan and target low-priced, price sensitive customer segments. They clearly establish what their singular competitive proposition is and consistently address what a targeted set of customers need. Direct Line cuts out brokers and agencies and offers lower-priced insurance, Private label suppliers avoid heavy advertising and marketing costs to provide lower-priced foods, apparel and other merchandise. All have established and consistently stick with a particular Price proposition directed to particular types of customers.

Such companies competing on low price often have no meaningful product performance differentiation, their service is not typically better than others and their branding is not the principal reason consumers buy. It is their recognisable low relative price position that is the fundamental form driving their business success

But it's not just about 'low price'. At another level, Marks & Spencer's strategy is based on a price value proposition which also combines quality + service (in our model's language, performance and service hustle). For M&S, all three forms of potential advantage need to work harmoniously together to provide and sustain its lasting and successful market position.

At another level still, Chanel, Armani, Rolls-Royce cars, Marlboro and others can adopt leading premium-pricing strategies. This is often without any meaningful product performance or service advantage but is linked into a more established recognition and set of values that these items can successfully command a relatively high and premium price.

Whichever of the paths is pursued, 'strategic pricing' often forms a necessary and fundamental part of any lasting and successful proposition in the market place. It helps establish the product's long-term value, overriding shorter-term competitive pressures. Surprisingly, too few companies treat pricing in this way but there is significant opportunity, as we shall see, in thinking and developing pricing more effectively.

Emotion

A new discovery! How can it be that all other strategy models have overlooked and ignored this extraordinary and compelling source of competitive advantage. Why choose Coca-Cola or Shell Oil or Canon copiers or Rubbermaid housewares or Citibank or Nokia? Why does ICI Dulux still have market leadership today when its paint performs without noticeable advantage versus its rivals? Why does Heinz babyfood outsell all competitors?

In these ever more competitive times, when many products are becoming increasingly commodity-like in performance, Emotion or the E-factor may be the only true distinguishing element. And many companies are beginning to recognise the value and opportunity that lies in this direction and in exploiting their E-values.

As we shall discover when we consider the third dimension of the model, this emotion-based form of advantage often builds off a degree of recognition or Branding, an historic track record of reliable reputation and trust. At other times it may simply be a reflection of fashionable, contemporary styles and designs such as the Swatch watch, the Filofax or a new TVR car model.

It is also important to point out at this early stage of description and definition, that 'emotion' is not an advantage confined only to consumer goods or service companies. It is a viable strategic option available to any organisation in any industry and we shall describe later for example how in chemicals, Du Pont, and in microprocessor chips, Intel, have set benchmark standards in developing the emotional values of their product offerings to provide a vital and additional source of competitive advantage.

Performance

This can represent the most physical and tangible form of advantage. Its core is about the basic functionality and reliability of a product – does it do the job it's supposed to do well and better than its rivals? Does the tyre provide better road-holding, does the drug treat the illness more effectively, is the crisp or potato chip crispier?

Performance in its elemental form is about this basic quality of the product/service being offered. It needs to perform at the essential functional level – does it do its principal job better in the customer's eyes than others? It also needs to do this consistently and reliably. Customers must be able to trust in the product doing its basic job and not letting them down. To be successful this minimum performance threshold is increasingly a *sine qua non*.

But in some industries now, such as transportation, financial services, and utilities, performance on the basics has reached a plateau and in the customer's eyes the product is often more commodity-like. In these situations, if companies don't push proactively themselves to find new ways to improve their product then their customers will drive them to it. Customers are now so demanding and discriminating that in some areas they simply assume the basics will be provided and have raised their expectations looking for something more. They are shifting their attention to broader more contemporary aspects of what the product can do. They're demanding a revolution in the levels of product performance being offered. The product must go beyond the basics and the focus is now especially on doing its job 'even more quickly' or being even easier to use to make the customer's life 'still more convenient'!

The emphasis now, in a number of industry sectors, is moving to performance 'speed' and performance 'convenience'. This is the new focus of customer and competitor interest. And where companies are still struggling with the basics, pressure is growing on them to fix those quickly, deliver them with total efficiency and now go on to play in the new, more value-added game.

This revolution in performance expectations has significant implications for how companies compete. Understanding the broader strategic potential in this area is going to be a vital part of using and applying the market commitment model.

We can find an illustration of this with one of our 'admired' companies, Procter & Gamble. For many years P&G was able to rely principally on the superior functionality of its products as its basic strategy in the market place. Backed up by heavy advertising and communication, P&G's 'washed whiter', 'cleans better', 'gets rid of dandruff more effectively' were persuasive customer propositions in their own right. A whole postwar generation grew up with P&G's side-by-side 'washes whiter' product demonstrations on television. This clear product performance competitiveness was convincing and often propelled the company's products to market leadership. But competitors, especially Unilever, caught up, the basic product performance differences on a number of products became much narrower, if even noticeable by consumers. To stay ahead, P&G has had to move on. It has looked for new types of performance advantage which are not based purely on the product's basic functionality. It has targeted new opportunities that better reflect and respond to consumers' search and emphasis on things being 'more convenient, easier and quicker to use'. So P&G's new Wash and Go shampoo specifically combines shampoo and conditioner in a contemporary style and in 'an easy-to-use one wash only' formula. The emphasis now is all about speed and convenience. When the product was launched it shot to market leadership.

Service Hustle

Service is no longer enough. I shall call it Hustle. What is the basis of success for the likes of McDonald's, British Airways, USAA, Nordstrom, Caltex (the Texaco Chevron joint venture), Ritz Carlton and UPS. It is not just customer service. It is extraordinary hustle. It is going beyond customers' expectations and creating levels of service and standards that had not been imagined.

When British Airways cabin crew carried out a life-saving operation on one of its passengers mid-Atlantic in 1995, it simply reinforced its reputation for doing everything that could possibly be done to serve and help its customers. Would any other airline have had the capabilities to harness the resources required so quickly to deal with a customer in that emergency?

It's about establishing a relationship with your customer that goes beyond the immediate transaction but builds into achieving a life-time commitment from that customer to work together with you to find mutual advantage and satisfaction. In highly competitive situations it can make the difference in customer purchasing behaviour, it can encourage the customer to stick with you even if your product/service offering is a little higher priced or performs marginally less well than a competitor's. So, for example, Honeywell beat Litton in a long competitive fight supplying navigation equipment products for the airline industry.[7] Its strategy – to 'assiduously court its customers' – provided the platform to enable it to continue to win orders, even when its products were no better than its rivals. In the same vein, First Direct Bank though it competes in the crowded, largely undifferentiated financial services sector, so understands its customer that it is able to consistently provide what the customer wants, when they want it, and in a form the customer prefers better than its rivals. Call up First Direct for yourself and experience the unusual pleasure of actually being satisfied in dealing with your bank and even in paying your bills!

When a company is really very good at doing that it's hard to beat!

The underlying sources of competitive advantage – the third dimension

The third dimension completes the market commitment model. It goes beyond the prime strategies of service hustle, price, emotion and performance. It sets out with greater specificity what the underlying sources of advantage may be. It provides the more detailed opportunities on which the strategy can be more particularly based.

It is deliberately more specific. It is intended to address the cry of strategy makers for a model which can be more practical to use and more obviously engage and challenge line managers in the organisation.

In practice I have found it provides a comprehensive set of underlying options. Again there may be some industry situations which are not covered here, but I would expect them to be the exception. Even with such exceptions the principal underlying sources of advantage are captured and described in this third dimension and should still form the basis and starting point for any specific strategy making investigation.

At this introductory stage, let's take one area of this third dimension of the model by way of example, referring to Figure 5.2. We will explore them all in detail in subsequent chapters. With 'Service Hustle', the four underlying sources that are defined represent the most powerful customer service strategies.

- **Comprehensive** – 'whatever I want'.
- **Available** – 'wherever/whenever I want it'.
- **Personalised** – 'tailored just for me'.
- **Symbiotic** – provided in a context of an enduring, mutually beneficial relationship.

Some organisations will be outstandingly better than their rivals in all four areas. For others, success in just one area may be sufficient. So leading hotel groups such as Ritz Carlton and Marriott, and leading airlines such as British Airways, Singapore Airlines and Southwest Airlines each push hard down the Comprehensive and Available options to demonstrate superiority. On the other hand USAA and, increasingly, Levi's exploit their systems and skills to focus on providing a 'Personalised service' tailored for each customer's different needs. And companies like Lucas Varity, Echlin, GKN and Rockwell put enormous investment and resources into working so closely and collaboratively with their automotive customers that they become joined almost umbilically as one entity working to each other's mutual, Symbiotic advantage.

We shall describe and illustrate the underlying sources of this third dimension in more detail in later chapters. But the greater specificity in the market commitment model is important. It is trying to point out for the first time in one model a more comprehensive view of strategy making. It is not just about commitment and advantage, it's not just about an overall strategy founded in performance or price. Companies must go on and find the most specific articulation of the advantage they are going to pursue in the market with a particular set of customers.

71

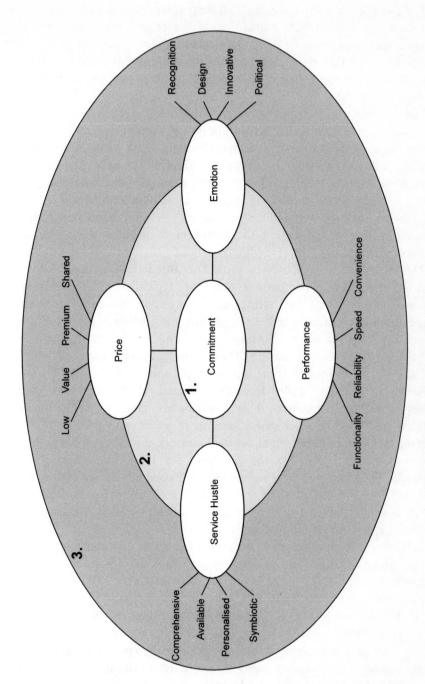

Figure 5.2 The market commitment model – in detail

The more specific the company's strategy the greater the motivation it can have upon the whole workforce of the organisation. It starts to provide that clear sense of direction – where are we going, what are we trying to do better than anyone else, what should be our operating priorities, what targets should we set, what's the core proposition in front of our customers?

For too long, many companies have failed to define precisely what their principal form of competitive advantage is. Yet winning organisations, by rigour and discipline and developed insight, have articulated their strategy and how they intend to win clearly and precisely. The market commitment model is intended to encourage that. Better committed than hesitant, better specific than vague, better clear plan and direction than relying on luck or the failings of others, better precise convincing communication and direction to employees than vacuous ambiguous mission statements.

There is plenty of evidence to show how this long-term commitment and this specificity of competitive advantage typically lie at the heart of successful companies. Their strategies reflect and incorporate these core building blocks. Let us consider the top ten 'most admired corporations' in the US from the annual *Fortune* survey[8] and see the extent to which their strategies reflect and capture these identified core strategy elements.

Table 5.1 takes four of these top 10 corporations and briefly lays out their stated strategies, taken from their annual reports, interviews and other working documents. It is immediately clear that they have established properly developed strategies as we have defined here. We can see their commitment, what are their strategic intentions, what is their future direction, what are the priorities for the organisation going forward. These are powerful statements of chosen advantage and future intent. Other top ten admired corporations such as Procter & Gamble, Intel, Hewlett Packard and Microsoft all describe their strategies in similarly clear and committed ways.

P&G looks to develop all four forms of possible strategic advantage, with especial emphasis and priority on the emotional driving force of its brands:

'1. expand our line-up of global brands and their recognition among consumers;
2. strengthen our ability to deliver breakthrough product innovation;
3. achieve extraordinary levels of cost effectiveness in order to meet demands for good value pricing;
4. work more effectively to build customer loyalty.'

Table 5.1 The market commitment model in practice

Top 10 most admired US corporations (examples)	1. Commitment	2. Prime forms of competitive advantages – priorities as stated	3. Underlying sources of that advantage – priorities as stated
Coca-Cola	'We have grown through a consistency in our approach.' 'We have momentum because we continue to remain disciplined and focused, no matter what the external environment might be.' 'We understand the universe of our business.'	*Emotion:* 'Make our brands clearly distinctive in every respect from every other item on the shelf, so as not to rely on price but to create value so people will pay more for it.'	*Recognition* of brand values. *Design* the 'famous contour bottle design.'
Rubbermaid	'43 years of consecutive sales growth in the same core product areas.'	*Performance:* 'focus on innovative new products of superior quality to improve living standards.' *Emotion:* 'develop and maintain the best recognised brands.'	*Functionality, Reliability and Convenience* 'products that are strong, reliable and are e.g. labour saving.'
Motorola	'Our future vision is a wireless revolution in the way people communicate and we will build on our technology platforms and invest as never before to maintain our position as the largest provider in the world.' 'We have increased our R&D investment every year for the past 20 years.'	*Performance:* 'leading quality products built on our core competencies.'	*Functionality and Reliability* 'our Six Sigma quality initiative has been a driving force in achieving competitive leadership.'
UPS	'Continuous investment in new technology to provide constantly better customer service ($1.1bn over next 5 years).' 'We will set the new standard for package distribution.'	*Performance + Service Hustle:* 'build on a basis of operations efficiency and reliability.' 'not just in the delivery business but in the customer satisfaction business.'	*Reliability + Speed* 'comprehensive information & tracking to ensure fast and timely delivery.' *Comprehensive + Available* 'Substantial investment to provide new customer services and delivery when the customer wants it.'

Hewlett Packard focuses more singlemindedly on its products' performance:

> 'create information products that accelerate the advancement of knowledge and improve the effectiveness of people and organisation . . . do this through higher performing products (that are totally reliable and effective) on the back of new product research and innovation . . . and exploring fresh ways to apply existing and new technologies.'

As we begin to describe successful companies' strategies we can not only identify some of the strengths of these strategies, we can also begin to see how the market commitment model easily and comfortably captures and encapsulates the different strategic options that companies must choose from and select for themselves in going forward.

The model can be much more specific than Porter's three generic strategies, for example, or the three alternative value disciplines of Treacy and Wiersema. It can prompt and guide and suggest with much more precision. It can generally offer a reliable and comprehensive tool for strategy development and advantage.

                              *   *   *

Before concluding this introductory chapter to the model, we can bring it further to life by describing a very real competitive battle that is even now still taking place, and in doing so further illustrate the practical applicability of the market commitment model. I'd like to examine the decades-old competitive fight between the two global consumer goods giants – Unilever and Procter & Gamble.

If we take their soap powder battle, especially over the past ten years, we can see how each company has – in effect – moved around the model in search of new sources of competitive advantage as market and competitive conditions have evolved. Both P&G and Unilever historically sought advantage along certainly three of the four axes, working on Performance, 'Emotion' brand values and Price to find the most competitive total market proposition.

If we had compared their relative competitive position in 1985, customer research would have shown them fairly equally appreciated and both competing along the same three axes as shown in Figure 5.3. Product performance was effective and reliable, there was a high degree of branding generating instant recognition and strong identity, with the whole effectively packaged at the premium end of the soap-powder sector. Neither company was putting any particular emphasis or effort in the service hustle area.

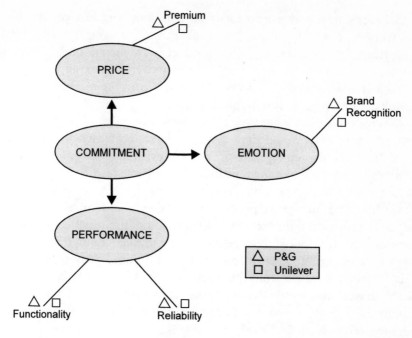

Figure 5.3 The model applied to Unilever and Procter & Gamble, 1985

Between 1985 and 1995 a competitive battle of extraordinary dimensions broke out. First, private labels began to emerge as a serious threat, especially in the UK with Sainsbury's Novon brand claiming similar performance levels at a lower price. Second, packaging innovation and product reformulations led to different forms of the product being introduced; for example liquid cleaning in concentrated form in easier to carry, and pour packaging. Suddenly a new source of differentiation and advantage opened up for the first time in terms of performance convenience and ease of use. But just as these product innovations might have been expected to allow Unilever and P&G to further reinforce their competitive strength and market positions, private labels began undermining that with aggressive pricing that challenged the premium position of the two giants.

P&G's principle response was to cut its own standard price aggressively, reducing its price on Tide (as well as other products) in the USA by 15 per cent in 1993. It also began working much more closely with its customers, looking to establish more substantial and mutually rewarding relationships with major accounts like WalMart on the back of new techniques in supply chain management and stock and ordering (which P&G called efficient consumer response).

Unilever's response was to focus on continued product performance innovation, coming out with 'Persil Power' in the UK in 1994. Unfortunately for Unilever, this product was shown under extreme washing conditions to be potentially too powerful, risking damage to clothes. It subsequently had to be withdrawn from the market just a few months after a high profile public launch.

As a result of this manoeuvring for competitive advantage, the market commitment model would show a very different customer-driven picture in 1996, with the emergence of serious private label competition a significant influence as shown in Figure 5.4. These leading soap powder organisations have searched around the market for new sources of competitive advantage as product performance and other differences began to erode. In doing so they have been, and are, in effect exploring the prime forms of advantage defined in the market commitment model. They have opened up new advantages in performance convenience which private labels have not fully matched. But P&G uniquely has pursued both service hustle and 'value' price leadership while Unilever has continued to fight on more traditional product performance and brand/emotion grounds.

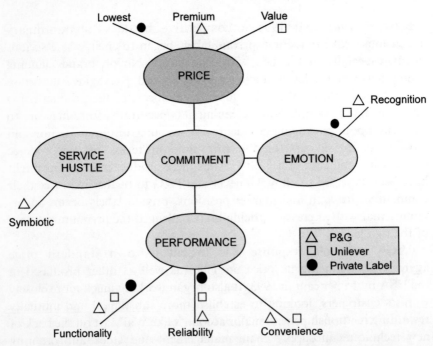

Figure 5.4 The model applied to Unilever and Procter & Gamble, 1996

Who will win this war? One thing is for certain – no two companies can demonstrate greater commitment to their core product areas than P&G and Unilever. Both organisations have established leading positions in soap powder around the world over many years, have continued to invest heavily and have shown an extraordinary ability to extract premium value out of an otherwise basic commodity product.

At this stage the slight favourite to win out may be P&G who have begun to develop a more complete competitive strategy, exploring all four forms of possible advantage to find those items of difference that can maintain value and influence both distributor and end-user purchasing.

The great advantage of beginning to use the model in this way is that companies can start identifying and measuring where they are competitively. A company can plot its competitive advantage relative to competitors. And it is possible to do this in a dynamic way showing how the competitive position is changing and even what is the future trend. We shall talk more of this later but a company can, in effect, work with the model to measure its competitive advantage gaps (its CAGs). It can determine how big the gaps are and whether they are significant enough to establish more recognised value with customers and sufficient to influence and switch customer purchasing.

For example, Unilever could work with a selective sample of customers to measure and score its levels of brand recognition and other forms of intended advantage versus the other brands in the market. In 1985, Unilever's Persil might certainly have equalled, if not outscored, P&G's major brand on positive emotional values and beaten private label products easily. By 1996, after its Persil Power failure, its Emotion CAG would likely have slipped noticeably and its Product Performance scores with customers may have reduced. Measuring these changes in how customers rated the product competitively and what are its CAG scores would begin to provide a quantitative basis for measuring competitiveness and customer-perceived value differences in the market place. It would immediately identify actions required to address any disadvantage or exploit any advantage. It could also highlight when there is a new axis of advantage, previously left unexploited, that a competitor like P&G is now busily pursuing as well.

The model becomes a live instrument of analysis. Its value can go beyond the identification of the best strategy. It can actually be used to monitor and measure relative competitiveness through regular research and analysis with customers. CAGs in a company's favour are the signs of success, indications that the product or service in its leading form is working, that there is a customer-recognised platform that can be built on and invested in to stretch that CAG so far that a competitor cannot easily catch up. Of course where the CAG analysis highlights a significant disadvantage, it is time for urgent strategic review and remedial action. (This measurement of competitiveness and advantage is discussed in more detail in Chapter 13.)

In this way, the market commitment model can go beyond strategy making. It can, as we have begun to illustrate, assist also in effective strategy realisation.

Because it is a relatively simple tool there is a greater opportunity for strategy makers to use it easily in practice. If this model can act to stimulate active strategic thinking in a company, then it will have been an effective catalyst. If it can also be institutionalised and adopted widely through the organisation, then a company might truly begin to realise the benefits of effective strategy making driving the direction and energies of the company into the future.

Addendum

I have chosen certain words and concepts for the Market Commitment model quite deliberately, born out of research and empirical observation. Some of them are immediately familiar, have been written and illustrated by many others and strike a knowing chord in all of us. We all know or think we know for example what service, price and performance mean. Most will be less familiar with 'hustle' or 'emotion'. We can read the specific definition offered but it can sometimes be hard to quickly internalise and embrace new concepts without other reference points and perspectives, without time to think about the ideas and see what they mean for each of us and so build our own understanding and interpretation.

For this reason I would urge the reader to be patient if some of the language used in the market commitment model appears unfamiliar or unconventional. Some will immediately recognise their own company's competitive position and the strategic opportunities it is pursuing. Their organisations will likely be using similar market and customer-rooted language and concepts. For others, perhaps used to a more traditional or asset-led approach to strategy, it may not be apparent at first sight where their company would fit on the model and so they may question how it should be applied to them.

The next few chapters aim to bring the market commitment model to life and put strategy thinking firmly in a late 1990s market and customer context. The aim is to explain these concepts and, with illustration and case study help define what they could mean for each and every organisation. We will explore how winning companies interpret these ideas and use them to drive their own strategy making. By immersing ourselves in understanding the model, the specific concepts should begin to clarify and provide a more rounded and up-to-date understanding of the strategic options that can drive a company's success.

6 Commitment: The Long-Term View

At the heart of the new model lies commitment (Figure 6.1). It's the stuff that successful companies are made of. It is the underpinning for lasting corporate success. It is hard to develop. It requires enormous determination and great leadership to gather the necessary understanding, set the long-term goal, convince others and then institutionalise it through the organisation. Once established, however, it provides the strength and momentum that, come what may, this organisation – like Microsoft for example – will have the best chance to win out and dominate its markets.

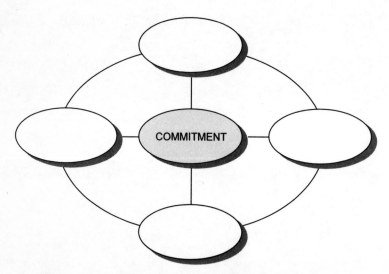

Figure 6.1 Commitment in the market commitment model

We described two key elements to effective commitment:

1 Developing a deep-rooted immersion in the market with customers.
2 Establishing the long-term horizon and determination to win.

In this chapter and the next I review each of these two elements and what it takes to become effectively 'committed'. The first element provides the basic market grounding and input, but I'd like to start in this chapter with the second. It provides more of a macro-overview and illustration of successful and totally committed organisations. It sets up more of the context before getting into the more micro-understanding of the detail and specifics of individual markets.

In terms of establishing the long-term horizon and determination to win, there are four success factors that lie behind this and characterise the successful committed company:

- Take a minimum 5 to 10-year view of market opportunities.
- Set clear measurable targets.
- 'Stick with it'.
- Focus.

We can explore each of these in turn and demonstrate what are the benchmarks and best practices for commitment in each of these areas.

Take a minimum 5- to 10-year view of market opportunities

Some relatively well-known examples and research highlight the power and importance of establishing the longer-term horizon:

- 'Our goal is to democratise the automobile.'[1]

    (Henry Ford, early 1900s)

- A hallmark of Nestle's success is to take a long-term view. 'The purchase of Rowntree must be seen as part of our long-term strategy. I'd have liked to have paid less but this was a decision made for the next 100 years', commented Nestle's CEO Helmut Maucher in a recent interview. 'We're in it to win the war, not necessarily every battle.'[2]

- 'I think in terms of decades', Michael Eisner CEO of Walt Disney stated in 1990. 'We've already figured out what we can do for 1997 and we've got longer-term plans set for 2005 . . . among other things our goal is to double the current numbers of visitors to Disney theme parks and we know what investment we require to get there.'[3]

- 'There is some pressure, even on a company like Boeing, to manage quarter by quarter but we just ignore the market noise and get on with our job.'[4]
(Boeing CEO Frank Shrontz)

- 'We want to become the most powerful, most serviceable, the most far-reaching world financial institution that has ever been.'[5]
(City Bank (now Citicorp) in 1915)

- 'Stocks outperform the market on announcements of long-term strategic investments.'[6]
(research conclusion by Professor Woolridge at Pennsylvania State University and by others)

There are numerous examples of successful organisations expressly taking a deliberate long-term view of their markets, and through their understanding setting stakes in the ground for the future. Many of these long-term players have been investigated in some detail and I'd like to focus on one particular piece of research describing their success which we considered briefly in the first chapter.

In 1990, Collins and Porras identified organisations that were widely admired, regarded as the premier institution in their industry, and who had impressed with their enduring quality and prosperity.[7] They described them as visionary companies who had set 'big hairy goals', audacious goals 'that – like Henry Ford's – were always long term and sometimes decades away from being realised.' But they were born out of a deep-rooted understanding of market opportunities.

The companies identified in this research included many of today's leading US organisations such as Hewlett Packard, Procter & Gamble, Merck and Motorola. All these organisations, the research shows, had made lasting long-term commitments to win out in their market place. The result was that these companies outperformed the stock market by over 15 times over the researched period of 1926 to 1990. Whereas $1 invested in a general market stock fund in the US in 1926 would have grown to over $400 by 1990, a $1 invested in these long-term visionary companies would have grown to over $6000 during the same period!

The key factor among these winning companies appears to have been 'a remarkable resiliency' over time in working at achieving their goals in the market place despite the twists and turns of market and competitive conditions.

Merck, for example, established a long-term plan to become the 'pre-eminent drug maker world-wide supported by substantial R&D'. Merck determined to build the best research capability in the industry to find breakthrough drugs, and went to extraordinary lengths to establish the most outstanding research centres and gather the best people in their field. Though by the mid-1980s Merck had achieved its main goal, the company unhesitatingly set yet new commitments for itself in the market. It targeted itself to become 'the first drug maker with advanced research in every disease category'. More recently, it has set new targets yet again with its $6 billion acquisition of Medco to solidify its distribution and strengthen its position with its end customers.[8]

If we look at Hewlett Packard, we see an organisation which had achieved tremendous success through the 1980s especially, but by 1990 it felt the need to reinvigorate its long-term plans in the market to reflect the changing market circumstances. Hewlett Packard went through a process asking: 'staying with our core strategy what can we do in the future better than anyone else?'

Hewlett Packard's now well-known position is summarised as '$HP = MC^2$' – to become leaders in the fields of measurement (M), computing (C) and communications (C) and the best at exploiting the cross-market cross-customer opportunities that the combination of these skills can bring.

Over the next five years following its 1990 review, Hewlett Packard doubled the number of product launches in its target M, C and C arenas, boosted earnings growth and transformed its PC operation from market laggard to become the second-fastest grower behind Compaq. As one inside commentator put it, 'Over time HP has sometimes needed a kick but we've had the same basic strategy and once we know where we're going there's years of experience driving things on.'[9]

This same research by Collins and Porras has also dramatised the advantages that come through long-term commitment by drawing comparisons between the 'committed' and the 'uncommitted' in the same industry, between the visionary and the near-sighted, between those who have become industry leaders versus those who are now just following on.

Examples of these comparisons include:

Boeing	vs	McDonnell Douglas
Citicorp	vs	Chase Manhattan
GE	vs	Westinghouse
Johnson & Johnson	vs	Bristol Myers Squibb
Marriott	vs	Howard Johnson
Philip Morris	vs	R. J. Reynolds

So while GE was talking about 'becoming no. 1 or no. 2 in each market it serves', Westinghouse for many years never seemed to move beyond vague statements about total quality or being 'technology-driven'. Equally, while R. J. Reynolds appeared to rest on its laurels as the then market leader, Philip Morris was targeting itself to become the 'General Motors of the tobacco industry and dominate world markets', even though at the time of this declaration it was the no. 6 player in its market with a share only a little over 5 per cent.

These more committed long-term players have also demonstrated a much greater appetite for continuous and significant investment than their more near-sighted rivals. **All** the more committed have outspent their rivals in research and development (indeed Merck's rate of investment in R&D for many years was an average 30 per cent higher on a percentage of sales basis). In addition they have shown a history of greater reinvestment of earnings for growth at rates of often two or three times their closest rival.

The success of companies like Merck, Hewlett Packard, Boeing and others provides compelling evidence of the need and value of taking the long-term perspective. It also challenges the view that short-term market pressures make such long-term commitments impossible, and that the only way to boost the share price is to keep pushing up next quarter's earnings.

This common perception – that the stock market in fact penalises long-term investment – is strongly challenged when confronted by evidence from a number of extensive market studies clearly showing that this is not the case:

1. A detailed study in 1985 across a sample of 658 companies in a range of industries concluded that share prices in fact rose when major capital expenditure programmes were announced, and in like manner there were significant decreases in market value when companies showed their planned capital expenditures were decreasing.[10]
2. A more recent study by Kalchas drew the same set of conclusions. UK companies like Tesco, BP and Reuters that announced major capital and investment programmes over future years saw their share price rerated upwards. On the other hand, companies like Grand Metropolitan, Christian Salvesen and Forte who failed to match sales growth with capital investment saw their share price downgraded.[11]
3. Further research in the mid-1980s by Randall Woolridge at Pennsylvania State University concluded, 'the consistently positive

stock market reaction to announcements of various types of corporate strategic investment decisions provides significant support for the proposition that these announcements are interpreted by investors as managerial decisions with expected positive net present value.'[12]

4. Finally, research in the late 1980s by Professor Rappaport of Northwestern University's Kellogg school sought to determine what percentage of a company's stock price is based on its long-term prospects. They examined the difference between the stock price and the present value of dividends expected by investors within the next five years. This study found the next five-year dividend stream did not account for all the stock price. It revealed a difference in every case and showed how, typically, the present value of the next five-years' dividends only accounted for around 20 per cent or less of the market value. The excess therefore had to reflect the longer-term payout anticipated by investors and it was typically market leading companies, as illustrated in Table 6.1, that enjoyed the highest long-term prospects rating.[13]

Table 6.1 Long-term value and expectations in stock prices

Company	Stock price at date of research	Present value of next 5-years' dividends	% of stock price due to long-term prospects
Boeing	$67.00	$7.23	89.2%
Procter & Gamble	$84.50	$11.44	86.5%
United Technologies	$42.00	$6.52	84.5%
Philip Morris	$97.25	$19.95	79.5%
AT&T	$27.50	$4.89	82.2%

Source: Alcar Group.

Perhaps it is less surprising then that companies who do buck the short-term market pressures and invest – consistently – do emerge as eventual long-term winners.

Indeed, a key characteristic of America's most admired corporations, as surveyed by *Fortune* each year, is their longer-term value to investors. Unsurprisingly, the more committed companies with long-term investment horizons – Microsoft, Hewlett Packard, Coca-Cola, Procter & Gamble – all figure consistently and strongly on the most-admired list.

Set clear measurable targets

'Before this decade is out, this Nation should commit itself to achieving the goal of landing a man on the moon and returning him safely to earth.'[14]

'Make my little Newport store the best, most profitable variety store in Arkansas over the next five years.'[15]

'Become as respected in 20 years as Hewlett Packard is today.'[16]

'Become no. 1 or no. 2 in every market we serve and revolutionise this company to have the speed and agility of a small enterprise.'[17]

'Become the world's largest passenger carrier over the next 10 years.'[18]

What President Kennedy, Sam Walton, Dean Watkins, Jack Welch and Colin Marshall and many others have done is to set out clear demanding long-term goals. Despite all the uncertainties of the future they put a stake in the ground as to what their organisation and resources should strive for. These weren't wild ideas. They were born of an understanding of their market places, of the way technology was developing and of the opportunities that arose. They were the far-reaching statements of future intent developed by true leaders. They realised that great success might only come by setting clear measurable targets and time frames to engender the will and commitment to making it happen.

Establishing the target and time frame is the action that keeps commitment grounded in reality. It has to be stretching, but still just about feasible and achievable. It becomes the catalyst for planning and investment and provides a milestone to work towards. Without this tangible expression of direction and intent it's too easy to keep postponing progress or to feel unconcerned if a year has gone by with little achieved. But such an act of boldness and daring can fuse together the various resources and energies in the company and channel them to work towards a defined goal.

Over the past few years companies have generally been quick to set cost reduction targets, but have been much slower in setting out future growth plans and goals. A recent *Wall Street Journal* article commented that after years of downsizing, 'executives are finding it hard' to set growth targets, uncomfortable with putting stakes in the ground into an uncertain future.[19] But there is no doubt in anyone's mind as to the value of identifying the cost reduction and re-engineering goals and time frames as specifically as possible to provide a focus and catalyst for the organisation. So too with future strategies; strategy makers and other senior executives must get into the mind-set of Sam Walton and others and search restlessly to find and define these more compelling strategic targets.

'Stick with it'

This is just as critical as the previous two commitment factors but in some ways the most challenging. This is because the rate and the pace of change in the market place is constantly rising, and companies are more frequently being confronted with uncertainty and unpredictability threatening to blow them off course.

We will, however, start with our champion of constancy and determination no matter what the challenges – Microsoft. What Microsoft has set out to do has won plaudits from many commentators who see their coming-from-behind investment plans to gain control of Internet-related software as a benchmark for future companies to look to. Of course such constancy to stick with it is hard, and there will be many doubters as to the success of the chosen course, but if we understand the markets and customers well enough – as most investors believe Bill Gates and his team now do – then we can find the greater confidence and certainty to continue.

Three examples illustrate well this third commitment success factor. These come from Seagate, Amoco and Sun Microsystems all of whom are hitting the headlines at the time of writing this book.

- Amoco discovered purified terephthalic acid or PTA from which polyester is made in the 1960s and has been building its market position in it ever since. The company currently controls 37 per cent of the 12 million tons per year global market. Amoco has recently announced its renewed commitment to this market place. It targets to double revenues within just four years, and plans to invest one-third of its $5 billion annual capital expenditure into PTA and related products.

  'No oil company is spending more aggressively' commented First Boston analysts. 'PTA has been developed by Amoco as one of the best options and they keep pushing hard with expansion to stay ahead of competition.'[20]
- For more than a decade, Scott McNealy of Sun Microsystems 'shouted himself hoarse' preaching the gospel of network computing.

Since the Internet explosion, Sun's mantra 'the Network is the computer' has finally caught on and businesses are falling over themselves to tap into Sun's products and expertise.

McNealy required plenty of staying power because by the early 1990s Sun's engineering work-stations still had only a small share of mainstream office computers, and sales and profits were flat. But now McNealy's vision of what customers would need and how the market would have to respond has been realized. His commitment to success with his plan has been proved right and Sun's stock after years of going nowhere tripled in twelve months.

Sun's Internet software Java has been adopted by all the leading names in computing, by Netscape, database leader Oracle Systems, by IBM and most recently by Microsoft themselves, and Sun now finds itself the centre of the computer universe – a total vindication of McNealy's foresight and determination to stick with his goal: 'The network has at last won out, the stand-alone PC is a time-waster.'[21]

- With $1.5m in start-up capital, Al Shugart entered the small disk-drive market for PCs back in 1978 and founded Seagate. While initially the company grew quickly with the growth in PCs in the early 1980s, brutal price wars nearly bankrupted the company. In addition, one of Shugart's partners left to set up Conner Peripherals in competition and took a great deal of business in the short term away from Seagate by linking up a distribution deal with Compaq. Conner soared and avoided heavy capital investment by outsourcing and assembling the various disk-drive component parts.

  However, Shugart was convinced that what was important was to build strong relationships with key customers and felt that through vertical integration he could control quality and service levels. And when PC demand truly exploded in 1991–2, it was Seagate that was able to keep up with demand and maintain service with immediate product availability. Meanwhile Conner, relying on outsourced suppliers, struggled to get all the necessary components. In 1995 Seagate bought Conner. 'It is a reward for Shugart's guts and how he saw the market. He was going to see it all the way through to the bottom of the ninth'. Revenues soared 104 per cent to $9.2bn and profits surged 130 per cent to $600m. Wall Street now trades Seagate stock at a multiple nearly double that of similar rivals. Shugart has driven Seagate from its early 1978 days with a consistent view of the market so that it now dominates disk-drives worldwide with an estimated 33 per cent market share.

Looking beyond these specific examples, a wider survey of the value and importance of sticking with it was carried out by *Fortune* magazine at periodic intervals through the 1980s.[22] They looked at companies who had averaged at least a 20 per cent return on stockholder's equity over the decade to 1983, and had maintained at least a 15 per cent return – consistently – through each year.

Fortune could find only eight companies in the top 500 who could meet this criteria **and** were still meeting this criteria five years later in 1988. The eight companies?

- Merck
- Coca-Cola
- American Home Products
- Dow Jones
- Kellogg
- Deluxe Cheque Printers
- Worthington
- Nalco

The analysis of this long-term and enduring success came down to one key feature which appeared to characterise all eight companies – 'persistent market penetration'. All the companies had set out to occupy core market positions and **over time** to dominate them.

Focus

The final commitment success factor is focus. Much has been written about 'sticking to your knitting' and focusing on core businesses, but it is important to review some of the more recent research and examples to illustrate the values of focus in our commitment context.

Kalchas recently conducted a survey of the top 500 UK and US corporations to determine 'what is the value of focus'.[23] There are numerous examples of companies without focus who have failed. But, more positively, can focus actually be shown to add value?

To test this we wanted to see if there is any relationship between the number of different businesses a company is operating and its success. We were looking to find if companies with fewer businesses typically generated higher earnings and whether they enjoyed a higher stock market rating. We measured earnings over a five-year period to take out the effect of one-off performances and to capture the underlying and

more enduring trend in a company's performance. We also excluded
certain companies such as UK utilities. (For several years after
privatisation water and electricity companies enjoyed soaring earnings
on the back of post-privatisation cost reduction and strong core cash
flow, but this disguised what subsequently proved to be disastrous
diversification programmes later shown to be significantly eroding
shareholder value.)

Our adjusted sample in each country was some 350 strong – still
substantial. What did we find? To our surprise, as Figures 6.2 and 6.3
show, there was a particularly strong correlation between the number of

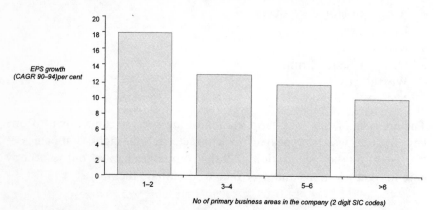

Figure 6.2   On average, focused companies deliver higher EPS growth

Note: *Averages of 353 companies.
Source: The Kalchas Group.

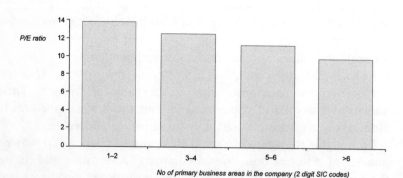

Figure 6.3   The market rewards focus with a higher P/E rating

Note: *Averages of 353 companies, P/E at 29 September 1994.
Source: The Kalchas Group.

different businesses and a company's earnings per share performances *and* with its stock market rating. The greater the focus, generally the higher the earnings per share (EPS) and price/earnings ratio (P/E). And while not every company fitted this relationship, the correlation was especially significant.

What lies behind focus and why are focused companies on average more successful? Put simply it **enables** an organisation to pour its total resources and investments into a few chosen areas without distractions of effort. With markets becoming ever more complex and competitive, surely greater focus is becoming a requirement rather than an indulgence. It is hard enough to get under the skin of any one market place and so understand customers and future trends that a company can stay ahead of the game. Trying to do this in the same market globally – as many companies now have to do – is even more challenging. Trying to do this globally in different businesses as well may well stretch the resources of any organisation. Even large multinationals do not escape this challenge as their 'big-company disease' (of which more later) makes it hard to co-ordinate effort and energies and harder still to do so in the detail and with the frequency that continued market success seems to require.

Two of the UK's most notable 'unfocused' companies – Hanson and BTR – who for many years had defied experience as to the pitfalls and potential weaknesses of being a conglomerate – have themselves recently announced the end of their conglomerate days.

The Hanson break-up, following hard on the heels of similar announcements by ITT and AT&T, stunned both the City and Wall Street. 'The granddaddy of them all is breaking up'. Hanson announced it was demerging into four 'reasonably focused' companies in chemicals, energy, tobacco and building materials. Like other conglomerates that have put themselves through such a wrenching break-up, Hanson no doubt hopes its move will boost the value of its shares which have underperformed for several years and in Britain have moved at 30 per cent below the market.

BTR too has announced it is accelerating its exit from 'non-core activities', with the proposed sale of 37 businesses including, for example, Dunlop Slazenger the sports goods company, and Tilcon the UK Aggregates subsidiary. Both were suffering from lack of attention in a large conglomerate, declining to relatively weak market positions and with a competitive disadvantage to their rivals.

Recent troubles at Daimler Benz and AT&T have been blamed on this same lack of focus, leading to an absence of any competitive advantage for the companies.

- Daimler Benz in 1995 revealed losses of DM 2.3 billion as its late 1980s diversification spree came home to roost. During the 1980s Daimler Benz moved into aerospace, industrial electronics, consumer goods and financial services 'to create a technological enterprise to rival the giants of America and Japan!'

  Yet this diversification did not achieve any critical mass in terms of market strength or competitive position. It simply plunged the company deeper into losses. It has now resulted in the 'most brutal shake-up of a German industrial group.'[24]

- AT&T has come in for some sharp criticism for its costly failure in computers and missed chances in the US and Europe. While state-controlled phone companies in Europe, for example, waited for an attack from the US giant, AT&T instead announced a $7.5 billion bid for NCR and a strategy to enter the computer business and challenge Compaq and Hewlett Packard and others.

  However the takeover of NCR has proved a debacle and is reckoned to have cost AT&T a further $5 billion in restructuring and integration costs, while still losing millions of dollars each year. 'This misconceived diversification has kept AT&T from moving more quickly on the telecomm front', commented the *Wall Street Journal*. So that by the time AT&T bought into cellular phone company McCaw the entry price had risen substantially to $12.5 billion.

  As analysts and others now pointedly remark: 'In the looming telecomm free-for-all AT&T will have to stay focused or it will simply lose out.'

Focus can operate at different levels too. For a company to develop a meaningful and potentially successful commitment it must not only consider focusing on a very few number of businesses. It must also challenge whether it needs to focus geographically, for example on a few regions or countries, rather than trying to dominate globally on a simultaneous basis. It must also consider focusing on a few customer segments rather than trying to win competitively with all customers no matter what their different needs.

British Airways for example – apparently one of the most focused companies in terms of being in only one major business – nevertheless still has a focus challenge when it considers its markets position across every region of the globe (see Figure 6.4). BA claims to be a global player but which segments are of greatest priority and importance to address? Can BA be strong in every segment? What's the level of investment required to address on a timely basis all the priority areas? Is that affordable? If not,

*Can British Airways succeed in **every** segment?*

	UK	France	Germany	Rest of Europe	USA	Latin America	Central America	Caribbean	Mid-East	Far-East	Australasia
Passengers											
Freight											
Holidays											

Figure 6.4 British Airways country/region opportunities by market sector

what currently weak market positions become vulnerable and what can be done about that?

Indeed, while BA races to try to dominate globally, with recent efforts to ditch US Air and link with American Airlines, it has identified a further focus challenge for itself. It is now examining what are the core skills its customers value and what should it do about the non-core areas. It has talked about becoming a 'virtual airline', whereby it focuses on only a few customer-valued activities such as sales, marketing and cabin crew, and outsources all the rest!

Focus, then, is an integral part of any commitment. It is the **enabler**. It enables the organisation to channel its energies, its investment, its research into so understanding a few markets and being so close to its chosen customers that it can achieve advantage and leadership and sustain it, despite competitor's challenges and future market uncertainties.

*   *   *

Through our understanding of commitment, we are arriving now at a more complete picture of the truly successful company. Long-term in its outlook, with clear measurable targets – stakes in the ground for the future, ready to stick with it come what may, and focused in its energies and direction.

Achieving this commitment in all aspects is hard to do. It is a sign of how important it is, though, that we have seen how winning companies have sometimes intuitively, often deliberately, embraced these key success factors. Those who can harness their organisation to achieve high levels of commitment will be giving themselves a head-start in the race to succeed. To recap Brian Arthur, Professor at Stanford, 'rivals will back off in a market . . . if they believe it will be locked in by someone else . . . [clear commitment] will discourage competitors from taking on a potentially dominant rival.'[25]

If the commitment is in place, then the ability to find and sustain competitive advantage in the chosen markets – though challenging – remains more feasible. As we saw with Seagate and Sun Microsystems, for example, Al Shugart and Scott McNealy needed extraordinary commitment to see-off rivals, stick with their beliefs as to how the market would evolve, and continue to motivate and drive their workforces against what at times must have seemed to others impossible-to-achieve goals.

Commitment is the required foundation for success. And it provides a rational way for a company to start building its strategy. It helps create the framework from which winning strategies can emerge. It need not be a leap in the dark. For Akio Morita, Shugart and McNealy – they **knew** they had a high chance of success. Strategy making must be seen as a series of steps that are rational and that enable a company over time proactively to develop its position in the market to its advantage.

For those who develop the arts and sciences of effective strategy making, success does likely beckon. For, as we have discussed, so many organisations have lost the skills and capabilities in this area, and yet it is the core competence that ultimately drives most winning companies.

I'd like to end this chapter with three illustrations of total and effective commitment – Mercedes, J. P. Morgan, and Gieves & Hawkes the Savile Row tailors. Each of these organisations demonstrates in their own way the four key commitment success factors we have discussed (Figure 6.5).

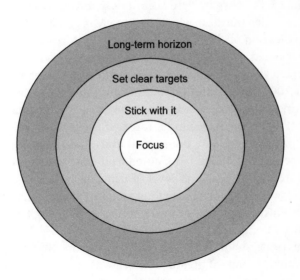

Figure 6.5 The four key factors of commitment

- Mercedes has announced a $6 billion investment in a fleet of smaller vehicles despite concerns that in doing so it is putting its luxury image on the line. Jürgen Hubbert, a Mercedes board member, in 1996 commented: 'as our competition heated up we faced a simple choice – move toward customers or lose them – we have chosen the first path. This is not a gamble. We have thought through what we are doing and are putting the investment behind it.'

  Mercedes has set 2001 as its milestone for achieving success with these new cars and expects it to represent 40 per cent of all its passenger car sales by that date. In addition, it has set a goal of a 12 per cent return on investment, higher than it has achieved in the past.

Customers, competitors, dealers and analysts are all querying Mercedes' market predictions, viewing them as aggressive and worried it will prove a diversification from Mercedes' core. 'But', continues Hubbert, 'we have overcome widespread skepticism in our own ranks and we will prove to the market that what we have targeted is achievable . . . for us it's about focusing on the needs of customers in premium segments – no matter the size or class or car – we want to continue to be the best at doing that.'[26]

- J. P. Morgan was the premier deal-maker in the US until the early 1930s. In 1933 the Glass-Steagall Act in the US forced the separation among US banks of investment banking from commercial lending. Banks like J. P. Morgan were accordingly forced to split, and it hived off its securities business which became Morgan Stanley.

  As application of the Act was relaxed, J. P. Morgan took advantage and determined to rebuild its investment banking capability. Starting in Europe it aimed to: 'recover our position as the leading adviser by the year 2000'. Its reputation and position in Europe have been built slowly and consistently and in recent years it has emerged as a dominant investment banking force. 'Success can lead to further success provided we stay committed and don't blow it', commented Terry Eccles head of the bank's financial institutions group after the bank scored its highest ever level of deals in 1995.

- Savile Row suits – not an obvious arena of fierce competition – but even this illustrious street of men's suits and tailoring has been feeling the heat of competition as sales plummeted in 1994 to £33m from £80m in 1991. Aside from recessionary factors that had an impact through that period, of greater concern was the fact that these tailors' long-standing and loyal clientele were getting older and buying less, while younger prospective clients were buying ready-to-wear elsewhere or visiting the more fashionable tailors.

  With suits taking at least six weeks to complete, and costing £2000 a time, Savile Row retailers were getting seriously out of touch with their customers. One firm – Gieves & Hawkes – decided to meet this challenge head on. It spent £2m on renovating and expanding its single shop creating a less intimidating but more modern and comfortable atmosphere. It has started advertising – something unheard of in its business – up from virtually nothing to 15 per cent of sales in 1996, and it has even mailed glossy catalogues to target customers. 'We've had to look again at our business and redevelop it

. . . we're not going to get side-tracked into other things . . . we've been in this same business for generations and we're dedicated to it . . . we're targeting wealthy men over 35 . . . we know the benefits aren't going to happen quickly but we're determined our business will remain attractive for the next one hundred and fifty years'.[27]

7 Commitment: Market Immersion

The late 1990s market place is like a jungle – a scene of ruthless struggle for survival. On the journey through it there will sometimes be a bewildering set of alternative paths and directions, unexpected twists and turns, daunting obstacles – all intimidating and inhibiting to the unprepared or the uncommitted venturer. Only the fittest will survive, only those who have planned and studied the environment and bring with them the right resources and energies will have the chance to master it and overcome.

Faced with a tough set of challenges some will give up trying to plan to win through. As we have described, some managers today will openly advocate a philosophy that eschews planning for the future. They will claim the market place is so uncertain that there's little point in trying to map a way through it. But the emphasis and mission of this book is not just to demonstrate the new competitive advantage model but to encourage and exhort management to embrace the necessary commitment that is its underpinning. Establishing a map and a path must be better than having no map or pathway at all. As we are demonstrating, those companies who are successful are the ones who have developed the extraordinary commitment to find a pathway through that jungle and reach the end goals and, if anything, anticipate the obstacles and have an answer ready for them, not simply to be pushed off course at the first obstruction.

If commitment to reaching the end goal is the critical first step, how does a company go about finding the best pathway through the market jungle? And once a particular path has been identified, how does it maintain a steady course, anticipate and overcome the unexpected threats and obstructions? How should a company go about finding its principal sources of advantage that will see off the various threats? How can a company ensure that it exploits its environment rather than is exploited by it, that it uses the 'flora and fauna' as shelter and nourishment rather than seeing them as obstructions and difficulties?

This chapter explores the other element of commitment – 'developing a deep-rooted immersion in the market with customers'. It suggests a way that the apparently impenetrable jungle can be penetrated, and shows that finding a successful path through it is not a matter of luck but a result of enormous preparation and planning and developed understanding of the environment and how to manage it.

To illustrate this, let us look at several case studies of well-known companies – including Marks & Spencer and McDonalds – where we can contrast their successes with their failures and draw out the lessons learnt.

Marks & Spencer

Marks & Spencer has dominated UK clothing retailing for several decades and not surprisingly in the early 1980s began to explore opportunities for expansion into new markets outside the UK. M&S developed a path similar to nearly all retailers expanding overseas at the time. It looked for opportunities to take its successful UK format – consumer positioning, merchandise, pricing, image and so on – and replicate that in new market places.

It carried out the traditional market research evaluating markets on the basis of their overall size, growth, demographics and so forth. It was like an outside-in view, walking around the outside of the jungle and picking one of the paths at the entrance because from the outside it seemed easier and attractive.

Essentially, Marks & Spencer in the early years of its overseas expansion took an asset-driven only approach. With relatively superficial external analysis it prioritised markets where it assumed its strengths and success could be replicated and where it appeared it would be able to largely repeat the same format and position that it had built in the UK.

But if we look at M&S's performance in Canada and in its first five years in the USA, it was extremely poor versus its high standards and its UK benchmarks. As the *Financial Times* Lex column pointed out: 'Marks & Spencer failed in Canada because it tried to export its unique UK store style to foreign consumers who had very different ideas about the shops they wanted to frequent'. And as the chairman Sir Richard Greenbury himself said 'it would have been difficult to get it more wrong'.

M&S had failed to fully research the North American markets. It had not build up any in-depth understanding of different tastes and preferences. It had not fully appreciated that what worked so well in one market might need to be substantially tailored to lead to success in another. It was not ready for a much more price-conscious market that was less aware of or influenced by 100 years of UK retailing heritage. It did not appreciate the full competitiveness of its new markets and the need to match rivals in promotion and educate consumers as to its value offering. It assumed that what was fashionable in women's clothing in the UK would be equally appealing to its new target audience.

Put simply, M&S had not immersed itself sufficiently in the market place. It had not got to the point where it so understood the needs of the local customers that it could identify the exact proposition that would be most welcomed nor the success factors for implementing it.

In contrast, the M&S expansion into continental Europe has been much more successful. In fact for many years M&S was the most profitable retailer on the continent with operating margins up to 11 per cent and more on sales of £250m and growing. It set performance standards none of the more established retailers in the region could match. In essence it had learned its lessons from North America, and as it expanded it identified what needed to be changed to deliver success. It embarked on a programme of 'local market immersion' – to understand local customer needs so fully that it could tailor its offering – so that it knew exactly how best to achieve its goals.

With these insights it has had the confidence to develop a long-term strategy to drive its business forward in this region. As with all good 'commitment-makers' it has established clear goals over the next five years, a target of doubling the number of stores, financial milestones and a clear understanding of what advantages customers will most value that will reinforce its competitive positioning.

Of course there will be uncertainties in its chosen markets, unexpected threats and obstructions, but the senior executives know precisely where they are trying to get to, can mobilise and enthuse their workforce with these targets, and it is hard to see what could truly throw them off their chosen path.

What is emerging is a way in which a company can effectively build on its commitment to a market and find advantage and success in it. That is to **immerse** itself totally in understanding the detailed market dynamics and needs of the customers in that market.

McDonald's

To illustrate this further let's look at McDonald's. Here is an organisation expanding overseas at a truly outstanding rate, opening two new branches every day somewhere in the world and growing from 10 000 units in 1989 to nearly 15 000 in 1995.

Yet with all its experience it has still largely operated from the point of view of exporting its successful US domestic format overseas into new countries. It has tried to overcome the need for any significant local market variation by continuously building its international brand name and reputation in an attempt to educate and influence consumers to enjoy what it offers rather than be overly responsive to their needs.

In many countries this 'export' approach has worked. For example, in the UK where consumers are relatively *Americanised* through a shared Anglo-Saxon culture, this approach has worked particularly well. But in Italy, for example, where attitudes to food are less globally homogeneous, McDonald's in fact came unstuck.

Opening in 1985 initially with ambitious growth plans for 44 branches in two years and 200 branches in five years, McDonald's struggled. Five years later they had only opened 40 and many of these were barely profitable. As the company began to review where it was going wrong, it found it had badly misunderstood the local market needs and conditions:

- Southern Italian tastes especially are based around salads, fish, fruit, olive oil, pasta etc., and had not at that point accepted 'foreign foods' with any enthusiasm.
- In terms of competition, Italy already had an extraordinarily well-developed pizza environment which catered for local tastes, met all the convenience aspects, was low-price and available.
- Government regulation refused McDonald's access to what it regarded as the key sites on grounds of preserving the local architectural and cultural heritage (a McDonald's in Piazza San Giovanni in the centre of Florence!).

All these items should have been obvious to an organisation used to immersing itself in local market conditions and tailoring its offering accordingly. But to an export-led organisation like McDonald's, it is perhaps less surprising that they missed this market understanding and made the mistakes they did.

Of course having made its mistakes and had its market immersion the hard way, McDonald's has since been able to draw on its vast resources, retrench and reposition itself in the Italian market, and rebuild its franchise in a more locally customer-sensitive and responsive way.

The triple-I model

In fact, case studies and the evaluation of the lessons from companies such as Marks & Spencer and McDonald's show there is a simple model which can guide a company through the process of translating commitment into continuous advantage in the market.

We can call it 'Triple I' and it is shown in Figure 7.1.

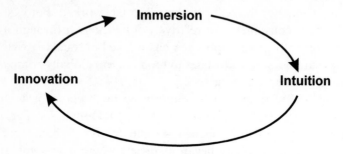

Figure 7.1   The triple-I model

By in-depth immersion, it is possible to develop an intuition – a feel about a market place and its opportunities – which combined with effective analysis and research can be a foundation of new ideas and innovation. 'Understanding can be the well-spring of life unto him that hath it'.

It is our experience that it is this process that can identify the right path through the market jungle. Short cuts or superficial external views in the manner of McDonald's in Italy, or Marks & Spencer in North America, will ultimately be the source of failure and disappointment.

It is constantly surprising how few companies have a rigorous institutionalised process – built into the core of the company – that goes through these Triple-I stages.

Typical examples of inadequacy here (do you recognise any parts of your own company?) would include:

- Repeating the same piece of market research year-in/year-out, with little thought to changing consumer needs.
- Having the market understanding done by the consumer research staff who are typically detached from 'coal-face' market issues and who worry more about statistical significance than about conducting continuous in-depth understandings of what is going on.
- A market research programme that is reactive to market needs as opposed to wanting to go a step further and also be proactive and

evaluate opportunities that would educate or develop new ideas and opportunities.

- A disregard for the views of those who have worked for a long time in a particular industry sector and have developed some of that intuitive feel for what is required. Alternatively, even if there is no active disregard, there is no structure for capturing it.
- A bottom-up only view of the world, where department managers just want to meet this year's budget financial targets rather than rigorously assess the market to identify threats and opportunities possibly three, five or more years away.
- Too frequently the asset-led approach – 'let's exploit what we have/ what we think we're good at' – instead of being market-led or even market-driving.
- A cavalier, 'we know it all', attitude generally to markets and customer needs (the M&S North American/McDonald's in Italy scenario is still being repeated in many different organisations every day).

Mintzberg has been one of the very few writers on strategy who has forcefully recognised the value of encouraging and formally integrating an intuitively developed view of the market place and the opportunities arising through it. In his view:

'The obvious conclusion is that to be effective, any organisation has to couple analysis with intuition in its strategy making.'

Mintzberg quotes Herbert Simon as follows:[1]

'Every manager needs to be able to analyse problems systematically (and with the aid of the modern arsenal of analytical tools provided by management science and operations research). Every manager needs also to be able to respond to situations rapidly, a skill that requires cultivation of intuition and judgement over many years of experience and training. The effective manager does not have the luxury of choosing between 'analytic' and 'intuitive' approaches to problems. Behaving like a manager means having command of the whole range of management skills and applying them as appropriate.'

In my experience there is a direct relationship between the degree of immersion that takes place and the ability to understand that market so intuitively that truly innovative ideas emerge. Somewhat crudely we can draw a simple conceptual graph as shown in Figure 7.2

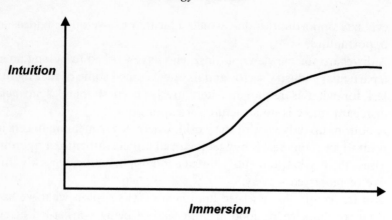

Figure 7.2 The relation between intuition and immersion

And it is like an S-curve. The value does not arise from one piece of research, it emerges from a deep-rooted and profound exposure to all the market place issues built up over time – not just understanding customers but what competitors are thinking of doing, what suppliers see as the threats and opportunities, what new entrants and products may come through, what 'commentators' and 'gurus' who have worked in a particular market environment think and believe. Absorbing all these factors, distilling the wood from the trees, reacting but also looking to anticipate and be proactive – that is going to be the key for uncovering sources of potentially sustainable advantage in the market place.

Yamaha

Look at Yamaha. By the mid-1980s it had captured some 40 per cent of the global piano market, yet demand was declining at a rate of about 10 per cent each year and cheaper imports from South Korea among other places were beginning to erode pricing and Yamaha's own market share.

Yet Yamaha is totally committed to the piano market and its team were utterly determined to make a success of it. It set about ensuring it had a thorough and developed understanding of its customers, of the way market trends were evolving and what people liked about pianos, but also what they disliked. How could Yamaha rejuvenate the piano and reach a whole new generation of potential purchasers and users? Options considered ranged from advertising piano-playing linked in with modern celebrities like Elton John, producing pianos in modern colours and designs, and introducing smaller sized pianos that could fit into a bedroom (to replace the guitar or drum kit?).

But what came out were two specific opportunities. First Yamaha launched a relatively low-cost digital electronic piano – the Klavinara – which was smaller but also produced many new sounds and could be programmed to play certain tunes. Second, Yamaha introduced the 'computer piano' which would play a recorded disk of your favourite piano artist or recording – and existing pianos could be fitted with this facility. Both products have been significant in boosting sales.

Innovation and R&D

Both Yamaha's ideas were 'Sony Walkman-like' in their innovation, offering products and ideas that were not obvious in market research but which could be identified as potentially attractive from the more intuitive feel that extensive customer research and immersion could develop. Both products have been great successes but could not have come about from the more typical general market overview which would have declared the piano market mature and declining, and encouraged 'harvesting' or exit rather than innovation.

Perhaps the more typical limited research approach is the main reason behind many companies' poor record of innovation. They simply fail to capture the insights that are available from the most rigorous and constant immersion in what markets and customers think and feel.

Few would dispute the value of truly innovative thinking and product development, yet many regard it as the equivalent of searching for a needle in a haystack, a matter of luck rather than planning, something elusive and ethereal that is nearly impossible to grasp. One result of this attitude is that R&D budgets have generally been reduced in the past few years as companies cut out pure research and focus more on development and on new applications of existing technologies. Indeed companies justify these cuts by talking about reducing 'blue sky' research; that is, the more open-ended project work with less certain payback. But in doing so they are eliminating those research projects which are searching for the new breakthroughs and the great new product ideas that can transform their companies' competitiveness.

Of course such blue-sky efforts – to be relevant and successful – must be grounded in the market and an understanding of it, but to eliminate such properly structured activity appears very short-sighted. As a result of such a policy the chemicals company ICI, following years of intensive cost-cutting and restructuring, found its level of R&D spending had fallen to only 2 per cent of sales in 1995 versus 4 per cent in its heyday, and significantly behind most other leading chemical companies.[2] Acknowledging that not all that 4 per cent was well-spent, how much more new product potential might ICI have today had it kept the same spending level but refocused that to be as market-grounded and efficient as possible?

Innovation need not be some elusive, random thing. But by an effective immersion process it is possible to intuitively identify new opportunities.

Sony had, long before the Walkman came along, set its sights and made its commitment to the market of consumer micro-electronics. As we have described, it had teams of people looking at ways of providing existing products in a micro-electronic form. It was driving down the path of consumer convenience – make things easy to use, accessible and readily available. With this sort of mission and resources long dedicated to these goals, it is less surprising that a product idea like the Walkman was developed.

3M and Raychem are other well-known examples of organisations that deliberately and proactively encourage innovation. And in that encouraging environment it is again less surprising that new ideas tumble out. So the well-known rule at 3M that technicians can devote 15 per cent of their time and budgets to any project they wish – provided it is in some way connected to 3M's core markets – clearly creates an environment where in fact lack of innovation and new product ideas is failure and under-performance rather than just bad luck.[3]

However, even within 3M there are critics of the way the 15 per cent rule is applied, with arguments for making it less up to individual whim and more structured around target-market needs. Some insiders view 3M's approach as 'managing in chaos', and claim the 15 per cent rule currently spawns projects that are so random that there is little leverage of existing market knowledge or of any developed market understanding.

'Structured innovation' – that ought to become the key for companies. Not random research or marketing in the hope of discovering the big bang but market-driven research and investigation focused on the markets chosen and prioritised by the company as its areas of long-term commitment. A proper history of many big new ideas can trace their origin and development to a logical and rational process of exploration, iteration and testing before the successful innovation emerged.

Sweet 'n Low

We can take as another example the development of Sweet 'n Low the low-calorie sweetner.

Lawrence Eisenstadt was of Russian Jewish parentage and born in Manhattan in 1906 in a impoverished family environment. Before the second world war he spent his life working in his uncle's cafe down by the docks, and when his uncle died he took over the coffee shop business.

Times were hard and to help bring up his own family Eisenstadt was forever trying different business ideas. One of his early efforts involved the repacking of tea landed at the docks into small tea bags. He was the first to do this and for a while he was a successful local distributor. But he was then soon outgunned by the big food companies who could beat him on both price and distribution.

Undeterred, Eisenstadt continued to explore product ideas that were developed in his coffee shop as he struggled to make that core business pay its way. One idea he tried in 1956 was to repackage sugar into small packets. His idea came about because he was forever throwing away the sugar in the usual sugar bowls left on the coffee shop tables which quickly became contaminated with flies, bits of food, stained with tea and so on.

And in this area of sugar sachets, at the time also a revolutionary idea, Eisenstadt made his mark. His little sugar packets – enough for one cup – quickly caught on and he was able to build up a thriving business. Though even here he was eventually and once again outgunned by bigger rivals – in this case the large multinational sugar companies.

Undeterred he kept exploring new ideas. He was finally inspired by a friend who suffered from diabetes but had a sweet tooth. Einsenstadt played around with some chemistry and tried out various mixes of saccharin. After much trial and error he found a mix that tasted right, held its consistency and was low in calorie.

Determined not to be outgunned this time, he patented his development established the brand name Sweet 'n Low, and went on to make his fortune. Random idea or structured innovation?

In fact Kalchas has researched 130 UK companies who were start-ups with new ideas in the early 1990s with the aim of identifying what characterises those that are successful.[4]

Of the 130, we looked at the 20 most successful who are performing outstandingly well today:

- They are making significant profits.
- They have built turnover to a multi-million pound level.
- They have broken through from a '1-person business' to being an established employer.
- They have professional management, systems and procedures in place.

What characterises these top 20 companies?

- The founder entrepreneur had a history of working in the industry in each instance for a number of years. A typical quote would be 'I'd spent my life in this and I saw the opportunity to fill a gap in the market'.
- The entrepreneur had a clear view of what the gap in the market was and had obviously researched the potential.
- The business was well-financed and supported by the banks who were clearly involved from the start and persuaded by the innate business logic.

'Despite mistakes and set-backs along the way we all along just knew there was a need for our speciality store products'

'I'd been a butcher all my life and I'd been experimenting with speciality sausages for years until I realised I could make a business out of that alone.'

'After years of experience of house building, I reckoned there would be little competition for low price easy-to-assemble home lodge units.'

Random ideas or structured innovation?

Summary

How can an organisation determine whether it has a sufficiently developed Triple-I process? How can it be sure it is diverting sufficient resource to understanding the market and customers and processing that information with rigour and discipline?

There are 10 questions that it can test itself on. A very strong 'yes' would score 10, a very strong 'no' would score 0, average scores 5. A score of less than 80 is inadequate.

1. Do senior executives spend enough time out in the market place talking with customers? _____

2. Would you say there is a significant amount of market research carried out which is properly updated at least every 6 months? _____

3. Are its findings fully reviewed within the business and its implications considered and actioned at senior management level? _____

4. Is there an established system, such as Lotus Notes, for local market intelligence to be systematically collected and shared throughout the business? _____

5. Does the company regularly access external objective perspectives about its effectiveness and plans in the market? _____

6. Does the company have a clear understanding, regularly updated of its competitors' and customers' future plans and expectations of the market? _____

7. Is new product development carried out on a proactive basis with joint customer and supplier teams integrally involved and inputting in the process? _____

8. Are the views and ideas of long-serving employees in the company in respect of market initiatives and opportunities systematically collected and rigorously discussed? _____

9. Is there an aggressive programme of continuous market place testing of new ideas and business opportunities? _____

10. Does the culture and environment in the organisation encourage discussion, evaluation and investment in future market opportunities five years out? _____

Ferrero

As a final example of an award-winning Triple-I company, let's look at Ferrero, the Italian confectionery company and makers of such international brands as Tic Tac, Kinder and Rocher.

Ferrero is an established international company with c. $4.5bn turnover. Its single-minded focus is chocolate and sugar confectionery. Each month its chairman and founder – Michele Ferrero – meets with all his senior executive team – some 15 other people. The aim is to taste that month's batch of new products coming up from the testing laboratories.

Products will be passed around and comments made informally on likely market receptiveness. The executives around the table are steeped in the industry with many years of work, and have often come up from the junior sales or marketing ranks. There is no question about their immersion, and their deep understanding of their consumers.

The whole organisational culture is geared to be product-innovative. Each laboratory team is expected to produce some new product, or redevelopment of an existing one, every two or three months. They are appraised and rewarded specifically on that basis. Each executive around the tasting table has engrained in his attitude and culture to be constantly searching the market for new ideas. As a result the company has grown consistently and has a unique record among customers for its product development and innovation.

It is less than surprising that the company is a success.

8 The Relative Commitment Audit

We have given a definition for commitment and have examined companies that have this 'right stuff' to win, as well as those that lack it and fail. But how can we tell if a company is committed enough, that it has a more developed understanding and determination to dominate in a particular industry sector than its rivals?

It's a question of keen concern to the many different constituencies of a company – to its investors, competitors, customers, its own suppliers and employees.

- To prospective investors, understanding the level of commitment in a company can influence, for example, whether it should be seen as a short-term play arbitraging some one-off situation or a long-term opportunity for capital growth.
- To competitors, a rival's particular commitment can be the signal that deters them from entering or putting further investment into a market. In the same way that no company today would enter the soap powder market to compete with Procter & Gamble and Unilever because these two companies' commitment levels are so high.
- To customers, one company's clear long-term commitment to success in their own industry may be a factor encouraging them to enter into a lasting relationship with it. Such determination from a company can give it an additional cutting edge and persuade customers to keep out apparently less-committed rivals.
- To the company's own suppliers, it may be a necessary framework to encourage them to invest in the company's future product plans and ambitions.
- To employees, it is a vital source of motivation. Microsoft employees will unquestionably go the extra mile because they know their company is totally committed to winning.

Measurement and audit

We can set out a path for better understanding a company's commitment because we can measure it. We can establish the idea of a 'relative commitment audit' which seeks to measure commitment both within the organisation and compare that externally to rivals.

This measurement draws on input especially from customers, employees, suppliers and competitors. These are the key market and organisational constituencies that see some inside aspect of the functioning of the company and have the ability to compare what they see with others in the industry and with what they intuitively know ought to be the target best practice.

It's an audit that needs to be objectively carried out. It needs a sense of detached appraisal to uncover protected turf and reveal whether what is going on is truly sufficient. It also needs to be representative so that it embraces internal and external views and captures the perspective of junior employees as well as the more senior.

The need to gather input on relative commitment from top to bottom of the organisation is particularly born out by recent Forum Corporation research.[1] Their research showed that there is an 'iceberg of ignorance' which they found as an almost universal characteristic among senior executives of large corporations. On average only 4 per cent of all the problems and opportunities known collectively to the junior employees in the company were found to reach the senior executive team! In this case how can any senior management hope to reassure itself about its relative commitment and whether it is doing enough to win in the market in the future, if it does not carry out the widest possible audit capturing as many perspectives as possible and being open to learning about both the good and the bad?

Recently Kalchas worked with Zeneca carrying out this sort of commitment test to understand the company's competitive strength and future potential in the market place. The management team had strained to put themselves in the most competitive situation in their markets but they were open and honest enough to acknowledge that while they thought they were doing all that could be done, they recognised the value of another more objective and representative check.

First, the internal audit at Zeneca revealed a significant difference of views, with the junior members of the company and the salespeople – all acknowledged as being closer to the market than the senior team – identifying some gaps in what competitors were doing versus Zeneca's own initiatives. So, for example, in Zeneca's pharmaceuticals business one of its competitors had been busily investing in an information database, tracking and evaluating different patient-treatment regimes for similar illnesses, recovery times and associated costs with the aim of identifying hospital savings. While Zeneca had a pilot project of its own in this area it found its rival was potentially ahead in exploiting this opportunity. Second, the external check carried out in-depth discussions with customers and competitors and suppliers that provided further evidence of the strength of this new competitor initiative, but also identified potential new avenues for Zeneca to explore that would strengthen its own position and reinforce its lead in its chosen sectors.

This was a quick and straightforward relative commitment audit that enabled Zeneca to reappraise its total market place planning and investment, check for any gaps and be as sure as it could be that it would be able to stay ahead of its rivals.

The relative commitment audit: key questions

We can describe here the ten basic questions for the audit. They should of course be added to or tailored depending upon a particular company's market situation and need. They should be addressed internally to representative samples of employees and externally to customers and suppliers. Input from and about competitors may need to be gathered in a different form but such insight is equally vital to providing a complete picture.

The detail of the audit will also be influenced by the amount and quality of information that is already in the public domain and accessible. In certain industries such as chemicals, retailing and consumer goods there are – at least in the West – substantial amounts of competitive relative data and benchmarking that can be easily captured and monitored. In other industries such as electronics, which is generally less mature and more fragmented with fewer large and long-established players, there is less public and comparable information and measuring relative commitment is harder to do. But even if not every question in the audit can be answered completely, recognising the need to measure, and actually measuring what is possible, has to be a positive step.

The aim is to score each question 0 to 10. Ten would indicate the highest level of commitment, 0 the lowest, 5 an average. Scores less than 70 here are inadequate, but I have rarely seen a score higher than 85.

1. Has the company firmly established and communicated
    what are its long-term goals and what it wants to achieve in
    its chosen markets?   _____

2. Are those targets found stretching yet credible and clearly
    motivating to the workforce?   _____

3. Do suppliers, customers, competitors and employees all
    rate the company as on the way to becoming the dominant
    player in its field?   _____

4. Does the company frequently and rigorously investigate its
    market, and in the customers' eyes demonstrably
    understand better than its rivals how its markets are
    evolving?   _____

5. Is there sufficient investment and enough resource and
    people with the right skills available?   _____

6. Does the company continuously fine-tune its plans to
    deliberately reflect changing market conditions as they
    happen?   _____

7. Is the organisation sufficiently focused on what are its
    priority businesses, geographies, customer segments and
    value-added skills?   _____

8. Are there monitors and measures in place which regularly
    capture the company's relative position in the market place
    versus its rivals, and are these monitors and measures given
    high priority and acted upon?   _____

9. Is the developed understanding of the markets resulting in
    high levels of new product introduction, and are these new
    products taking a growing share of total revenues?   _____

10. Can you describe the understanding of markets and the
    determination to win as something that 'courses through
    the entire organisation'?   _____

This sort of audit is not a one-off exercise. A truly committed
organisation would want to carry out some version of it at least once a
year, if not some parts of it – especially with customers – more frequently.
Not only can it reassure the company that it does have the foundations
for effective strategy in place, but it can highlight any shifts in its relative
commitment score. In doing so it is providing the early warning signs,
pointing up areas that are falling short, highlighting opportunities and
providing an agenda for action.

Over the long term there is likely to be a strong correlation between a leading relative commitment score and market success as the following example shows.

Case Study

Procter & Gamble

In its 'diaper wars', after P&G's initial launch, rivals were quickly able to see the enormous market opportunity that was developing, and were able to come in with their own versions of the technology. Barriers to entry were low as the costs of simple plant were not high and retailers private label provided a distribution channel for many 'cheap and cheerful' products. P&G's share as first in the market was initially high but began to slide, and for example in the UK fell from around 30 per cent to about half that against private label penetration. Despite this, a relative commitment score would have shown P&G a league ahead of its rivals on all dimensions. If a company is ever looking for comfort or reassurance when markets get tough then this is one source to provide the confidence to stick with it, to keep on investing and sowing the seeds because ultimately this will outweigh less committed and dedicated competitors.

P&G had a raft of technical developments to the diaper on test to further improve its product performance. These were already scheduled into a next 5-year new product to market pipeline. In addition, it had a substantial cost reduction programme underway so that it could reduce its price difference versus private label, and it was beginning to build substantial brand awareness via significant advertising investment, higher than all competitors put together, creating a better understanding of its product excellence.

Not surprisingly, over time P&G has seen off all its rivals, from smaller private label operations to bigger branded products from Colgate, Boots, Kimberley Clarke, Peaudouce and others, and has re-established itself as the clear branded market leader.

To contrast this, let's look at a stark example of commitment failure. This particular illustration is to be found in a mid-sized medical equipment business that suffered and eventually collapsed because of a lack of commitment from its parent company, who was involved in a number of different businesses. Here was an organisation selling diagnostic medical and associated equipment which required significant on-going investment in plant, R&D, sales and marketing to stay competitive.

Pressure of short-term earnings persuaded the parent to put a stop on this sort of investment for a while. Of course in year-1 there appeared to be little harm to the business, the market share had not changed and earnings increased. Encouraged, the parent withheld investment in year-2 and, while there was growing complaint from the employees, again the company's market position still held up. By year-4, not surprisingly the cumulative lack of investment began to tell as the company became unable to match competitors' new products, and its manufacturing plant had become higher cost and less flexible than its rivals who had continued to automate and improve. Customers started to put pressure on the company, hit prices and started switching to obviously more successful and committed suppliers. Workforce morale declined. The inevitable happened.

Sadly this sort of scenario is not rare. Good businesses are allowed to run down through insufficient investment and either get sold cheaply or go bankrupt. Yet the parent company could have been measuring and monitoring its commitment score and could have accessed customer, competitor and other input. It could have identified early-on the likely level of investment required to continue meaningfully with this business, and taken a decision on whether it was prepared to make that investment or not. Immediately a no-invest decision is made, the company is vulnerable to falling behind. If this is repeated a second year, the more positive approach is for the parent to recognise its unwillingness to support or invest in this particular market sector and get out now while the market value of the enterprise is still significant.

The key is to understand the relative commitment level and either put in place what will be required to succeed or recognise that the company does not have the requisite appetite and act accordingly. The worst situation, as too many organisations find themselves in, is to be in the middle – wanting to succeed but never quite putting enough in to get there.

*   *   *

This relative commitment audit can be a simple tool to evaluate where the company stands on a broad range of basic measures. It provides a straightforward measurement system and an agenda for action. As we've seen, it's the foundation stone for strategy making. No company can hope to effectively move on and explore the specific forms of advantage that it can pursue in the market place if it has not first built in the critical understanding of that market place and set a determination to win.

9 Competitive Advantage through Performance

The most tangible and physical form of competitive advantage is in the basic performance of the product or service. Does it do its job well, is it reliable, are the basics being carried out proficiently and effectively?

This is the starting point for any customer decision-making. Does the product perform its underlying function efficiently? It is the *sine qua non*. It's the entry point into the market. Unless the product or service achieves at least threshold levels of acceptable performance it cannot compete. It's what Motorola, Toyota, Rolls-Royce and others are all especially striving for.

In most industries this basic product/service performance is still a key battleground of competition. (This is commonly described as 'quality' – achieving excellence in the fundamentals or the basics of a product's performance.) Companies are working hard to continuously improve the underlying functionality and reliability of what they offer. But in some other industry areas now a revolution is slowly taking place. In computers, telecommunications and household consumer goods, for example, basic quality performance is often already at acceptable levels and the customer is now demanding more, something additional to 'turn them on'. Finding advantage through performance is shifting to something more exciting and contemporary. It's got to be more relevant to the ever-more demanding and sophisticated late 1990s customer. There's a revolution in performance taking place and we must explore it.

The challenge now is to build on the basics and go on to improve on **how** that performance is delivered. The pressure increasingly is on how speedily and how conveniently the product or service performs. Can it now do its job 'even more quickly', can it be made even 'easier to use', to make the customer's life even more convenient?

This new performance focus is very much driven by customers. It's about performance speed, and about performance convenience. (The concept of Performance is used in the model to take us away from just thinking about basic quality or reliability. Performance is a much more

117

active expression of value delivery. It encapsulates broader areas of product potential and opportunity that we shall see can be exploited.) The place of performance in the market commitment model is shown again in Figure 9.1.

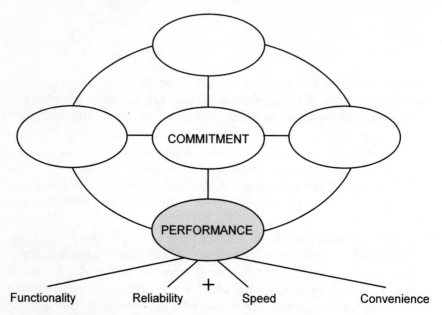

Figure 9.1   Performance in the market commitment model

This performance focus is also about setting a pace and standard that will become ever more important benchmarks as we move into the next century. Customers will force companies to sort out with still greater effort any basic quality/reliability issues with their products. Customers want to move beyond that and join in the new performance speed and convenience game. This new focus does not undermine the importance of getting the basics right and continuing to improve on them, but it's a reflection of growing customer expectations to step up from basic quality and now see a broader and more developed performance offering.

This chapter explores the performance revolution. As we shall see:

- The basics still remain critical . . .
- . . . but the Performance goal posts are moving . . .
- . . . the revolution has started – customers want more.

The basics remain critical

It was the PIMS framework back in the mid-1970s which best demonstrated through its empirical database that 'quality is king'.[1] It captured the notion of 'relative perceived quality' – that is, how customers view the product performance offered – and showed unequivocally that it is a key driver of a company's profitability. In the PIMS view, performance quality was found to be: 'the most important factor affecting a business unit's profitability'.

While PIMS demonstrated the overall importance of improving the performance quality of products and services, it was the Japanese who created the biggest shock and catalyst. Only a few decades after digging themselves out from the rubble of world war II, Japanese companies transformed themselves from making 'rusty tin cars' into an economic powerhouse with a single-minded obsession with quality – delivering products that not only did their basic job well but did so with increasing reliability.

As J. M. Juran, the noted American quality consultant and others have commented:

'In the 1960s 30% of Japanese products were failures, by the 1990s it's down to 1% or even 0.1%, now we're actually contemplating zero defects – and they have shown the way'.[2]

On the strength of initially a vastly superior quality offering, the Japanese as is well known have gone on to build market leading positions across the globe and to establish themselves as major players in a number of industries.

- Through the 1970s and 1980s, Japanese merchant ship builders were responsible for 50 per cent of worldwide tonnage.
- Japanese steel had a 20 per cent global share of steel through the 1980s.
- Today they also have high global shares in, among other things, automobiles, TVs, high-fidelity equipment, motorcycles, sewing machines, cameras and semiconductors.

The surge of Japanese products into new overseas markets created an awakening among western companies to the power of performance quality, and initiated a desperate attempt to catch up. This has been seen most particularly in US business where substantial efforts have been made to embrace quality and start matching the close-to-perfection standard set by Japan.

Business schools began to emphasise this new thrust, expeditions were sent to Japan to learn about this quality revolution, Deming's work and ideas – originally acclaimed in Japan – were spotlighted, the Malcolm Baldridge quality award was set up, and in Europe the 1S0 9000 standard was created. There was a widespread realisation that basic product quality had to become engrained in the way companies did business with their customers. And this has been recognised with increasing force.

'We say we want to be number 1 or 2 in the markets we choose to operate in but how are we going to do that? Quality is our best assurance of customer allegiance, our strongest defence against foreign competition and the only path to sustained growth and earnings.'

(Jack Welch, Chairman of *GE*, in 1980s)

In 1985 at one Hewlett Packard factory, 4 out of every 1000 soldered connections were defective. 'We could still get away with that in those times but we gradually realised it just wasn't enough. We've now cut the defect rate down to under 4 per *million*.'

(John Doyle, VP manufacturing Hewlett Packard)

'The ultimate aim is total customer satisfaction. Our original goal was to slash component defects to the six sigma level – that's 3.4 defects per million components. Now we're close to that we're looking at a more ambitious goal – 60 defects per billion. We're establishing these demanding standards on our processes as well as our products.'

(George Fisher – Chairman of Motorola in 1993)

'GM now needs a different paradigm of quality to prevail against growing global competition. We need a *pharmaceutical mentality*. If the pharmaceutical industry can produce and sell pills by the millions and they're all perfect, car manufacturers and their suppliers should be able to do that too. We're moving in the direction where we will refuse to do business with suppliers that exceed zero defective parts per million. That parts per million as a measure has to disappear.'

(Harold Kutner, head of worldwide purchasing at General Motors)

'We can't point to any one thing that we do, but all the little things add up to a more loyal and more profitable customer base. We aim to get the basics of our operation right every time. We can't begin to think about customer service if we haven't got the basic operation in place.'

(Bruce Hammond as Vice Chairman of MBNA America Bank)

Achieving quality product performance is now demonstrably high on the agenda of most companies. But even though the performance revolution has begun and customer demands are moving higher, the focus still in most industries is still on getting defect rates down, improving reliability, getting the product to function and perform to a higher standard – trying to adopt 'the pharmaceutical mentality'. It's largely still about the basics and it remains a vital stage most companies have yet to totally master and complete.

As a result basic functionality and reliability are still critical sources of competitive advantage. In many situations there is substantial competitive opportunity for the company that gets the basic detail absolutely right.

- A recent survey by the British government's DTI (Department of Trade) showed that a product's 'functional performance' – its 'quality' – was still the most important factor in providing the platform to compete.[3]
- A 1996 report on the success of Germany's Mittelstand group of mid-sized companies concluded that the critical factor behind their success was 'product reliability'. In over half the companies it was seen as the main source of competitive advantage.[4]
- 'Gillette's future hangs on its commitment to maintain the technological supremacy of its products. We are investing hundreds of millions into research every year to improve the way our products perform.'[5]   (Alfred Zeien, CEO Gillette)

And getting these product basics right still pays back. It's not just 20-year-old PIMS research that shows this, but a number of more recent studies too.

Most comprehensively, a recent McKinsey report rooted in the automotive supply industry showed that companies achieving the highest levels of quality in terms of defect rates achieved significantly superior profit returns and also established much higher sales growth rates.[6] Best performers achieved on average **twice** the profitability and growth. This survey mirrored recent findings in the well-known J. D. Power customer satisfaction index, which shows customers explicitly rewarding manufacturer basic quality performance with higher sales.

Furthermore, the emphasis on improving performance has led to increases in productivity as companies make renewed efforts to increase efficiency and reduce process complexity. Andersen Consulting suggests a rule of thumb that reducing product engineering and production defects by one-third can increase profits and growth by a similar factor: 'simpler processes and fewer parts means fewer things can go wrong, product reliability is bound to improve, customers are happier and if you can do more of this then your market sales will go up.'

So we see Motorola's drive for six sigma; Du Pont initiating a process of continuous improvement to boost product quality; Alcoa introducing a benchmarking process to measure its quality gaps and target an increase in yield of 'good quality aluminium sheet from 70 per cent to 80 per cent' to match Japan's Kobe Steel; one of Germany's smaller machine tool companies, Index, leading the way in product quality by redesigning its products using a modular approach to cut down on the number of different parts; Nissan, NEC and Toshiba leading a consortium of 200 Japanese companies figuring out how to jump to the next plateau where defects and errors disappear entirely!

The list of initiatives and initiators is long as companies search for improvement and competitive advantage in this direction. But it's also clear that there is a surprisingly long way to go for most companies to achieve a level of basic product performance that is completely satisfactory.

The McKinsey research referred to earlier, showed that the Japanese still maintain a vast performance reliability lead over US and European rivals. Over 85 per cent of the Japanese companies surveyed were achieving better than average performance quality scores, with 55 per cent at a near perfection level. This contrasted with only 31 per cent of European and 44 per cent of American companies scoring better than average, and only 7 per cent of European and 9 per cent of American companies in the 'near perfection' category.[7]

This sort of relative competitiveness has also been shown in a report put together by the authors of *Lean Thinking* Womack and Jones,[8] as shown in Table 9.1. Other studies have found that still only 26 per cent of US companies were putting in place an effective quality programme that did yield results (Rath & Strong), and that as few as 15 per cent of companies surveyed were investing sufficiently in quality improvement (Gunnerson Group and Britain's Federation of Small Businesses).

Table 9.1 Average relative performance in auto assembly

	Japan	USA	Europe
Defects (ppm)	193	263	1373
Deliveries (% late)	0.2	0.6	1.9

Source: Womack and Jones, 1996.

These performance gaps naturally need to be fixed and there is growing pressure to do so quickly. The late 1990s customer is becoming impatient for the basics to be delivered and for the product to be reliable. And business is responding by pouring ever increasing amounts, for example into R&D spending and investment, to develop technologies for new and improved product performance (see Table 9.2).

Table 9.2 Percentage increases in corporate R&D investments, 1991–95[9]

Country	%
Denmark	45
France	35
United States	31
UK	27
Germany	25
Switzerland	11
Japan	6
International Average	23

Source: Department of Trade and Industry, 1996.

Although the percentage increase for Japan is the smallest in Table 9.2, Japan continues to lead the way on a percentage of sales basis, despite the catching-up efforts of western rivals (see Table 9.3).

Table 9.3 Average R&D spending as percentage of sales, 1991–95[10]

Country	%
Japan	5
Germany	4.5
United States	4.5
Italy	3
UK	2

Source: Department of Trade and Industry, 1996.

In electronics, six of the top biggest spenders are Japanese – Hitachi, Matsushita, Toshiba, NEC, Sony and Mitsubishi, with the bulk of US and European companies coming half-way down the list. In computer software, however, US firms now dominate occupying all of the top 10 places in terms of level of investment. And in chemicals, it is Germany's

Hoechst and Bayer that lead the way, spending more than £1.5bn each in 1995 with Japanese companies well down the list.

Business is going to need to do more than just spend and invest to catch up, though that must be the catalyst. It must also better link that investment into its corporate strategy and direction. A study by Booz Allen & Hamilton of 800 European managers showed that two-thirds felt their companies 'were doing a poor job of harnessing the investment and technology to corporate strategy'.[11] Too much of the investment and spending is being done in a vacuum. There remains insufficient collaboration across departments or functions to most effectively leverage any new potential, and spending is still often carried out without sufficient reference to what customers will need and will rate in terms of improved performance.

With the product quality performance battle still to be won, we can list a group of five success factors which have been shown by winning companies to characterise their effectiveness and which are the main reasons behind their victories and improvements in this performance arena.

1. *Link performance initiatives and investment to what the customer needs.* W. Edwards Deming emphasised that 'the consumer is the most important part of the production line. Quality should be aimed at the needs of the consumer present and future'. In fact Deming's 'production line' starts with and ends with customers and consumers as the driving influence on what standards to achieve and which performance attributes to measure[12] (see Figure 9.2).

2. *Involve the whole company.* Continuous improvement is best achieved when the entire organisation is dedicated to that task. Studies have shown that without this, the typical cross-functional/departmental barriers slow things down and lead to a set of compromises to meet differing vested interests and priorities. Where the organisation is working harmoniously, it is because the competitive opportunity that the performance improvement represents has been clearly communicated and has mobilised everyone in the workforce to break down any remaining barriers that might slow or impede the necessary pace and direction of change.

3. *Involve suppliers.* Suppliers have their own core competencies and centres of excellence which can be drawn into the customer value delivery process. The more progressive companies are increasingly pressuring their suppliers to open up their skills and share them, to

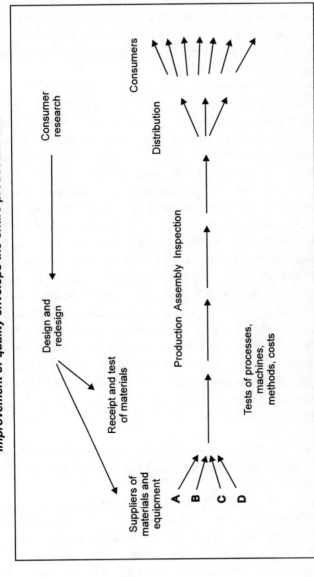

Figure 9.2 Production viewed as a system

Note: Deming adds: 'in a service organisation, the sources A, B, C, etc., could be sources of data, or work from preceding operations, such as charges (as in a department store, deposits, withdrawals, inventories . . and the like)'.
Source: W. Edwards Deming.

provide a better product performance platform. For example, Motorola now insists that all its suppliers apply for the Baldrige quality award, establish their credentials to meet its criteria, and assist in every product quality improvement programme.

4. *Involve customers.* The best companies now have joint working teams with their customer, often involving full-time dedicated resources with the goal of continuously developing and improving upon product performance and reliability.

    By involving customers it also helps to ensure that efforts in performance improvement are customer-relevant and meaningful, and can work to deliver advantage and competitiveness and avoid being just improvements for their own sakes. So first-tier suppliers to the automotive industry, like Lucas Varity, work hard with their customers to design-out faults and defects and improve their products' performance on their **customers'** production lines.

5. *Institutionalise a learning environment.* There are now numerous quality tools such as Kaizen (continuous incremental improvement), KaiKaku (radical improvement), Poka-Yoke (mistake-proof production processes by inspecting at source), Taguchi (design by experimentation), SPC (statistical process control in measuring process performance) and many others. All these tools have been well-documented and are increasingly well-understood. But it is less the tools themselves than creating an environment that encourages learning and adaptation and teaches and trains in the new skills that are necessary. Some organisations like Boeing, Raychem and Xerox have set up special learning/training centres where the necessary skills can be constantly improved and developed.

There are no doubt other success factors, but the five described here come up in research and observation time and again as the drivers of quality and performance success.

With all this it's clear that the basics of product performance remain as vital today as ever, and there is a substantial effort both required by customers and being put in by companies to narrow performance gaps, improve upon reliability, push further toward zero defects and generally aim for the highest possible standards on these most basic of product attributes.

Yet even as US and European companies race to catch up on the Japanese lead, the goalposts are moving.

The performance goalposts are moving

While we have shown that in general the basics are still critical today, in some industries we are fast arriving at a time where improvements in basic product functionality and reliability will no longer provide a source of competitive advantage. Performance reliability will be assumed, it will be a given, the minimum threshold to compete, simply the gate money to enter the game.

What's changing? Why is the basic performance advantage eroding?

- Performance life-cycles are shrinking.
- The rate of successful imitation is increasing.
- Technology is now mature in some industries.
- Some companies are already achieving, or are close to, performance perfection.
- There is increasing cost and risk deterring substantial investment in new technology.
- Customers are not what they used to be – their needs have moved on.

Performance life cycles are shrinking

Radio and film took 40 years of incremental improvement and innovation before they became relatively mature products. But the portable telephone has taken just four years to shift from being a cumbersome novelty to a micro-light easily portable and relatively mature product. Sony say that they expect any performance advantage over competitors to last 'six months – at best'![13] The time to introduce new car models has fallen from five or six years, to only two to three years today.

Any performance advantage that is established is now unlikely to last a long time. Products are being developed at ever increasing speed, companies are ratcheting down time to market, and technologies, markets and organisations are more dynamic than at any time in history. Products based on an innovative technology or approach can emerge, even gain prominence, but be replaced and virtually disappear in just a few years. Look what's happening to products like Lotus Symphony, Laser disks, Rover's metro, Apple, Netscape and others.

This erosion of performance life-cycle is being fuelled not just by new technologies but also by new approaches to business such as process re-engineering, the explosion in information availability and the erosion of patent protection. Re-engineering, for example, is especially focused on reducing things like product development time. 'Simultaneous engineering' and other time-to-market techniques have achieved dramatic results. Automotive companies, computer companies and others have been at the forefront in exploiting and capitalising upon this, rushing out new improved products with increasing speed to beat back any competitor initiative.

The availability of information has exploded in the last few years enabling all sorts of organisations to find out about other companies' products and ideas and if they can copy them. Thanks to solid-state electronics and the microprocessor, and even more recently the Internet, there is little or no information that cannot now be discovered or accessed. It can all be done very quickly and at least in the Anglo-Saxon business world almost nothing is kept secret – all is open to the keen-eyed investigator.

Whether it's politely called benchmarking or more explicitly 'finding out what your competitors are up to', information gathering is now a developed science capable of providing immediate insight on how one company might be achieving a performance advantage versus another and thereby showing how any gap can be narrowed. And as competition globalizes, there is now no barrier preventing access to this information and understanding – whether the investigator is the largest western multinational or the smallest and newest 'Asian tiger'.

The final barrier that might have kept performance life-cycles from shrinking and resisted these trends is also now being threatened. Patents are designed to protect performance innovation and advantage. Unfortunately, companies are becoming ever more adept at finding ways around them, undermining their value, reducing their reliability and threatening the amount of time they can provide any sustainable market advantage.

This is not only a comment on sometimes less-disciplined companies operating out of LDCs, where western rules and general legislation may not always be enforced with the same rigour and effect. It is also true for large western multinationals and we have already seen how adept Kodak was at getting round Polaroid's patent protection, and how Fonar, though first with the product, actually lost its patent battle on MRI scanning technology to the greater guns and resources of GE and J&J.

So in this world without barriers it is not surprising to see the next force and change that's moving the performance goalposts. . .

The rate of successful imitation is increasing

We have considered the success of imitators already, but it's worth reminding ourselves of the bare facts:

- 60 per cent of all patented innovations are imitated on average within four years.[14]
- It is estimated that counterfeit copies steal $20 billion a year from US business.[15]
- The top 1000 US companies on average expect new products to provide 30 per cent of profits in the next five years.[16]
- The Lexus car has been accused of being a blatant copy of Mercedes, and the Mazda Miata a design copy of the English Triumph sports car.
- 47 per cent of pioneers – first movers in the market – failed. According to a 1992 research study: 'let other firms pioneer and explore [it may be better] to enter after learning more from others'.[17]
- In at least 20 per cent of case studies, competitors knew details of the new product R&D of their rivals within six months of the initiation of their rivals' projects.[18]

Increased process engineering skills, benchmarking, wider and instant information availability have all created an environment where competitors can reverse-engineer a rival's offerings and successfully bring a similar performance or lower priced product to market with increasing speed.

- 'We don't try to reinvent the wheel . . . we try to leapfrog from someone else's ideas.'   (VP of Uniforce Personnel Services)

- 'There are companies that systematically avoid being the first. They don't have to get the first bite of the apple, they let others pioneer, if the idea works then they'll quickly follow suit.'[19]   (Theodore Levitt)

For companies that are pioneers, that are driving out the boundaries of performance advantage, these threats from imitators are increasing. They are undermining their product performance thrust because it's not delivering the sustainable value-added that was hoped for.

The consequence is that in a number of industry areas today competitors have caught each other up in product performance and are in a position to quickly imitate any improvement a rival makes. From the customer's perspective the different product offerings, at least in terms of basic functionality and reliability, appear similar. There is no obvious difference. In the absence of anything else, purchasers can quickly turn to price and move into treating the product as a commodity.

It's at this point that the manufacturer/supplier has to start looking around the market commitment model for other means to compete effectively. The search is on for new or additional advantages. This may require a shift to a new prime form of advantage altogether. Or it might still be in the performance arena looking for other sources of performance advantage at the third-dimension level.

This is a good example of where and how the market commitment model can become a practical guide to strategy development. It can encapsulate the principal strategic options. Companies can explore and try to exhaust the various opportunities identified and defined. They can measure how they are doing down the paths selected. If their competitive advantage in one performance area is narrowing or even disappearing, and if there is no obvious way to improve that then new options need to be selected (Figure 9.3).

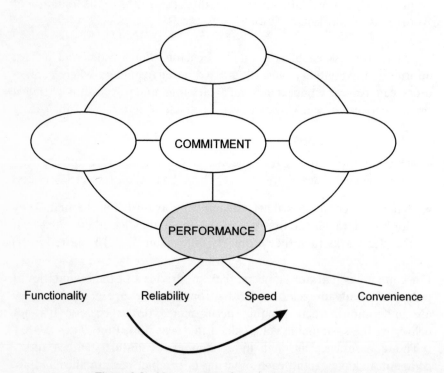

Figure 9.3   New sources of competitive advantage

Technology is now mature in some industries

Not only are performance life-cycles shrinking and imitators becoming more successful eroding any advantage gaps, but we find a third force moving the goalposts. In some industries technology has reached a level of maturity where there is limited further basic product performance improvement to be had.

A technology will eventually reach its limits with respect to accepted measures of progress. A technological threshold will come about where meaningful customer-noticeable improvement ceases to exist. For example, the technology threshold for conventional propeller-driven aircraft was reached at a speed of around 500 mph. In metrology, the threshold of existing mechanical measurement technology is now also being reached. The speed and efficiency of mechanical measurement has ceased to advance. Technological thresholds appear in other areas such as cellular phones, the walkman, watches, calculators, high-fidelity equipment, and household consumer products like soaps and cleaners.

In all these situations, companies must either find the new technology breakthroughs or, while maintaining the threshold, look for new areas of performance or other advantages. Where technological maturity is approaching, it is yet another reason for companies to be proactively searching out how to continue to excite and be more competitive with their customers. Anticipating these thresholds is critical. But through benchmarking, accessing all market information, involving suppliers and customers in product development discussions it might be possible to avert any 'commoditisation crisis' and precipitate the next competitive move.

Some companies are close to perfection

As Womack and Jones have commented:[20]

> 'On July 27, 1994, something remarkable happened in the assembly hall of the Porsche car company in Stuttgart. A Porsche Carrera rolled off the line with nothing wrong with it. The army of blue-coated craftsmen waiting in the vast rectification area could pause for the first time in 44 years, they had nothing to do. This was the first defect-free car.'

Over a period of years, Porsche had vastly improved its operations efficiency, cutting defects in supplier parts by 90 per cent, reducing first-time errors in-house by more than 55 per cent, cutting parts inventories by 90 per cent and shortening lead-times from raw materials to finished vehicle from six weeks to three days. What a performance promise to be able to offer to customers – absolutely no defects, complete reliability!

This achievement by Porsche, however, still lags Toyota who **consistently** win out on every measure of product reliability and performance benchmarking. If Japanese companies in general still lead American and European companies on defect rates per million parts and in the race to perfection, then Toyota leads all Japanese companies by similar margins. Its parts per million defect rate is now getting down to under one per million, closer to perfection.

As Deming has pointed out, 'if it can be measured it can be improved', and with developed statistical process controls, sophisticated manufacturers are now increasingly able to measure and so monitor performance in all the critical process steps and move towards total error elimination. This is as true for manufacturing as it is for service companies. Organisations like MBNA or Joban Spa Resorts in Hawaii who won the Deming Award succeed because their continuous measurement of everything has enabled them to improve upon all the basics of their operation to deliver near-faultless service. Their measurement systems enable them to track progress and eliminate errors in all things that matter.

As companies learn what to measure and get better at it – like Joban Spa, MBNA and another constant customer measurer, British Airways, so they realise that perfection is not such a crazy idea. They can see the process of continuous improvement to reduce defects, waiting time, complexity, mistakes and costs to start offering a product which is ever nearer what the customer actually wants.

Providing products on a consistently 'perfect' basis is regarded now as only a few years away. *Business Week* predicts the first 'perfect factory' to come about around the year 2005, and while it's certainly still a hard slog to get there, advances in technology and information-sharing and measuring are hastening the day.

Perhaps consistent perfection will only be achieved by a few companies in a few industries in our lifetime, but the fact that it's even on the horizon is remarkable and it is setting both new targets for manufacturers/suppliers and also new expectations among customers.

As a result, we are already seeing the leading Japanese companies shifting priority attention and effort away from product performance quality to try to find new performance leaps and advantages. 'The issue is now less quality *per se* but about how to deliver it more quickly or in a way that better meets individual customer needs', was the conclusion of a recent Deloitte and Touche survey. One consequence has been the establishment in the USA of the Agile Manufacturing Enterprise Forum to promote improving flexibility and responsiveness in the production line to deliver products more quickly and more attuned to the customer.

With perfection in sight, the game is moving on and investment is starting now among the leaders so that they can continue to stay ahead as the goalposts move into the new performance era.

There is increasing cost and risk

As improvement in performance and the race to perfection becomes an ever more sophisticated exercise, so investment costs rise and with that the associated risk.

For example, a pharmaceutical company in the 1970s and 1980s had a relatively proven and established process for bringing new drugs to market. Thousands of chemicals would be screened in a routine manner for therapeutic effect; they would be approved through standard clinical trials and then promoted to physicians with consumers having to pay whatever price was set.

Competition has eroded that settled world where investment cost and risk were more predictable. Now there is increasing difficulty in coming up with the blockbuster product. It's almost as though the only guarantee is the total level of R&D spend, and even then it's a bit of a lottery. More sophisticated biotechnology tools need to be employed. The FDA is interested not only in safety but also in cost effectiveness. Managed Care organisations make price a key issue in the launch of any new products. Dedicated generic drug companies are waiting in the wings to mirror the developed technology or find ways around the patent.

All these pressures make performance success harder to come by, and the cost of sustaining it that much greater. In response, some pharmaceutical companies have acquired aggressively to spread the investment load, such as Glaxo or Ciba Geigy who acquired Wellcome and Chiron respectively. Others have started moving into new areas to find new sources of profit growth or ways of shielding their position, as Merck did with Medco and SmithKline Beecham did with Diversified Pharmaceutical Services.

For pharmaceutical companies as well as for all business, increasing cost and risk has become yet another factor forcing companies to look beyond the more traditional performance areas of functionality and reliability to explore new forms of advantage that might be more attractive and accessible.

Customers are not what they used to be

The final force moving the performance goal posts is also the most fundamental. Customers have changed dramatically. Consumers of today are typically better educated and more sophisticated than their predecessors. They are more affluent and they are better informed. They are more aware of what is available and what to expect. It's easy and quick to shop around and compare and they can search knowledgeably for the best value. They can surf the Internet, have goods delivered within 24 hours and send them back if they don't perform. They know their rights, are more discriminating and are no longer persuaded just by price or a label. They know the 'customer is king' and the 'customer is always right' and they enjoy their influence in setting the agenda.

They have expectations that they can have any product, any-place any-time and at a lower cost. Look at Safeway's philosophy: 'what customers want, they get.' They are more readily promiscuous, more than ever willing to shift loyalties and experiment with new and differing product offerings. They have become more individualistic in their behaviour, each ready to assert his or her own preferences and needs and even if their tastes may vary only slightly they expect to be catered for.

Yet while the consumer now has the luxury of choice there is chronically less time to indulge. People are working longer hours, frequently both spouses or partners in a household are at work, the demands of parenting seem ever more taxing, and holidays are a snatched week or two instead of a leisurely break. Time is more precious. But on the plus side incomes in many households are larger and there is more free cash after commitments.

What does all this add up to for the suppliers and manufacturers to these late 1990s customers and consumers? What is the impact of this revolution in expectations and purchasing sophistication and information?

This sea-change among the buying public comes on top of the other shifts in the performance goalposts we have been discussing. Performance life-cycles are shrinking, imitators are increasingly successful, performance technology is becoming mature in certain industries, some manufacturers/suppliers are even getting close to perfection. Future investment in basic product performance breakthroughs are becoming higher-cost and higher-risk, and the big breakthroughs themselves are becoming harder to find.

Performance, in terms of basic product functionality and reliability, may still be a critical goal for many suppliers and providers, but for consumers the game has already moved on.

The revolution in performance has started

In this new game, the emphasis now more than ever is to deliver the product performance faster and easier, and if possible cheaper. Time and speed of delivery are of the essence. Product convenience and ease of use are now especially desirable.

It's no longer just about basic performance. If we want to label it, the shift is from 'quality' to 'delivery'. 'Companies are recognising that elements such as quality and functional performance are no longer sufficient in themselves', reported a recent British government DTI and joint CBI survey,[21] 'in fact such elements are now seen by an increasing number of firms only as necessary qualifiers to survive in the market. The emphasis now is on initiatives for example in delivery time, service, customer support and style'. The goal is to find out how to **deliver** basic quality performance now more quickly and more conveniently.

> 'In today's pressured environment people suffer from 'time poverty'. They want products or services that help save time or make it easier to do things.'   (Henley Centre research)

> 'At GE we've always talked about product quality but now we need to move to the next stage. We need to shift from Manufacturing . . . the product you sell is only one component of your business . . . as product life cycles shorten and technology becomes easier to emulate there are few real competitive advantages. . . we have to move on.'
>   (Jack Welch of GE, 1996)

The shift in emphasis has been recognised most recently in a telling study reported by Womack and Jones on the attitudes and priorities of German management teams. Mittelstand companies generally believed for decades that the product itself was the most important factor. The voice of the engineer prevailed and trade-offs between product quality and product price always traditionally fell in favour of quality – at whatever the cost resulting in whatever price. Now there is 'a growing sense of panic' as German companies realise much of the last few year's efforts in improving quality were made without reference to the customer. Product costs, reflecting the engineering investment and associated employee skills training and sophistication, have risen in some areas to too high a level to justify the customer-perceived value-added. Now there is growing awareness of the need to listen to the customer and understand that the customer, while demanding product quality, is not so obsessed about it that they will pay any price for it. Now they have other interests and demands which are also growing in importance and need to be addressed.

In our new customer-sophisticated world, any new product will be judged on these new performance dimensions in addition to the previous ones. If we look at some of the leading NASDAQ 100 companies in 1996, many of the fastest growers are providing products which 'assume the basics' and focus directly on these new performance options. They look specifically to deliver speed and/or convenience or ease-of-usage advantages.

- Parametric Technology supplies software aimed at automating mechanical product development processes, and its products are used by nearly 10 000 companies today to increase process speed and reduce time to market
- Altera markets programmable logic devices that offer significant advantages over customer logic chips by helping customers shorten time-to-market and reduce development costs
- Adaptec's goal is to 'make information move between computers and the world as quickly and easily as possible.'
- Page Net is one of the world's largest wireless messaging companies and expects to soon introduce 'the revolutionary product Voice Now which will be a pocket-sized easy to carry lightweight answering machine.'
- Xilinix commands the market for programmable logic, and its products make it possible for its customers to reduce product life-cycle risks, reduce costs and get faster time-to-market production. 'Our technologies make it easier for designers to program our chips to perform specified tasks.'

Let us look more closely at performance speed and convenience as underlying sources of competitive advantage

Speed

There are in fact two aspects. It's not only about getting the product to the customer more quickly. It's also about providing a product or service that can help the customers themselves save time or do things quicker.[22]

1. *Time to customer* Getting it to the customer as speedily as possible and responding to customer needs more quickly is the most vigorous response by manufacturers and suppliers to today's changing customer needs. Some examples are as follows:

- Levi's are endeavouring to retool and rework their entire business process so that they can turn around a customised pair of jeans in record time.

  They have put in place computer links between each Levi's store and the nearest factory whereby an individual's measurements can be specified and sent to the factory at the same time. There, computerised fabric-cutting equipment cuts the cloth and sews to meet the specification.

  At present, Levi's can offer the supposed 'perfect fit' within three weeks at a cost of just 12 per cent more than the normal rack price. They expect their three week deadline to constantly reduce.
- Panasonic are moving down a similar path looking to provide 'semi-customised' bikes with a fast turn-around time. Based on a series of modular production techniques, they are targeting delivery 'within days of order.'
- A few years ago it took Bell Atlantic two weeks to connect customers to their preferred long-distance carriers; now they can do it in a matter of hours.
- The FAST Electronic Broker aims to provide both a faster service and save the customer time. FAST is an automated broker for standard, off-the-shelf items like electronic and optical parts and components, and also for laboratory testing equipment. Business is transacted electronically through the Internet or commercial networks. FAST automatically analyses the request to identify appropriate vendors, electronically requests a quote, and settles a price often all within a few minutes and substantially faster than traditional distributors and brokers.

2. *Helping customers themselves save time* This can be seen more explicitly in these illustrations:

- Thanks to credit cards, point-of-sale systems, on-line services, home-shopping programmes such as QVC and HSN, and eShop which allows users access to personalised on-line stores and malls, today's customers find it easier to save time and better utilise such precious time as they have.
- Furthermore, CD Rom catalogues, interactive television, or accessing web sites are all making available more easily but also more quickly any specific information that is needed.
- Samsung's new 256M DRAM improves operating speed to 40 nanoseconds.

- AT&T's new structured cabling systems claim speeds of up to 155 Mbps.
- *Concorde* may currently get passengers across the Atlantic from London to New York in just over three hours. The Japanese are so keen on the benefits of speedier travel that they announced in Spring 1996 that they will build the successor to *Concorde*.

Convenience

Like speed, there are two aspects to exploiting convenience as a source of competitive advantage. This is in delivering products that themselves perform easily, that are easy to use. It is also in providing products that make the customer's own lifestyle easier, that get rid of hassle or remove impediments from operating and working more effectively or living more comfortably.

1.   *Ease of performance and use*   Some specific examples of products/ services that are successful because they are themselves more convenient and easier to use are the following:

- SAP is seeing serious competition from Baan software which claims to be offering an easier to use/less complex product.
- Motorola's award-winning new StarTac cellular phone scores because of its small size and ease of carrying.
- Fujitsu won market share among America's fast-food outlets with a counter-top terminal which was specifically designed to be simple to use, recognising many of the employees in these food outlets are not as well-educated.
- 'Videoplus' is an easy 5-step product that can be used to programme the VCR without fuss or complexity.
- Rockwell International and ViA Inc. have developed computers you can wear. They are strapped to the waist and use headgear with a monitor that flips down over one eye and is controlled through voice-recognition software. The units are easy to work and could be used in operating rooms and by inventory-takers.

2.   *Lifestyle enhancement*   Some examples of products that provide lifestyle or business convenience are:

- Much of the innovation in electronic information is also aimed at providing convenience, making life easier. EDI and the Internet are two obvious examples.
- ATMs.

- The Sony Internet Terminal, often called Web TV, has already given birth to the 'web potato'. Web TV, accessible through new Sony or Philips devices, represents the first experience in which ordinary consumers can easily connect to the information highway without effort, and can spend an evening like a 'couch potato' surfing the Internet within the comfort of their own home.
- Ernst & Young have recently established a Business Solutions Centre based in Chicago which is intended to provide a more convenient means for senior officers of the company to meet together and develop solutions to business problems. Typically a three-day exercise in workshop format, it is intended to be intensive but provide a convenient forum to address critical business issues.

Summary

We have now described the performance revolution. We can see how the basic quality aspects of product performance – the core functionality and reliability – can still provide competitive advantage and be a viable strategic platform. But we have also discussed the warning signs of change. In some industries today, winning companies have already been forced to move beyond the basic performance attributes. In other industries, the performance revolution is not far away.

The more sophisticated and demanding customer is but one of several forces that have caused this revolution to take place and accelerated its impact. There is now growing pressure to improve on the speed and convenience with which the performance is delivered.

Yet we are still at the early stages in the development of these newer forms of performance advantage. Unlike with quality, the 'technology threshold' has not yet been reached in these speed and convenience areas. There still aren't that many companies really good at them and most are still exploring the limits of what can be achieved. They have only more recently come to the fore through the sophistication of information technology especially, and so there is substantial further opportunity. Most encouragingly, once achieved, advantage in these newer performance delivery areas may be more sustainable and better able to provide a customer-recognised and lasting barrier against competitors still racing to catch up on the basics.

One last illustration – Toshiba's planned assault on the US personal computer market – shows how well one organisation in particular is recognising this performance revolution and adapting to it competitively.

──────────── **Case Study** ────────────

Toshiba

In Spring 1996, Atsotoshi Nashida, the general manager of the company's PC division announced major plans to launch desktop systems in the USA and worldwide by the end of the year, targeting first the home market and then moving into the corporate sector. These launch plans, especially in the USA, were described as aggressive assaults on American computer companies' domestic strength, where Toshiba at the time was the only major non-US player and with a leadership position in notebook PCs. Following Toshiba's announcements, several other Japanese companies also described new plans to compete in PCs, with Sony, Hitachi, Fujitsu and NEC all issuing statements in the first half of 1996.

Toshiba will be up against the major US competitors like Hewlett Packard, Compaq, IBM and others. How did it expect to compete?

In interviews, Toshiba's Mr Nashida described how first and foremost the product's performance must function superbly and consistently well – 'We want to be known for our reliability'. To support this it will have leading-edge technology in PC components such as memory chips, CD-ROM drives and audio-visual technology – 'there will be a product story to tell'.

Recognising also that this product ' functionality and reliability' may not be enough by itself, Nashida has also talked about making his PCs generally easier to use with freshly-designed keyboards, lighter weight and simpler instruction manuals for example. In addition, significant effort is being put into speeding up product development and production to ensure forecast demand can be met without disappointment.

There will be other aspects to Toshiba's competitive positioning, too, such as attractive value-pricing (not necessarily going for the lowest price), as well as aiming to build off its already strong reputation in notebook PCs.

What has clearly emerged from Nashida's launch plans is a very clear view on what forms of advantage Toshiba would pursue and what role each would play. Product performance aspects would contribute the underlying message and there would especially be functional, reliability and convenience aspects to that. There was also recognition that the intensely competitive PC market would mean the customer-perceived performance advantages, while important to establish, might still not be enough to win significant market share. Hence, Nashida set additional plans on price and brand exploitation.

Overall, Toshiba put together a competitive package of product substance and additional elements that gave confidence the plans would succeed. They have proactively thought through the performance advantages they could gain and realised they needed to move well beyond the performance basics that they used to rely on exclusively to be able to meaningfully compete.

Toshiba's planning is clear and simple. The market place competitive challenges are precisely identified. There is recognition of what can be realistically achieved with the competitive weapons at hand. If we were picking winning stocks, this sort of clear strategic thinking and competitive programme would certainly encourage us to invest.

10 Competitive Advantage through Service Hustle

The next prime form of strategic opportunity that can be defined is Service Hustle (Figure 10.1).

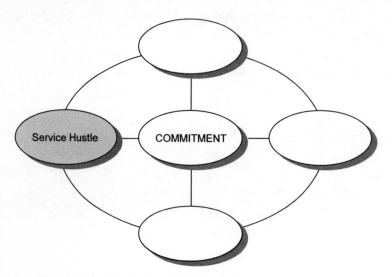

Figure 10.1 Service Hustle in the market commitment model

In today's competitive environment it's not enough just to provide a service, to answer the phone, to send the goods on time or be open from 8 till 6. It's now about something that is much deeper and more pervasive. It involves establishing a relationship with the customer that hustles to do every little thing that can enhance and make pleasurable the experience of dealing with each other. It's about creating a culture and an understanding and a desire among employees to go above and beyond the call of duty, to do things that the customer might not even dare ask for, and to deliver it with enthusiasm and commitment.

A few companies immediately stand out as ones who excel at not just serving their customers but providing what we can call Service Hustle.

They are constantly challenging themselves and enquiring: how can we do better, how can we make the difference, what things can we do today that will make dealing with our company more pleasurable and fulfilling for our customer than dealing with a rival?

Body Shop provides the first illustration, and Anita Roddick's service hustle philosophy is clearly spelt out:[1]

'I want to create an electricity and passion that bonds people to the company and to our customers. You have to find ways to grab peoples' imagination. You want them to feel they are doing something important, that their own actions will make a difference to how our customers feel.'

Another retailer, WalMart, is also an organisation which has led the way in stimulating a customer service culture and setting a standard and benchmark which others struggle to imitate. Sam Walton's 'promise' is a striking way of establishing this service hustle standard:[2]

'Now I want you to raise your right hand and remember what we say at WalMart – a promise we make is a promise we keep – and I want you to say after me: "from this day forward, I solemnly promise that every time a customer comes within 10 feet of me, I will smile, look the customer in the eye and greet that person, so help me Sam."'

British Airways, Southwest Airlines, and Nordstrom are other organisations who excel in this field. They have broken through the complacency that often surrounds customer service and have turned it into something exciting. They have created cultures and workforces that truly believe that their own individual interaction with the customer can make the difference. They have been trained and persuaded that their personal contribution can be quantified, and add backup to the company's total corporate profit and growth objectives. Each customer kept happy is likely to stay loyal, each customer won is an important initiative, their purchases can be quantified. Each customer lost is revenue and profit out of the door.

For these companies, customer service is not just a phrase trotted out at the end of annual reports, next to comments about concerns for the environment and responsibility to the local community, it's on page 1. Pick up the annual reports of Home Depot or The Limited or Southwest Airlines – it's all about people – about the company's employees and the thing's they've done for customers. These companies recognise this both formally and informally with awards, 'customer initiatives of the month', and link it to bonus and wage rates.

These companies are 'hungry' with their customers. They have intuitively or expressly been around the market commitment model and realise that it is in Service that they must make their mark. They have so understood their customer needs and wants that they have seen that competitive advantage can be found for the one company that can truly excel at it. They have seen that customers are dissatisfied with existing service activities, and quite often that competitor suppliers are either complacent or unable to transform their own organisations to the necessary levels of awareness and service hustle action.

For some organisations there will be no choice in terms of choosing the service axis. The basic performance of their core product or service offering may be seen as largely similar to others, and there may be little immediate opportunity to improve upon that. They may be in a near-commodity product situation where they are forced to find other things to differentiate themselves or suffer the constant push down on their prices and there may be limited brand or E-values to exploit. Other organisations may have more choice in the matter; their products' performance may still be superior but they do not want to sit still. They want to continue to challenge and find new avenues of competitive attack to strengthen and reinforce their customer position.

The companies that push successfully down the service hustle path tend to be the ones that develop the strongest customer orientation, who get to know their customers better than any other, who build the strongest relationships that last. But **every** company, whether a service hustler or not, must still be totally immersed in its markets and its customers as we have described so that it can deliver not only what they want, but also anticipate what they will need. It's a step beyond that to establish service and hustle as a prime form of competitive advantage for the company. Service hustlers go on to translate their basic understanding and immersion into a specific service direction for their employees, a principal area of investment and training, a major focus for the way they think about their business. For some markets and customers, service and hustle may need to reach only acceptable threshold levels, for example because the customer's principal concern is that the product performs with utmost reliability. Those industrial manufacturing companies whose success might rest principally on technical performance are likely to be in that camp. On the other hand, service organisations especially, such as hotels and airlines dealing with the mass consumer base are often likely to find establishing excellence and advantage in service hustle a prerequisite.

Let's look at some examples of Service Hustle success from the service industry:

- One of the philosophies behind 1-800-FLOWERS is to 'be hungry' about its customers. 'In the "contact economy" humans crave connection and anything you can do to boost that connection, those units of social intimacy, is going to be widely successful. We want to foster belonging rather than alienation.'[3]
- In this highly competitive world of food retailing, Sainsbury sees the emphasis on service as another stage in the evolution of supermarkets. There is talk of 'super service' and 'efficiency plus' in service standards. 'With any service initiative it's not going to work unless we get all the elements in place to make sure we can deliver our promises.'[4]
- 'Our commitment is to offer the best customer shopping experience, the best merchandise, the best merchandise presentation, the best customer service, the best value, the best everything that a customer sees and experiences. To achieve this goal we must maintain a restless, bold and daring business spirit noted for innovations and cutting edge style. We are determined to surpass all standards for excellence in retailing by staying close to our customer and remaining agile.'

  (The Limited Inc. 1994 Annual Report, p. 1)
- Ritz Carlton claim that more than 90 per cent of customers return through their outstanding customer service programme.[5]
- Over the five years between 1990 and 1995 MBNA, one of the largest credit card providers in the USA, increased their earnings per share on average by 18 per cent per year and has achieved returns on equity in the high twenties. 'In our view, success is about getting the right customer **and** keeping them.'[6]

But where are OEM manufacturers, for example, in this service hustle game? Despite all the management literature and case research, manufacturing companies who are not selling or in some way interacting with end-user consumers never seem to figure on any list of service-excellent organisation. Though manufacturers who are in consumer goods, such as Procter & Gamble, Heinz, Philip Morris, are becoming increasingly skilled in the service arena, the more industrial the company the further away they still appear in terms of effective service hustle orientation.

Is service hustle unnecessary for such industrial companies, do their customers care less about these things, can they rely on product technology alone to win orders and always beat out rivals, is price the only other weapon when technology begins to mature or others catch up? Let's consider the service challenge in the more industrialised arena.

- In Zeneca, the large pharmaceuticals and chemicals group, until a few years ago if you listened to executives talk and read their published literature then notions about customers were clearly low down on the list. It was all about technology, manufacturing-excellence and treatment regimes. Even through the early 1990s these core competencies were probably still just enough. But, for example, the historically unsophisticated hospital customer base for pharmaceuticals has of course now begun to exercise its muscle, and not just in the USA but across Europe too forcing the company to get real about customer management. And while Zeneca is now responding hard, in some areas it's still got some catching-up to develop the organisation-wide learning and experience of customer-excellent companies.
- In ICI, there are many efforts at establishing greater market and customer awareness but it's just not yet institutionalised in the culture or in the bones of the workforce. Here again most executives will talk first about research, products, technology or logistics. That's always been the root of success. Customers bought because the products were unrivalled in their performance. But those forms of advantage are eroding. To be customer-driving rather than asset-led has not historically been a natural ICI approach. Again things may start to change here with the arrival of a new CEO in 1995 from consumer goods group Unilever. But it will be a battle to change the orientation of a decades-old approach.
- Compare the strong page-1 customer profile of the Limited with Shell: In the 1995 Shell annual report we have to wait until page 14 until the word customer is even mentioned. It's the only mention in the whole report. There's talk about 'building for the future', but it's all in the context of Shell's organisational structure, or its investment plans or its cost management. Even in sections dealing with marketing and retailing the customer is not referred to at all. For how long can Shell continue to keep its customers at a distant arm's length? Was the way it handled its Brent Spar disposal in 1995 and the public challenges it found symptomatic of a company with too insular an approach?

Without the pressure from sophisticated customers as we see in food retailing, for example, or high pressure/high demand situations as we find with airlines or hotels, many manufacturers have been let off the hook in the past by less-demanding customers. But as opportunities to achieve lasting competitive advantage diminish in other areas such as product performance, so even OEM manufacturing companies will need to examine their service hustle options with increasing intensity.

It is most particularly in the automotive industry where we have seen some of the more successful ventures by OEM industrial manufacturers into the service arena. This is especially so in the efforts of suppliers to form long-term lasting relationships with their customers that go beyond the basic product offering. Such supplier initiatives are looking to develop a total business system relationship, focusing for example on ways to improve the whole supply chain for mutual benefit and profit gain.

We can categorise such initiatives as more than just relationship building. They are about achieving a 'symbiosis' where supplier and customer interact and even fuse their supply chain with a view to each other's mutual advantage.

We can see this development in pharmaceuticals too. Groups like Glaxo are trying to serve their customers in a way that is so mutually beneficial that it locks out rivals. In their case, they are striving to provide 'total disease and treatment regimes' in conjunction with their hospital purchasers. They too are looking for such a deep and intertwined customer relationship that there is a symbiosis between them. But achieving this requires highly developed operational as well as customer-service skills. While many aspire in this direction, few companies have really got there.

For industrial manufacturers and the many others who want to excel in service hustle we need to step back now and characterise what are the success factors and experiences of winning companies. What do aspirants need to do, what are the specific skills they must develop, what are the keys behind this service hustle approach which make it a success? There are four particular factors to highlight:

- Measure the right things.
- It's not just serving, it's keeping.
- Getting the right customers.
- Doing it.

Measure the right things

Each year ICI Paints used to conduct a customer survey in the UK. It mailed out the same form with the same questions to all its customers.

The survey was three or four pages long with some 20 questions. About 15–30 per cent bothered to reply. The survey results typically showed ICI Paints was well-rated by its customers and perceived as well as its major rivals in most areas. The management team took this as confirmation that it was doing OK and went on about its daily business in the same way.

For many years it did not challenge whether the 15–30 per cent who replied were representative, whether those who did reply had taken trouble to really think through their answers, whether the overall aggregate scoring system ('score ICI one to five on how well it's doing') was sufficiently insightful, what did four out of five really mean, and what did it mean to always score around three or four out of five on most questions?

The search was superficial and the data response that was received was superficial. Yet it gave comfort to the managers and in the absence of any crisis encouraged complacency.

All that's changed now. It had to, because this ICI business did go through a minor crisis in the UK in the very-early 1990s. It came as a surprise, and in the aftermath the company began to realise that its means of gathering market and customer intelligence was inadequate. It hadn't read the signs properly, it hadn't measured the trends effectively, and when problems arose they came as a shock.

AT&T had a similar learning experience. They carried out research that showed that most of their customers claimed to be satisfied with AT&T's service. However, when customer retention rates started dropping unexpectedly they dug further. They found that some 40 per cent of those who said they were satisfied would still probably buy from competitors instead.[7]

What's going on here, don't customer satisfaction scores mean what they say? TARP (the Technicians Assistance Research Program based in Washington) has shown that in fact only 4 per cent of dissatisfied customers actually do complain, and that for every one complaint received by a company there are typically 26 more complaints that are never filed or communicated.[8]

How many times do you promise to write in to complain but never quite get round to doing it? How many complaints communicated to the junior clerks we talk to on the phone or in a retailer actually get written up and passed on to senior managers? Further research by The Forum corporation, which we will refer to again, has shown that only a tiny proportion of the issues and problems including customer problems and complaints that are known to the junior staff find their way up to senior management.[9]

In fact a completely satisfied customer and a completely pleasurable purchase experience is still the exception rather than the norm. A recent study by Bozzell found that 89 per cent of American adults polled were dissatisfied customers.[10] Service incivility and manners were rated a major problem in the poll. Professor Berry at Texas A&M University concluded, 'there is generally a customer respect defect'. His research found consumers are commonly treated to rude, impersonal and unhelpful service.[11] He characterised a number of examples:

1. **Broken promises**. Not showing up as promised; careless, mistake-prone service.
2. **'I just work here.'** Powerless employees who lack the authority, or the desire, to solve basic customer problems.
3. **The big wait**. Waiting in a long line because checkouts or counters are closed.
4. **Automatic pilot**. Impersonal, emotionless, no eye-contact, going through the motions, non-service.
5. **The silence treatment**. Employees who don't bother to communicate with customers who are anxious to hear how a service problem will be resolved.
6. **'Don't ask.'** Employees unwilling to make any extra effort to help customers, or who seem put out by requests for assistance.
7. **Lights on, but no one at home**. Clueless employees who do not know (that is, will not take the time to learn) the answers to customers' common questions.
8. **Misplaced priorities**. Employees who chat to each other or conduct personal business while the customer waits.

What's clear is that there are many dissatisfied customers still out there. There must be many ICI Paints and AT&T type examples of companies conducting research which is just too superficial to unearth the real need. There must be plenty of 90 per cent customer satisfaction scores encouraging complacency while the underlying service needs, as ICI and AT&T discovered, in fact remain unsatisfied.

And it's poor service that appears to be the principal cause of concern and complaint. Further research by The Forum corporation indicated that 70 per cent of the reasons why customers switched their business away from a supplier had nothing to do with the product itself. 15 per cent claimed they switched because of price, another 15 per cent claimed they switched because of poor product performance, but the 70 per cent majority switched specifically because of poor service.[12]

As a recent American Society survey showed, many of today's major companies are failing in the customer-service stakes:[13]

- In telecommunications, MCI is ranked well-down on customer-satisfaction scores and way behind AT&T.
- In insurance, Farmers and Aetna are also relatively low-rated and lagg behind State Farm and Prudential.
- In banking, Citicorp doesn't even match the average score in the banking sector.
- As for public administration, the IRS got one of the lowest scores of all!

All this should be telling organisations that there's still a major customer service problem – and more importantly, opportunity – out there, and that standard research techniques aren't enough to uncover the real issues or point out the real potential.

Success in service hustle is all about going beyond the standard and the ordinary or the routine, beyond the basic research or the basic service.[14] It's about breakthroughs. And the breakthroughs need to come in finding ways to learn more deeply about customers' service needs – as well as in actually meeting those needs and achieving excellence.

In order to move onto this higher plane of learning and achieving, it may be that the senior management of a company need to stir up a service revolution and do something to shock the complacent and change the culture.

Xerox, for example, transformed its thinking in this area in the late 1980s. It moved from a principally profit-driven organisation to a customer-driven one. Instead of talking about return-on-assets as the primary goal, it talked about customer satisfaction. Instead of mostly rewarding on profit contribution it started recognising customer development. Now the company puts customer satisfaction as its number-1 goal. Its philosophy is that through success in the customer arena it will drive market strength and gain and thereby generate the profit targets it's looking for. Of course for the organisation in general, talking, rewarding and measuring customer service can be more readily identified with and understood and is intuitively more motivating than an overall return on asset target.

Archie Norman tried to do something similar in his turnaround of the Asda supermarket chain, with a simple message that 'shopping should be fun' and the company must put the customer first. To signal that to the workforce, the desk **next** to his in the head office was the customer complaints desk. It was not stuck three floors below in a tiny back office producing reports with limited circulation that clog up in-trays. Norman would get a sample every day of the complaints coming through to the company. He could immediately see even without analysis whether any of his customer service programmes were working and whether the customer base was truly satisfied.

At a different level, USAA has institutionalised a customer-service measurement system that goes to the heart of what the company is trying to achieve.[15] Like Xerox, service is set as an objective ahead of profits and growth. It teaches and trains all its employees in what it calls its 'Family of Measures' to track the effectiveness of its employees' interaction with customers. These measures include:

- Overall customer satisfaction.
- Right first time query resolution.
- Service timeliness.
- Number of transactions handled.
- Quality of interaction.

Each unit of employees in USAA has the responsibility to develop the full set of service and other measures which monitor the effectiveness of what they particularly do and which reflect their role in the company. The measures are not the same across the company, but tailored to influence each unit's service interaction. But whatever measures a unit selects, it must be able to show that (a) it involves some form of data that can be collected, (b) the collection is within their control, and (c) they can easily analyse the results.

This measurement system works because it is disciplined but fair, rigorous but simple. It wasn't rocket science to set up and is not complex to implement. It's built on what the employees **themselves** see as important, and so is motivating to them more than any set of top-down-imposed across-the-board measures.

USAA and Xerox are good customer service measurers. They are joined by a handful of others like British Airways and Ritz Carlton hotels. But these organisations – excellent in this service field – do remain an exception rather than the rule. They are the leading organisations where customers are so well-understood, where what the company does well and badly is so closely monitored and measured, that the customer gets to experience pleasure in dealing with them. And in an environment where there still is a 'customer service defect' problem, if excellence is truly achieved it will be lauded and acclaimed and become widely known.

The first lesson for those who wish to excel in the same way is kick out the standard surveys; start right from the basic customer service needs instead; open up a clean sheet of paper to approach the situation afresh. Given there are relatively few who truly satisfy and meet the service hustle standards, then for the organisations who get it right there must be plenty of potential and profit in this area of competitive advantage.

It's not just serving it's keeping

In this increasingly competitive world it's not enough to think about customers in the context of a one-off transaction. A business cannot afford to lose customers at all, nor can it just serve them once and care less whether they come back. From the moment contact is made, successful service hustlers are thinking about a relationship, a connection that can last a lifetime. The art of keeping customers is akin to a marriage, the cost of losing them now the equivalent of a divorce.

As competition increases it's too easy for customers to switch away. Alternative sources of supply are often just a telephone call away. As performance advantages erode, alternative products are increasingly able to provide similar reliability or convenience. In today's environment customers find it easy to be promiscuous (see Figure 10.2). For many products and services it is easy for the customer to indulge in the luxury of a wide range of alternatives, there's no cost in switching and alternatives are widely available. In consumer goods for example, with cars, PCs and packaged foods, the customer has become sophisticated in shopping around, comparing value and trying new things. Research has shown that most companies will suffer defection rates, as customers try out alternatives, of between 10 to 30 per cent a year![16]

How to stop this natural customer instinct? Can it be resisted? Can companies develop a lasting and truly satisfying customer relationship that defies the forces tending to promiscuity? The answers now lie in developing a better understanding about loyalty, about how to retain customers to keep them completely satisfied, not once but on every occasion that they might require the product or service on offer.

Achieving this customer loyalty unquestionably delivers value. There has been a stream of research during the 1990s exploring this notion as companies have become increasingly concerned at losing customers, too many and too easily, and more determined than ever to find ways to keep them. Reichheld and Sasser in their analysis found that, typically, a 5 per cent increase in loyalty could lead to a 25 per cent plus increase in

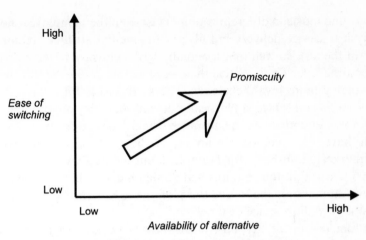

Figure 10.2   Customer promiscuity

profitability. A similar study conducted by Price Waterhouse suggested that as little as a 2 per cent increase in customer retention can have the same profit impact as a 10 per cent reduction in overheads.

The profit benefits from keeping customers can come in a number of ways. 'Acquisition costs' for new customers are reduced as there can be less need for new customer selling effort and advertising. The more satisfied existing customers, the more referrals of new customers. Loyal, stable, satisfied customers are more likely to increase their level of purchases over time. Northwestern Mutual, for example, claims that more than 50 per cent of new sales now come from existing customers and in insurance generally premiums are reckoned to grow at nearly 10 per cent a year among customers who stay with the same company.

But achieving these profit gains and breaking customer promiscuity is hard to do. It requires an extraordinary effort and sense of purpose through the whole organisation to deliver the customer service that makes people want to keep coming back for more. Xerox call it achieving 'total satisfaction' as distinct from merely 'satisfying' customers, in a concerted attempt to stretch the thinking and the service standards that their employees aspire to deliver. At Ritz Carlton hotels, where they won the Baldridge quality award in 1992, they talk of achieving '100 per cent customer satisfaction – and we don't mean just satisfied, we mean that they are excited about what you are doing for them . . . and even if you have 100 per cent customer satisfaction, you still have to make sure that you listen just in case they change'.[18] At Joban Spa Resorts in Hawaii they measure and analyse every single customer interaction from waiting in-line at the check-in desk through to enjoyment of different types of background music in different rooms. They train their employees not just in physical service delivery but also in the mental attitudes required to perform the task so well that it actually 'gives pleasure to the customer'.

Providing specific incentive has become an important device for encouraging more loyal behaviour. The more successful service hustlers will often have in-place sophisticated loyalty-building programmes. The best known of course are the air miles schemes developed by the airlines which have been copied by hotels, credit cards and more recently supermarkets. Sainsbury, for example, launched its Reward loyalty card in 1996 and within four months had 7 million cardholders. If we assume one per household, that's one-third of the UK households signed up within a very short space of time!

Customers appear responsive to these schemes despite the often negligible bonuses and benefits made available. For example, the trade press criticised both Sainsbury and its rival Tesco for the small size of loyalty bonuses offered on their cards. But for relatively limited cost it does appear possible to significantly influence customer purchasing behaviour and affect the intention to repurchase from the same provider.

The more a supplier can create value for customers the greater the loyalty it can probably generate. In turn, the stronger the business base it can establish for future growth and profitability. Keeping customers is a hard-won battle. There's no substitute for instilling a total dedication to that goal that must run throughout the organisation. Marketing and incentives schemes are all part of the weaponry at hand. But they can only be truly effective and start generating that valuable loyalty if there is a decision and determination to win out long term in the service hustle game.

Getting the right customers

But a company cannot satisfy everyone. It can't necessarily meet every customer's needs. Its customers may vary significantly and there may be a group for example who would never stay loyal, who are always impulsive or difficult if not impossible to please. There are other customers where the cost of serving them satisfactorily might outweigh any profit or value the company can derive.

Every business must go through a process of selection. It must determine who are the right customers for it, which are the ones where it can have most leverage and impact, which will be most responsive to what it can offer. Trying to retain chronically unhappy customers can actually be not only expensive but also a mistake. They will distract, they will undermine a value proposition which might be totally satisfactory to others, and they can affect morale, discouraging employees and putting other customers off.

Determining who are the right customers is a matter of segmentation (see further on this in Chapter 13). It's a matter of determining who all the customers are, understanding their different needs and buying factors and defining which ones are the most attractive to service. It's a necessary step not only for service hustlers but in fact across the board for all strategy making: determining where and with which set of customers the company can achieve a recognised competitive advantage. Importantly, this process is not only about prioritising the most attractive, it's also about deselecting those the company cannot easily satisfy. (Though a word of caution needs to be injected; customers cast aside need still to be monitored and assessed in case needs change and they can be brought into the fold. What's more they must be watched to ensure they do not attract in a new competitor who could become a major rival to the core customer base.)

Case Study

BET

BET, when acquired by Rentokil in 1996, were right in the middle of a process of determining who were the right customers for them. One of the building services businesses was the pioneer. They had begun the task of conducting extensive interviews and research across their entire existing and potential customer base. They had identified four factors that distinguished those customers who were both more responsive to the business's proposition, and at the same time more profitable. The four factors were (i) customers who were themselves large in size (> £30m turnover), (ii) had at least one significant market leadership position in their own product lines, (iii) had a good IT capability – for example EDI links with their own suppliers, and (iv) were themselves profitable with a reasonable track record of earnings growth. Such customers were relatively sophisticated. The BET research found that in general the longer the customer relationship the more profitable it was, and that customers who especially matched these four factors were certainly the most attractive.

As a result they developed a simple segmentation of their
customers which helped them quickly and easily point to the ones
they needed to focus on, as shown in Figure 10.3.

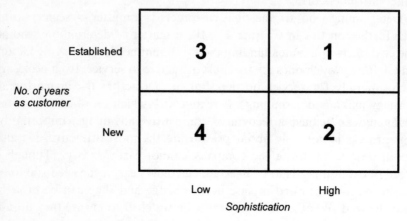

Figure 10.3   Customer segmentation

Category-1 customers generated most of the business and even
more of the profit. The investment and business priority was to
ensure they were 'totally satisfied' with the service and could be
counted on for the next five years. Category-2 customers were the
next most attractive as these represented the 'future stars', the ones
who could be led, by encouraging repeat purchase and loyalty, into
joining the category-1 base. Category-3 customers were loyal but
their lack of sophistication made them less responsive to service,
more interested in price and so ultimately produced very little
profit. Customers in category 4 were to be 'deselected'. Category-1
and 2 customers were to become the focus of a substantial
investment in customer service, doubling the sales force, upgrading
the systems links, involving other departments in the supply chain,
and striving to be rated the best in what mattered.

This sort of segmentation is relatively straightforward but is a
vital step in helping an organisation focus its service hustle efforts.
It helps to think through who are the right customers and to
develop the most persuasive proposition to that group. It avoids the
mass customer approach trying to be all things to all people and
failing to satisfy any one group on the way.

Doing it

We have already discussed how hard it can be to actually deliver the service-hustle standard of excellence. And perhaps the principal road-block is that service more than any other form of competitive advantage, depends on a large number of often relatively junior employees. It is the desk clerk at the hotel reception, the stewardess on an airline, a young salesperson fresh out of school.

Even with all the best training in the world, sometimes these people can be hard to motivate, difficult to get excited about lifetime customer relationships when their own horizons and ambitions may be more limited, or when their poor education or environment handicaps them. Yet it can be done.

A key insight comes from a move made some years ago now by the airline SAS.[19] They realised that success in service to their customers was only going to come through their people, through the vast ranks of front-line employees. So they put them first. They turned the standard organisation chart on its head and put their front-line employees at the top to symbolise their recognition. It was they who were going to deliver this service hustle success (Figure 10.4).

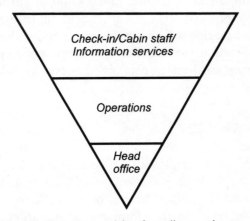

Figure 10.4 Recognising front-line employees

Others have taken this same sort of thinking to heart:

- Southwest Airlines is a dedicated achiever in service hustle. Right at the front of a recent annual report it boldly stated: 'We honour our employees who daily go above and beyond the call of duty to ensure legendary Customer Service. We salute these true heroes of the heart.'

Southwest Airlines has put substantial investment and training into its employees. It knows they are its 'front line' with the customer. The airline has won the US airline industry premier award – the Triple Crown – more times than any other for best passenger performance and was recently voted number 1 in a *Fortune* survey of 'America's best companies in which to work'.

- Nordstrom ascribes its success to its employees. Its philosophy is that every employee is an owner empowered to make their own decisions in serving customers. 'If we take enough care of our people they'll take care of customers, the two go hand in hand'.[20]

  As one Nordstrom employee described the company: 'Here at Nordstrom I feel I can be the best that I can be and I want people to love to shop here'.

- Home Depot aggressively advertises its employees' commitment both to the organisation ('the orange culture') and to their customers. As one employee was recently quoted: 'By giving 100% to customers I'm helping to write the success story of this company'.[21]

- John Lewis, the UK department store, had compound sales growth of c. 15 per cent from 1970 to 1990 and remains a leading retailer. Its success is built on its partnership involving its whole workforce. It is the largest employee-owned firm in the world.[22] 'Partnership for us is not just about pay and perks, it's also about not letting the side down, being decent and honest between ourselves and with our customers.' Last year all staff on the shop floor got a bonus of 15 per cent of their salary. They appear to be as committed as ever to making the retailer a success.

These sorts of companies with this sort of employee-led approach to customer service appear to have found a winning and sustainable formula. But, for sure, employee loyalty is as hard to get as customer loyalty. Achieving it requires the same focus, effort and determination and may also need the same culture shocks that Xerox, Asda and SAS went through in order to transform the organisation into this more effective way of thinking and behaving.

In summary, a clear path is emerging for the would-be winner in service hustle:

- Measure the right things; don't be satisfied with standard customer research but breakthrough to uncover a true measure of customer satisfaction and intention to repurchase.

- It's not just serving, it's keeping; the thrust now is toward retaining customers for their lifetime, finding ways to break customers' natural tendencies to be promiscuous, and motivate and incentivise them to keep coming back.
- Get the right customers; don't try to be all things to all customers but segment the ones where achieving advantage is most sustainable and most leveraged.
- Do it; get the workforce – each and every employee – to own the service hustle challenge and feel individually committed to delivering it to their customers.

If this provides a pathway toward building this form of strategic advantage, then let's look further and in more detail at the possible underlying sources of service hustle, at what customers are more particularly looking for in this arena.

The third dimension of service hustle

The market commitment model sets out the more specific third dimension of service hustle opportunity as shown in Figure 10.5.

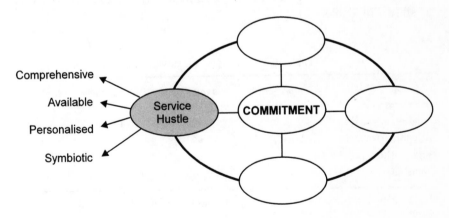

Figure 10.5 Service Hustle: its third dimension

We can further define these concepts as:

- **Comprehensive** – 'whatever I want'.
- **Available** – 'whenever/wherever I want it'.
- **Personalised** – 'tailored just for me'.
- **Symbiotic** – provided in the context of an enduring, mutually beneficial relationship.

These third dimension options are intended to provide a more specific guide for strategy makers. They represent the more detailed sources of this service hustle advantage. By presenting them in the model, experience and analysis has suggested these four sources are the principal types of service hustle and are the main ones that an organisation should explore. As we've said before, there may be some situations where there is some additional type of service not captured here, but that is likely to be the exception rather than the norm.

These third dimension options should not be seen as alternatives. In many ways the more options an organisation can pursue, the stronger will be its competitive position in the market. Typically, however, companies will find there will be one or two of the sources that are most relevant to its customers and which it is most capable of delivering on.

In fact a number of the winning organisations we have featured in this service discussion do score especially competitively in more than one area as shown in Table 10.1.

Table 10.1   Service hustle advantage

	Comprehensive	Available	Personalised	Symbiotic
1-800-FLOWERS		✔	✔	
British Airways	(✔)*	✔		✔
Ritz Carlton	✔	✔	✔	
Sainsbury	✔			(✔)*

*A tick in parentheses suggests the company still has further to go in establishing this area competitively.

So Sainsburys, Tesco, Nordstrom, John Lewis, Home Depot and Andersen Consulting, for example, have the widest possible range and selection of goods and services in their chosen market sectors and attract customers because of it – the most comprehensive service. British Airways, UPS and First Direct have put substantial investments into providing services to the greatest extent possible wherever and whenever the customer wants it – the most available. Levi's, 1-800-FLOWERS, USAA, Hertz Gold Card, Singapore Airlines are moving fast down the road of providing a totally individual personalised service distinguishing each customer, recognising and greeting each customer personally by name, understanding and responding on a personalised basis. And as for those searching for that mutually beneficial relationship and symbiosis, let's consider some more specific illustrations.

- The major automotive companies lead the way. Ford, GM, Chrysler, Toyota and Honda are all leading examples of companies that have required their suppliers to invest in them as customers. While the initiative here is coming from the customer base, nevertheless some component parts suppliers such as Echlin, Rockwell, GKN and Lucas Varity have responded to the challenge and now have exceptionally strong links built on mutual investment in research, systems, automation, supply, design and other areas where they must interact.

  Chrysler, for example, as a customer of its suppliers has benefited substantially by developing strong relationship links with its major suppliers. By working together they speed up product development, reduce development costs, reduce procurement costs, sort out production line defects, and also now pool marketing and promotion resources to increase sales in the market.

- Procter & Gamble has developed very close ties with its major US customer WalMart. Instead of the traditional 'supplier is separate from retailer' philosophy, these two companies now share an integrated supply chain in which, among other things, P&G is increasingly taking responsibility for store-ordering and inventory management. The rationale is for a shared understanding and service leading to reduced supply chain costs and working capital, greater product availability, and generally a larger profit pool to generate between them. The changing relationship is shown in Figure 10.6.

- Baxter International shares business risks with some of its major customers by jointly setting cost reduction targets, establishing joint teams from supplier and customers, and then sharing the savings. Equally, where investments are required there is joint sharing of the investment cost to underline the mutual benefits both parties target. It's the equivalent of establishing a joint Profit and Loss account.

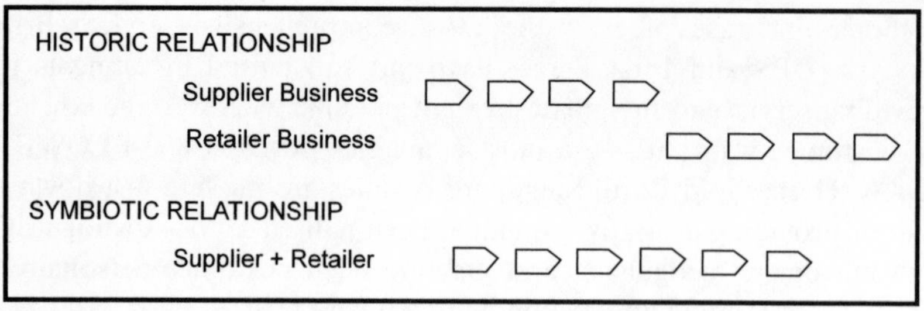

Figure 10.6 Changing relationships between supplier and retailer

- 3M seconded a number of its own people in 1993 to one of its key customers – Boise Cascade – and on its customer's behalf worked at reducing inventory and speeding up Boise Cascade's own customer delivery systems. The two companies had specific cross-functional/cross-company teams that worked together to the same set of objectives.
- Weyerhauser the newsprint manufacturer, and Deere & Co. the agricultural equipment manufacturer, are both examples of companies who require each employee to spend a period of time working in their **customers'** operations, seeing first-hand how their own products and services could be reconfigured to improve their customers' operations.

                    *   *   *

Service hustle can provide a rich source of opportunity for companies striving to find a lasting and competitive advantage. Especially in service industries it's commonly a necessity no matter how strong the core product/service proportion. Consumers are more sophisticated, discriminating and demanding and their expectations have been heightened in recent years. The service organisations described in this chapter are outstanding examples of companies who have risen to this challenge and done so mightily.

For industrial companies, service excellence is not yet common. The automotive industry has forced its suppliers down the symbiotic-relationship path and aerospace is following. But in, say, chemicals, metals and engineering, companies generally still have a long way to go to interpret and institutionalise for themselves what being an excellent service hustler is all about, either through their suppliers or with their customers. Such industrial companies may, however, be forced to accelerate their initiatives in this arena as historic product performance advantages erode and they are compelled to find new forms of advantage to compete successfully.

Service hustle has become a hot topic in the late 1990s. There is much comment and debate in this area and excellent companies are interviewed and paraded as benchmarks and lessons to others. Where one company has achieved a lead in its industry it's going to be hard to catch up. It's not easy to mobilise the workforce to 'give pleasure to their customers', but once institutionalised it can become a strong and sustainable foundation for competitiveness.

11 Competitive Advantage through Pricing

'We're going to democratise the automobile and build a car for the great multitude that everybody will be able to afford. We will price it so that no man making a good salary will be unable to own one.'[1]

(Henry Ford, 1907)

'We exist to provide value to our customers – to make their lives better via lower prices and greater selection – all else is secondary.'[2]

(Sam Walton, WalMart, 1977)

'The purpose of Motorola is to provide products of superior quality at a fair price. We're aiming to sell 100 000 TVs next year at the price of $179.95.'[3]

(Paul Galvin, Motorola, 1949)

'We take a long-term view about our growth and our core skill is the ability to produce massively at very low cost so we can get to the best price for our customers . . . we have a calculatedly aggressive view about price that fits our long-term vision.'[4]

(Woo-Chong Kim, Chairman Daewoo, 1996)

'Our strategy is to price to reflect the product's perceived value to the customers. When we came to price Zantac in 1983, SmithKline Beecham Tagamet was market leader. But Zantac performed better, it had to be at a premium position. We set the price at a 50% premium and it was market leader within 4 years.'[5]

(Glaxo VP, 1996)

These are some outstanding examples of companies who have put Pricing into a long-term context, who have taken a view about the pricing that will underpin a product's positioning in the marketplace for all its life. For these companies, pricing is not just a short-term marketing tool, it's an integral part of their long-term strategy. In some instances it will even be their main strategic focus (Figure 11.1).

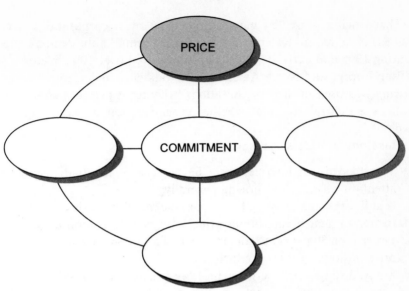

Figure 11.1   Price in the market commitment model

Such organisations stand out as among the few who have shown a mastery and sophistication around Pricing. Companies like Coca-Cola, John Lewis Partnership and Great Lakes Chemicals, and others we will investigate, have deliberately developed a long-term reputation with customers for a particular price position for their products which reflects their **perceived** value. They have understood both the macro-economic environment[6] of their chosen markets and have rigorously evaluated at the micro-level the individual competitiveness of each product, what it is worth in its customer segments and developed its future pricing strategy.

But our research has shown that for most companies pricing remains an unexploited tool. It is rarely used in a sophisticated way and is misunderstood. It's typically treated as part of the marketing tactics, a short-term lever to boost volume sales, for example, rather than an integral part of a company's long-term competitive positioning.

Why is pricing treated in this way? The intention of this chapter is to explore pricing as a prime form of long-term competitive advantage and to examine the roadblocks that cause its more tactical than strategic profile and exploitation. I want to encourage strategy makers to see pricing as a positive long term means for signalling value in the marketplace; to establish its place – not relative cost or scale – as a meaningful and prime form of strategy.

That pricing is treated inappropriately in most corporations is not denied, as a recent Kalchas pricing survey remarkably demonstrated. During 1995 and early 1996 Kalchas interviewed over 100 directors and VPs in Europe and North America.[7] We wanted to understand how well pricing was used in their organisations, whether it played a strategic as well as a tactical role and whether executives felt it was adequately exploited.

Our findings were surprising:

- The majority of interviewees – 63 per cent – felt that insufficient attention was given to pricing generally.
- A still larger majority – 71 per cent – acknowledged that pricing was treated in their organisations principally as a short-term tactic.
- Fewer than 30 per cent claimed they had a three-year-plus view on the price position of their products.
- Many distinguished between the way pricing was considered at the time of a product launch and then its subsequent treatment. With a new product introduction there was often considerable input and discussion as to the product's appropriate market pricing prior to the launch. However, as one VP put it: 'As soon as it's handed over to the Sales Department we seem to lose control, they start discounting or whatever and they never want to put the price up, only down – from then on we've lost it.'
- Of greatest concern was that 56 per cent felt that inadequate treatment of pricing in their companies was leaving millions of dollars of shareholder value on the table: 'I wouldn't be surprised if there were several margin points not being captured.'

Getting the most value out of pricing is becoming ever more critical. Growth in revenues generally within the more established and mature western markets is increasingly difficult. So intense and capable is the competition that companies commonly find themselves fighting over only small incremental gains in sales and market share. New products that might have been expected to drive future revenue growth are often quickly copied and any sales impact dissipated. Pressure is kept on pricing through the constant stream of new suppliers from LDCs. The 'cloak of inflation' that had previously enabled many to disguise price increases has now been firmly removed in the West. In this environment companies cannot afford to give insufficient attention to their top revenue line or ignore the pivotal role that effective pricing can have in underpinning any long-term revenue growth. It cannot be treated as only a short-term tactic. Its full potential must be exploited.

This Kalchas survey plus other research and observation has shown there are four roadblocks which need to be removed:

1. To date there has been no adequate tool for thinking about pricing strategically.
2. Pricing responsibility within companies is organised poorly.
3. The right information is generally not available to senior management to enable them to treat price more appropriately.
4. There is a widespread feeling that 'pricing is outside our control'.

Inadequate strategy tools

We have already discussed how most available strategy tools look inward and talk about cost or scale or operational excellence. Yet today's customers care less about the manufacturer's costs in making a product. What they will care about is the price that's charged and what other benefits or advantages they perceive are in the product proposition for them.

Costs anyway should never be the sole determinant of price. They are an input into formulating the company's final pricing strategy, not the arbiter. Of course a company must make some trade-off between the price the customer will pay and its own financial needs, but it is the benefit the **customer** recognises that must remain the principal driver.

So the strategy frameworks that encourage management to focus on their scale economies or their operational excellence or their cost position are unhelpful in this respect. They actually take no account of what product/pricing proposition should be put to customers. Where is the customer benefit in all this 'denominator management'? Looking to build competitive strategy on internal strengths instead of on what the customer values is, at worst, a waste of the efforts and energies of the workforce and likely to lead to a destruction of shareholder value.

Ironically, the company that sets prices from the perspective of its own internal position generally foregoes the very profit it seeks. If a company's internal focus leads it to price below what customers will pay, it will fail to realise its full profit potential. If it prices above what customers will pay, the product will also fail to sell and again the opportunity for profit is lost. Pricing based or driven exclusively off the company's own internal perspectives is inappropriate and ineffective.

Unfortunately, even those strategy and management tools that do focus on the customer and can be described as more market-based, curiously overlook pricing and the role it should play. For example, a recent study on customer loyalty by Reichheld scarcely mentions price, yet the thrust of the argument is all about ways and means to retain customers for life.[8] There is plenty of discussion about customer relationship management, exploiting employee productivity and improving quality, but no apparent role for price as part of the total customer proposition. Given that pricing is commonly the first or second item on the customer agenda, this omission on pricing is all the more surprising.

Similarly, Treacy and Wiersema's work on the *Discipline of Market Leaders* gives a vigorous account of the value of 'customer intimacy' and the importance of developing a product proposition that meets customers' needs.[9] They do talk powerfully about relationship management and the role employees must play in building that, but the role of price is largely ignored. In fact it is only mentioned to point out that successful companies can charge a premium for their value-added. It is treated as a consequence of some other activity instead of a driving force in its own right.

In fact, as we can illustrate, for many companies pricing does play a leading if not the defining role in building successful relationships with customers.

Food retailer Aldi's customers know the company is 'low price no frills'; it's what they expect and trust Aldi to deliver. It's Aldi's consistent promise and it's been delivered successfully over many years. Low pricing is Aldi's principal form of strategy and its main form of competitive advantage. It's a strategy that drives its whole organisational structure, resulting in an especially lean low-cost logistics system and a set of values amongst employees that while positive and enthusiastic accepts a no-frills few-perks environment.

Chemicals company Great Lakes has established an outstanding reputation with its customers for superior performing products, and its price premium positioning is an important signal to the market. Like Mercedes, customers have come to appreciate the superior performance and reliability and are willing to pay for it. Managing and sustaining that price premium reputation with their customers is a major part of Great Lakes' efforts in the marketplace. Like Bang & Olufsen, there is a specific corporate commitment to avoid depreciating perceptions of their quality image with any significant price discounting. Indeed, the premium price image is deliberately reinforced by explicit promotion of the company's long-term commitment to technical excellence.

For other companies like Marks & Spencer, Raychem and Procter & Gamble, price positioning is an integral part of their overall market proposition, and maintaining that relative to competition is a delicate and continuous juggling act – but a critical one that cannot be overlooked. It is treated proactively and with great attention.

Companies must ask themselves: can price serve as our primary strategy for attracting customers, as it does for Aldi and Fujitsu? Alternatively, can it serve as a consistent signal of quality as with Great Lakes or Rentokil or Rubbermaid? Will price serve to deliberately restrict the company's market to an exclusive segment, as it does for Gucci and Paccar trucks? Will it act as a value-reinforcing function as it does for Marks & Spencer, Ford and Swatch? Or will pricing become a joint decision made with the customer, and a catalyst for deeper win–win customer relationships, as it does for example between automotive manufacturers and their suppliers?

For all organisations, a company's long-term pricing position is a critical element in the way customers perceive its products and services and react to the overall product/service proposition put before them. Especially in these very competitive times, that long-term position must be monitored and fine-tuned as appropriate. Suppliers are never going to become successfully 'intimate' with their customers if they only manage the Performance or Service or Emotion side of the relationship.

That is why the Market Commitment model does treat Pricing as in fact one of the four prime forms of competitive advantage. It is incorporated in this way because it reflects the realities of the late 1990s marketplace. Pricing is the number-1 or number-2 question on every customers lips in any product presentation. In all research it's a major influence on customer decision-making. Reacting to that on a short-term tactical basis will, in today's environment, most likely lead to continued pricing pressures and a downwards spiral of pricing levels. On the other hand, determining a long-term pricing position that drives to or supports meaningful customer advantage in the marketplace, and working deliberately and proactively to reinforce that position, can be a platform for success.

Poor organisation of pricing responsibility

Given the findings of the Kalchas pricing survey referred to earlier, we wanted to explore further the reasons for the 'inadequate attention' given to pricing. What emerged particularly strongly was that pricing decision-making is poorly structured and relegated to tacticians rather than owned by strategy makers.

- In over 80 per cent of the companies included in the survey, pricing was the responsibility of the sales department. But 'I have never seen a salesperson yet who wanted to increase price'.

  When challenged, nearly all agreed that the sales department would be most likely to treat pricing as a tactical and short-term tool, with the emphasis being on managing volume sales rather than long-term profitability.

  > 'We appear to have handed over one of the key levers in the business.'

  > 'If we haven't got a total company input into Pricing how can we hope to get the most profitable mix?'

- In only 14 per cent of the companies was the finance department specifically involved in the price decision-making process.

  > 'It's hard to get the balance but at least we're thinking about our long-term profitability rather than next month's sales.'

- In less than 10 per cent of companies did the CEO feel close enough to the pricing decisions.

  > 'It's just too low down on my agenda.'

  > 'My problem is even when I feel in my bones the pricing is wrong I'm too removed from the market and our customers to really challenge the sales people.'

If pricing is delegated to one function in this way, and to a function rooted in a short-term and tactical perspective, then it is no surprise that in such organisations pricing is treated ineffectively and inappropriately.

If a company can acknowledge that pricing must play a long-term, as well as a short-term role in the business, then that long-term pricing responsibility must be restored to the long-term thinkers – that is, the senior management of the company and especially to the strategy makers.

It calls for some reorganisation but not a structural revolution. Sales departments can continue to take a lead on tactical pricing, though even that responsibility is better managed if it has proper input from finance and marketing departments for example. But the long-term positioning calls for a different approach; it's more fundamental to the way the entire company must operate and requires much more detailed consideration and evaluation.

If we take Glaxo as one possible role model, that company has a Market Strategy department that sits between sales, finance, medical and the more traditional sales marketing departments. Its role is to think and plan for the long term. One of its prime objectives is to develop the long-term strategy for its products. This role has become all the more critical as traditional product-performance gaps versus competition erode, products come off patents and lower-priced generics penetrate markets and customers. In these circumstances, this strategy unit is thinking about alternative forms of competitive advantage and has among other things a responsibility to maintain the long-term premium pricing position of the product. In doing so it acts as a counterpoint to sales department who see the price down, volume up short-term benefits, and to finance who may see the opportunities to milk certain product situations while they can.

As an alternative approach, at the UK utility London Electricity the concern and need to manage supply pricing is so great that they have considered establishing a specific pricing function. The aim would be to co-ordinate all pricing decision-making in one department. The team would become highly skilled in pricing, understanding the elasticity with each customer, carrying out conjoint analysis to review the effects on pricing of additional add-on services, for example, and generally leading in a crucial area of the company's market competitiveness.

Perhaps strategy makers in other organisations can adopt one of these structures or reinvigorate an existing one to guard and nurture pricing's longer-term potential.

The right information not available

A further roadblock highlighted by the pricing survey was that often information about market pricing within the company was generally poor.

- Only 28 per cent of companies rigorously monitored pricing information of their products versus their competitors.
- Less than 20 per cent actively reviewed the drivers of their product price sensitivity and fine-tuned the price within any sort of long-term framework to maintain the price vs value-added relationship.
- Only 15 per cent of organisations had any institutionalised system for measuring the profitability of each of their product or service lines, or

had a mechanism in place for incorporating that understanding into price decision-making.

Why did Marlboro experience such unexpected share loss on Marlboro Friday in the spring of 1994? Put simply, having established a premium price position for its cigarettes it had failed to monitor that premium. The customer price–value equation which made the customer ready to pay an extra 50¢ a pack versus 'discount smokes' had been severely undermined by constant incremental price increases. But no one was monitoring this at Philip Morris as the premium crept up to a $1 a pack. At that level Marlboro was nearly twice the price of some deeply discounted basic cigarettes. Not surprisingly, when Philip Morris pushed things too far volume began to tail, distribution was cut and the brand was forced into an embarrassing 40¢ price cut. Share has now come back for Marlboro but there was a harsh lesson for the organisation – failure to manage the long-term pricing positioning of the product can destroy it, and it's critical to have the right information to enable the company's decision-makers to manage that positioning.

In contrast, Procter & Gamble did monitor its pricing. Its premium on Tide was moving up too high versus discount private label whose own product performance had also been improving significantly. P&G, however, did not wait for another 'black Friday', but its keen observation of its price–value position enabled it to anticipate customer concerns and by cutting its price on Tide restore the value proposition to a more persuasive level.

Getting the right information together is not that difficult. Today's software packages, the experience and sophistication of activity-based cost accounting, the amount of research and information generally published or obtainable in the marketplace, especially in western countries, enables companies to collect and analyse product pricing data relatively easily. If a company acknowledges this need for information and the importance of understanding its price position and managing it, then the steps in processing that information need not be especially time-consuming nor require significant investment.

Effective information management is directly within a company's control; just as organising how pricing decisions get taken is something a company can address relatively quickly. That few do it well enough today is disappointing, but more positively that provides opportunity for those who do. If we accept the role of pricing as a long-term driver of business success, then relatively straightforward internal information management and organisation steps should be high on the list of priorities.

'Pricing is outside our control'

A common roadblock in talking about pricing effectiveness within a company is the widespread feeling that: 'it's outside our control', 'the customer is always pushing prices down', 'we can plan what we want but if our major distributor insists on a price cut basically we've got no choice'.

Is pricing truly as one-sided as that? If a company really has lost control of pricing in that way then it must also have lost control of any value-added the product might bring. To reach a point where a company's long-term pricing proposition can be so undermined, the product must have lost any form of recognisable competitive advantage in the market and become a complete commodity in the customers' eyes. As companies battle to establish their preferred pricing position in the market, they must confront those who claim 'its outside our control'. Is the product really that weak, is its pricing position in the market really completely beyond our influence?

For some products this may indeed be the case, but for many products in a company's portfolio I find deeper investigation shows that there does indeed remain some form of advantage. It may not necessarily have been fully exploited but there is often potential to begin to challenge a customer's 'price-down' view. In addition, not all customers will be as price sensitive as others. Some will see the added value more clearly and as more relevant to them.

What's important is for the organisation to push aside the 'outside our control' attitude and to encourage debate about what is the value-added with the customer, what advantages are there, are we communicating that to customers, can we exploit it better or differently?

To start this investigation, what is helpful is to unravel and unbundle the whole product–customer portfolio and start thinking about each separately and distinctly, distinguishing the less price sensitive or more customer responsive areas (see Figure 11.2).

While a company must set an overall long-term pricing position for its products to establish its core value proposition, that pricing position can be fine-tuned for these different customer segments. An understanding of different customer buying needs will help not only establish the right level of pricing, but provide continued insight as to how each customer or customer group is measuring the competitive value-added of the products they can choose from in their area.

If the supplier or manufacturer can develop the detailed and slightly different market understanding for each main customer box or segment

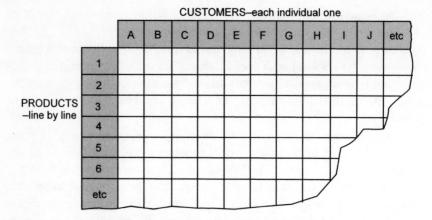

Figure 11.2   The product–customer portfolio

of Figure 11.2, then it can take a more precise view as to the different pricing opportunities and needs in each.

For a company like Glaxo such analysis is critical. Like all pharmaceutical companies it is generally under increasing pricing pressure, but Glaxo's leverage is very different in each market with different customers. Even though its antibiotic drugs, for example, are largely similar in performance to some of its rivals, in some countries some customers are found to value their longer-term contact and relationship with Glaxo more, and are less concerned about the absence of any noticeable product superiority. In such cases Glaxo can build on and manage that relationship and still maintain a premium price. With others it may have to price differently.

Glaxo has determined to take control of pricing for itself where it can. It has unbundled its different customer segments or 'boxes', researched each different customer and so immersed itself that it can target **individual** pricing opportunities within the portfolio and go after them.

If a company is able to succeed here, to knock aside these various roadblocks of internal organisation, information management and attitude, and is willing to reappraise its long-term pricing propositions, then pricing can begin to play its more vital role as a prime form of competitive advantage.

As we evaluate the exploitation of pricing in this way, we can further explore the third dimension of the market commitment model and the underlying sources of pricing advantage.

The third dimension of pricing

We can define four specific underlying sources of pricing strategy as shown in Figure 11.3. They are rooted in what markets generally demand and in what customers more particularly are looking for. Observation and experience suggest these are the principal options that a company can investigate and pursue in setting price as its main strategy or as part of a wider competitive proposition. And, to repeat, while there may be other options in some industry situations they are likely to be the exception, and certainly any evaluation of pricing should start with these four specific sources of opportunity.

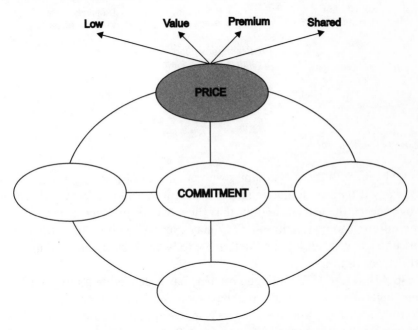

Figure 11.3 Pricing: its third dimension

Choice of pricing option will inevitably vary with the total value-added the supplier is able to provide. The greater the perceived value in the customer's eyes, for example, the more opportunity to price adequately to capture the full product investment and what it is worth.

We can draw a simple illustration of this, as shown in Figure 11.4, to indicate how the customer's perception of relative value is a pivotal influence on the specific source and option of pricing strategy to be pursued.

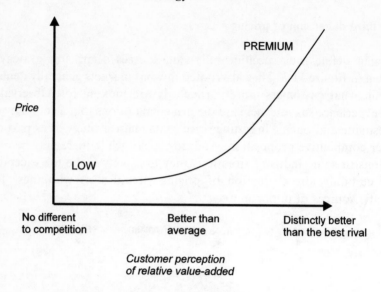

Figure 11.4 The perception of relative value

Low price strategies

If we begin with those companies who pursue a low pricing strategy, then typically if they are managing price deliberately and proactively they will not concern themselves unduly that their overall product proposition is 'no different to competition'. They may expressly choose to adopt a low price strategy as a result, and determine to be the best and most consistent at delivering that.

So Argos, the UK catalogue retailer, has a deliberate strategy of 'pile 'em high, sell 'em cheap' and has successfully developed a powerful consumer proposition in selling reasonable quality household goods at low prices. Its approach is different from Rubbermaid which continues to push its product quality, branding values and reliability in the same arena but is pursuing a different pricing course. Yet even with low prices, Argos has built up a strong profit base and shown consistent growth through the 1990s

'Fujitsu shokku' was the term applied to Fujitsu's determinedly low-price strategy for its PCs through the early 1990s. They were certainly no better than those of Compaq or IBM, but Fujitsu had deliberately chosen to price at a low level so it could maintain and build its market share. To sustain this low pricing position, Fujitsu had overhauled its supply network and sourced components from overseas making a 20–30 per cent saving. At that stage it viewed PCs as being largely a commodity, 'but business is about survival and our prices are our hope', Fujitsu's President Tadashi Sekizaura commented at the time.

Successful exploitation of low price platforms also appears commonly in the airline industry. The major airlines have long been challenged by determinedly low-price operators who see the opportunity to price low, undercut their larger more established higher cost higher price rivals, and carve out a customer segment where their value proposition is especially persuasive. Laker and People were among the earliest to make a meaningful impact achieving high profile with cheap transatlantic fares. More recently, Europe has seen the emergence of many small regional airlines such as AirOne, Noman, Air Outre Mer, Air Liberté, Spanair, Air Europe and Easyjet. These newcomers charge low fares and they make this profitable by keeping costs low, being less unionised and having a more flexible workforce. As Robert Crandall, Chairman of American Airlines, has commented recently: 'the market is telling all airlines that they must now learn to compete in a low price low cost world'.

Low pricing provides many clear examples of single-minded companies who have built long-term successful strategies on that specific platform. Can we find similar effectiveness and success at the premium pricing end?

Premium price strategies

A premium price by itself is a signal to customers. It implies some additional value. It's suggesting this product or service is not necessarily for everyone, perhaps not all can afford it, and it encourages perceptions of exclusivity and aspiration.

Sometimes that signal by itself without any other validation or substantiation can create the perception of higher quality and persuade customers to buy. Wine is a good example. Many consumers lack other information enabling them to evaluate the quality of the wine before purchase. They tend to rely on relative price as a cue to a product's relative quality, commonly assuming that the higher price could not long survive unless justified.

In fact there are examples where a new car wax made no headway in the market till its price was raised to a premium. In healthcare, many professionals successfully set deliberately high prices to encourage the notion of a higher quality more exclusive service. There is the well-known example too of Loctite glue which had been struggling for market share. The same basic product was repackaged in a more attractive way and a new price set at a premium of nearly 100 per cent to the rest of market. The product became highly successful.

Setting a premium pricing strategy without any further validation or substantiation does however potentially leave the company vulnerable. More commonly a company will develop that premium positioning on price along with and linked to some other form of advantage. This might be founded in the emotional values, brand image or reputation built up around a product or service the company is offering. It might rest very tangibly on some customer-recognised superior product performance. Or it might be linked to some service hustle proposition which the customer especially values. Let's consider each of these linkages in turn.

Premium pricing is often linked to emotion as a validating form. Chanel, Versace, Marlboro, Coke, Ferrari and Dulux all command premium prices which are principally supported by their image and reputation. While in some cases there is some additional product performance value such as with Ferrari, the performance difference alone does not support the size of price premium. But that premium is easily commanded in the market place and established by consistent support and investment in emotional and branding values around the product.

These premium positions need to be carefully nurtured however; a brand will carry a premium but the question is how much? As we saw with Marlboro and as happened to Dulux paint, the price:value-added equation can fall out of line unless it is carefully monitored.

Where the price premium is linked to product performance there is typically a more tangible and sometimes economically rational justification for the premium positioning. Increasingly, in pharmaceuticals for example, suppliers to more sophisticated western customers are able to consolidate their product's position by providing an economic rationale based on the product's performance advantage to justify the price premium. This might be based on the time the product saves nurses, or the labour saving from more convenient easy-to-use packaging, or reduced patient in-hospital time. Whatever the basis, customers in this environment are demanding but can be persuaded by evidence along these lines to justify and enhance the price positioning.

When Procter & Gamble introduced its disposable diaper it went to great lengths to demonstrate and quantify for consumers the product performance benefits and related cost savings of using disposables versus the towelling system most households then employed. It was in a position to provide a compelling argument to validate the price premium by reference to these performance advantages. In practice, for the average consumer the cost savings arguments were too sophisticated, but it didn't matter as there were still other more immediately recognisable product benefits to link with the price in the general convenience and emotional baby-care values the product additionally offered.

Other premium price/product performance-linked positions may less easily provide a clear economic rationale, but nevertheless still establish a value-added that customers recognise and desire. For example Good-year's Aquatred tire was priced at about 10 per cent more than Goodyear's previous top-of-the-line tire, the specific performance advantages were not that significant but it was positioned very effectively to provide 'better traction on wet roads' and sold with great success. Great Lakes, Du Pont and Raychem all seek to develop superior performing products which meet specific customer needs. They aim to do this so much better than anything else available that they can command a price premium often beyond what any economic rationale could justify. SAP, for example, can push its price premium up to 50 per cent for its software because it is perceived as so much better than its rivals, even though there is sometimes insufficient economic justification.

The final aspect of premium pricing is where it is linked alternatively to a service hustle proposition. This is a combined form of advantage which we are seeing with increasing frequency as customers become more demanding. It may be the premium to Fedex for guaranteed delivery before 9.00 a.m., or the premium to sit in British Airways club world or first class and be offered premier service, or the additional services provided with the American Express gold card which are deemed worth the extra price.

However premium pricing is established or linked, this examination of it as a strategic option is helpful too in understanding how the market commitment model can best be used. Is pricing a prime strategy in its own right – as it might be for low price providers – or is it a complementary linking form of advantage that works alongside Service Hustle or Performance or Emotion to combine into a most competitive customer proposition? Provided the strategy is being built on the foundation stone of commitment, then the model sets out a clear set of options for strategy makers.

Before we leave price we must finally explore the two other specific themes of underlying advantage – that is value pricing and shared pricing.

Value pricing

This is defined here as a price that customers would deem reasonable or appropriate given the level of perceived value-added of the associated product or service. It's generally neither a high price nor a bargain, and would lie comfortably in the middle of our pricing curve as shown in Figure 11.5.

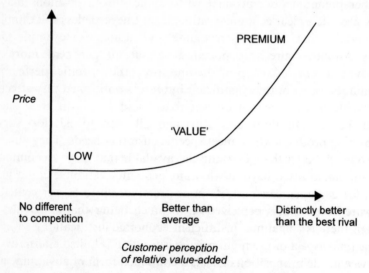

Figure 11.5 'Value' on the pricing curve

In many competitive situations today a company will often have some small value-added to offer its customers, but it will not commonly be perceived as **distinctly** better than the best rival. In such situations its 'better than average' proposition – if recognised as such by customers – lends itself properly to a value-pricing strategy. There's enough in the proposition to resist low price rivals and price more fairly to reflect the extra value added. This value pricing opportunity is also typically reinforced by small advantages in performance, service or emotion.

Value pricing is becoming increasingly attractive to companies. It provides a positive alternative to the more traditional cost plus approach that reflects the old asset-led view of the world. Instead it encourages the now more appropriate customer-driven perspective. As a VP at General Motors Chevrolet division commented recently, 'we didn't use to do it this way but now our Marketeers set a value price customers can afford, then we say our profit is so much and we back down into cost'. As Compaq have put it more succinctly, 'we design to price'.

Marks & Spencer and Swatch are two classically recognised masters of a value pricing strategy. Marks & Spencer has long pursued a strategy which combines 'quality, value and service'. The whole organisation is geared to being the best volume retailer and its pricing is typically just a little higher than the average of its rivals. It doesn't seek to be low price, or 'never knowingly undersold' as its rival the John Lewis Partnership would claim. Yet it's not at the higher fashion, exclusive department store end such as Selfridges or Harrods.

Swatch's overall proposition is that a watch can be more than just functional, it can have a fun design as well. Its basic model sold at the same $40 price and did not change in price for ten years: 'price has become a mirror for the other attributes we try to communicate . . . it's different from an ordinary watch . . . but it's deliberately affordable and approachable'.

For Marks & Spencer, Swatch, Chevrolet, Compaq and others, their value pricing is at the core of their total competitive strategy position. It's a part of a service or product or brand value mix, and managing each element effectively is a critical requirement for success.

Increasingly, other companies are joining this value pricing band as their 'distinctly better than the best rival' position erodes and they are forced by the market to adjust their premium position to something that better reflects the level of recognised value added. Most noticeably and recently, Procter & Gamble has dramatically cut its price on Tide and its other leading brands to restore its price value equation with its customers.[10] P&G will never be a low price company; it provides too much additional value in the form of its branding, its continued stream of new products, and its constant search to improve product performance. But the company no longer sits arrogantly as a premium priced branded manufacturer and pays much greater attention to its value price position.

Shared pricing

The fourth underlying source of advantage that has been defined here is termed 'shared' pricing.

This represents a completely different approach to pricing. Instead of the supplier setting the price – albeit in a market-driven way – the supplier deliberately engages and involves the customer in the price decision-making process. Pricing becomes a shared responsibility and goal. It's a way of locking into a deeper customer relationship to the exclusion of rivals. It's increasingly being pursued as a strategy where there are no other advantages, where pricing is the main purchase criteria and the company is searching around to find some other way of resisting low price pressures and still add value and differentiate itself. Here a company can find a different way to stand out among otherwise price-sensitive customers by turning pricing into a joint decision instead of one company trying to impose and negotiate a view of price on the other.

A simple example of this is open-book pricing. It's the way suppliers to the automotive industry, for example, must work if they are to build some lasting and effective relationship with their customers. It does indeed require the supplier to open the management accounts and cost ledger to the customer, review the drivers of cost, time and margin and work together to set a price which the customer regards as appropriate and suppliers feel they can live by. Historically it's usually been the customer who has been the proactive demander of a shared pricing approach, but increasingly it is the supplier who is taking the lead and turning it to advantage.

Shared pricing as an approach to build customer relationships is given greater authority where it is established on as broad a base as possible. Typically this now involves consideration of the whole of the supply chain including the joint system economics of both the supplier and the individual customer. In this context, 'sharing' or open-book becomes more convincing as it develops a more complete business rationale based on a full view of the joint costs of doing business together and the future potential. Such an arrangement is not only based on simplifying and streamlining supply chain costs, but can go well beyond that into joint collaboration on new products or even mutual investment in each other's businesses.

In food ingredients, Dalgety has established a very strong relationship with its customer McDonald's in the US. Each year a new contract is jointly discussed and agreed, with pricing set on a transparent open-book rational basis. It's significantly different from the fraught emotional negotiation which used to characterise the relationship between the two parties years ago and where neither side really wins. It's taken significant investment by Dalgety to get to this position. It's not just in the systems to track the costs, or in the major cost and supply-chain improvements that have to be delivered each year, but also in building up the trust where this shared pricing approach is respected and not abused.

Procter & Gamble has been a leading exponent of price transparency in its dealings with its customers to the extent it has become another source of advantage for it. It stands out from the pack because its product pricing and discount structure is set on an open rational basis. The price the customers pay becomes a shared decision and responsibility. Customers know that depending upon a set of agreed supply chain efficiencies the price to them can be reduced, for example by the use of EDI, a linked stock-order system, cross-docking and so on. Instead of the annual round of adversarial discussion there is now an institutionalised and accepted rational platform of pricing debate.

Recent research by British consultancy firm Silverman Associates has highlighted this opportunity for suppliers.[11] It has investigated how suppliers can find advantage in otherwise commodity business areas, and has looked at some form of shared pricing as a way of breaking down adversarial supplier–customer relationships and building a different more attractive approach:

'At the root of the problem in relationships between retailers and manufacturers is the tendency for the supplier to compete on low price and so find margins driven down to almost nothing. Our research shows retailers are crying out for their suppliers to take a shared partnership approach. Instead suppliers' often overlong and erratic delivery times, chaotic invoicing methods, reluctance to fully use information technology and their generally adversarial approach seriously limit the volume and quality of business they can do. Consequently there is plenty of opportunity to work closely together to reduce price sensitivity.'

Despite the fact that many customers are crying out for their suppliers to operate more in this way and that the automotive industry especially has been pioneering in this area, most suppliers do not pursue this avenue of opportunity. They generally fear that such shared pricing will open the way to further erosion of margin. But in situations where their products or services are no different from their rivals then it can provide a breakthrough with customers. And if the company can in addition show commitment to its market and to improving its customer relationships generally this might be enough to give it competitive advantage versus other less proactive rivals.

*   *   *

In summary, we have urged a reappraisal of the long-term role of pricing as a form of strategic advantage rather than a tactical tool. This requires not just a recognition within the organisation of the potential of thinking about pricing in this more leveraged way. It also requires a number of organisational and structural changes to enable pricing to come centre-stage and be managed proactively and effectively from there.

The Market Commitment Model provides a framework for working with pricing in this more strategic way and suggests four principal underlying sources which research and observation indicate are the most likely types of advantage available.

Armed with this greater understanding on pricing and building on the right level of commitment, a company can develop a long-term pricing strategy and vision that sets or reinforces its competitive position and establishes a greater chance of finding the lasting success that especially its investors and employees demand.

12 Competitive Advantage through Emotion

Our description of the Market Commitment model has so far taken us through three of the major strategies influencing customer purchasing in the late 1990s. We've looked at Product Performance – how well a product or service does its job. We've shown how breakthrough Service, in support of the core-product proposition, can transform customer loyalty. And we've discussed the Pricing of the product either as a long-term strategy in its own right or as part of a wider value proposition.

These three strategies – Performance, Service Hustle and Price – combined with a commitment to the market and the customer present clear primary routes to finding customer advantage and success in the market place. But are they complete, is there anything else, any other strategic option we also need to capture?

As we have already highlighted in laying out the Market Commitment model, there is one opportunity that is missed by these three. Something that is so important, so fundamental to many companies that it has to be recognised as a prime form of competitive advantage in its own right.

The missing opportunity and our fourth strategic option that we capture in the model is 'Emotion' (Figure 12.1). We mean the emotional and image values that have been created for a particular product or service – the E-factor. We are describing those emotions and feelings that are intimately associated with a product and which can make it stand out from the crowd. They can be compelling. They can create desire. They can persuade the customer to choose a particular product even when all other things between it and its rivals – Performance, Service and Price – are otherwise seen as equal.

This Emotional force can come in different forms. It might be the recognition and appreciation that is generated by an established Brand, the product or service being in some way marked or branded in an emotionally distinct way. It might be in the recognition of a company's proven track record or an appreciation of the importance of a long-term relationship or a company's commitment to innovation. It might be the appeal and aesthetics of a design or style. It can even be about encouraging emotional feelings of patriotism to buy British or 'made in

185

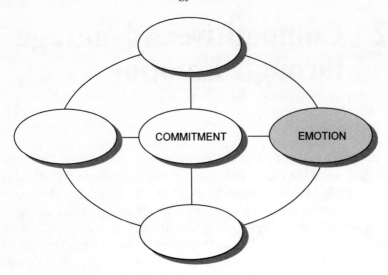

Figure 12.1   Emotion in the market commitment model

the USA'. In whatever form, Emotion must now be recognised as having the potential to be as major and lasting an influence on customer purchasing as any of the other three strategic options.

We will explore the specific types of E-advantage in more detail later in this chapter but before that let's better understand its overall potential. 'E' drives the success of some of the world's leading companies:

• Coca-Cola is the world's most valuable brand. It is the world's most widely-recognised expression after 'OK'. It is a 'global affirmation recognised everywhere'. A core focus of what Coca-Cola is about is to 'rapidly add strength to the world's strongest brand . . . we're talking about the brand's ability to inspire people . . . to become the preferred beverage everywhere'.

  Each year Coca-Cola spends up to 30 per cent of net operating revenues on selling and marketing – an extraordinary ratio and significantly ahead of other packaged-goods companies. Since 1980 the share price has grown at an average annual compound rate of 24 per cent, twice the level of the Dow Jones Industrial average. Consistent and continuous commitment to building the brand values has been at the heart of Coca-Cola's success. They summarise it themselves with this stark assertion: 'If our company burned to the ground we'd have no trouble rebuilding based on the strength of our trademarks alone.'[1]

- Procter & Gamble are setting their plans to 'win in the twenty-first century'.

  'First we will need to expand our line up of global brands. We have a solid foundation to build on. *Brand Week* magazine's ranking of Super Brands shows P&G led the list of companies in the categories in which we compete. P&G is listed as having 17 "Super" brands, our next closest competitor has 8. The real depth and breadth of our business is reflected in this list of our brands . . . brands that are winning the loyalty of consumers around the world.'[2]

- Rubbermaid, voted America's most admired corporation, proudly proclaims its reputation as 'America's No. 1 Household Brand.'

  'Across the country shoppers reported that the one brand they knew and trusted most was also the one they would buy and amongst all its competitors Rubbermaid was acclaimed the best.' [It was voted ahead of leaders like Black & Decker, General Electric and Hoover in independent trade research on brands' consumer value.]

  'Our vision is to delight customers around the world with Branded products which are responsive to their trends . . . and make their lives more enjoyable and productive.' [Building leading Brands is Rubbermaid's major goal.][3]

'E' lies directly behind the success of luxury goods companies like Bulgari, Gucci, Hermes and Tag Heuer. What else other than their deliberately created powerful emotional and image values is driving customer purchasing? It certainly isn't the basic performance of the products that's any better than cheaper rivals and the support services are rarely outstanding. It is the trust and recognition they have generated over years of consistent advertising and promotion-building, the sense of exclusivity and desire.

In fact as the bull market for stocks stays strong through the mid-1990s and consumers put the recessionary fears of the beginning of the decade behind them, we have seen a surge in luxury branded goods companies' shares. Tiffany and Bulgari's stock price doubled through 1996 and P/E ratios of 30+ in the sector were common. Newly rich Asians, Latin Americans and Russians rush to indulge and demand is forecast to grow 10 per cent plus each year on average through to the end of this century.

Building emotion as a prime source of competitive advantage is becoming a major thrust now for many companies and developing as the core of what they do. They can see the success of, for example, Coca-Cola, Procter & Gamble and Rubbermaid. Those companies excel at exploiting their products emotional and brand values. They develop recognisable differentiation in the market place, sustain price premiums versus other similar products, and continue to generate growth in sales and earnings even when their basic product performance is often no better.

In fact as many market sectors approach a commodity-like status as basic product performance advantages erode, so companies will be forced to consider alternative strategies, with E among them. If they stick to their historic product-technology orientation, they might find the more agile of their rivals stealing a march in the service arena, or very possibly in developing and exploiting a more competitive set of emotional values that make a difference with customers.

Look how the following company is trying to break the mould:

Case Study

Citicorp

Citicorp's boss John Reed has recently announced a new platform to drive the bank's continued recovery and global growth.

Reed proposes to turn Citibank into a worldwide consumer brand to become 'the Coca-Cola or McDonald's of the financial services world'.

Reed has said his intention is to distinguish Citibank from its competition through brand building and thereby cut through the commodity nature of the banks' products and services and either be able to charge more, or, through increasing the pull effect from the consumer, sell more. Reed has also said that one of the secondary objectives is to capture and take advantage of the latent value in the Citibank name and to exploit some of that 'Brand equity'.

While Citicorp's P/E is around 10/11, Coke's P/E is around 35! (1996 market valuations). Reed's aim is to 'turn the Bank into a consumer goods company'.

While this new strategy and platform for growth may at first sight seem a surprising turn, market commentators suggest it is sound and with high potential. 'Citi's long-standing focus on the consumer, now two decades old – gives it a real leg-up in knowing how to establish a worldwide brand.'

'Citi already has the technical ability to sort and manage data for a large customer base and to segment that customer base for different products . . . Citi is already ahead of its competitors in exploiting its consumer brand franchise.'[4]

Unless a company explores these other options it could end up with no differentiation and be forced by its customers down the ever-spiralling price negotiation and reduction path. How often have we heard the cries, 'our customers only think about price, there's nothing else we can do, it all comes down to who can offer the lowest prices'.

Yet in such circumstances in the next breath I have equally often heard managers say: 'but we've got the best reputation out there in the market, our brand has been around a long time, we've never let a customer down, our customers tell us they like dealing with us'. If this is the case then surely it represents an opportunity to build and develop those reputation and relationship strengths, to understand what they might be worth and find ways to exploit them. E is not something that can be achieved overnight, it may take years of investment and deliberate action but it may be the route to sustain an otherwise unviable position.

How else have Procter & Gamble and Unilever maintained price premiums, profitability and growth in that staid commodity, soap powder? How has Monsanto maintained the sales position of Nutrasweet despite the emergence of similar rival products, and why do a majority of UK investors still put their money in low-returning Building Society accounts where their funds barely keep pace with inflation? These companies have made something out of nothing. They have established a lasting value with their customers in otherwise commodity or unappealing products and services.

In some industry situations now a company has no other option but to develop E as aggressively and successfully as possible.

- Hitachi were one of several Japanese companies talking through 1996 of their plans to relaunch their computer product lines into the already highly-competitive US market. Hitachi, however, are talking about a different approach this time to winning business. While it is clear they will certainly be price competitive, they are planning substantial advertising to create awareness and consumer pull-through. Hitachi have talked of spending $40 million to market a new line of notebook computers and of maintaining high levels of activity to build the brand. Fujitsu have also planned to attack the US market but it too is now intending to spend significant sums (it is talking of \$20–30 million) to brand its PC products.

Both Hitachi and Fujitsu have prepared their market launch in this way because they say they realise that US PC-makers have 'established strong brands, which low prices by themselves won't erode.'[5]

- Harley Davidson's record of growth over the past ten years has, so the company claims, been on the back of vast improvements in product reliability and functionality which has enabled them to fend-off 'cheap Japanese bikes'. These product improvements have not given Harley Davidson any competitive edge by themselves, however, but critically they have given the company the credibility to then go on and exploit its very unique image in the market and 'the intense brand loyalty' that exists for their bikes.

'The Harley audience is granite-like and we recognised most buy on emotional and image issues. We had to get product quality up to the mark so we could be in a strong position to build market share through the brand and that's become our core strategy. In summary we've been blessed with a heritage and a mystique and providing we protect that image we can continue to grow . . . and get high mark-ups on the price.'[6]

'E' opportunities are not restricted to consumer goods companies. There is no reason why an industrial manufacturer should also not try to seize this form of advantage. Any organisation has the potential to exploit its reputation and its products more aggressively to create a stronger desire for them.

We can characterise this as developing a 'pull-through' for products and services as opposed to the more traditional push. Instead of pushing products down the supply chain toward the end-user, there is the opportunity to create demand, to get customers asking for your particular products because they perceive them as more desirable. P&G, Rubbermaid, Compaq and Nike, for example, are companies who typically sell to disbributors yet have become highly skilled at creating this end-user consumer demand and pull-through.

Why don't more industrial manufacturers do the same thing? A few are trying and the best of them is Du Pont. Du Pont's products all have a 'branding' which gives them a high profile, and this is deliberately developed to establish a pull-through via its distributors.

Du Pont's 1995 annual report contains a valuable story:

'To consumers worldwide, the name Marks & Spencer is synonymous with quality and value . . . But even that name . . . can use an ally in the highly competitive retail business – especially when that ally is Du Pont Lycra brand spandex. Marks & Spencer was one of the first retailers to recognise [be persuaded?] that using the Lycra brand name would create an extra edge. Over the years the Lycra brand has become a further assurance of quality.'

Du Pont has 'branded' or developed the image and emotional value of all its product lines. So it has established Classic (a premium herbicide), Conoco's Jet, Zytel (a nylon resin), Teflon (which has developed sub-brands of 'SilverStone for mass market segments and Autograph for high-end gourmet workware'), Ti-Pure (titanium dioxide), Suva (refrigerants), Formacel (foam expansion agents), Dacron . . . the list goes on.

'What makes Du Pont different from the many other major companies? . . . I respond that Du Pont starts with strengths others don't have and then we build on them. We have a broad range of outstanding products, a superb reputation for market-driven innovation and outstanding people. And these all contribute to the power of the Du Pont brand which benefits from generations of credibility, trust and quality.' (E. S. Woolard Jr, Chairman DuPont)

There are some, but not many, other examples of companies who have not allowed their indirect contact with the end-user or their ingredient/component-only role to inhibit their building the emotional values and reputations of their products to create demand and differentiation.

- Intel has made its Pentium chip a recognised mark of quality and differentiation in the market place. 'Intel inside' has been a remarkably successful campaign, requiring massive investment in end-user TV and other advertising, even though Intel has no direct selling contract or contact with those end-users.
- Nutrasweet too has become a household name by promoting itself as the preferred low-calorie alternative to sugar, tying up an exclusive deal with Coke with its logo displayed on the can, and also investing in direct end-user advertising.

'To the consumer Nutrasweet is not Aspartame (the chemical name), other people sell Aspartame, we sell Nutrasweet. Our product is a combination of an ingredient and a customer image which gives us an advantage in the marketplace.'[7]

- What De Beers have done with a commodity product (diamonds) has in fact been to create an entire culture which makes diamonds a token of love and esteem. Through continuous public relations and advertising campaigns, De Beers with its cartel has re-educated public awareness and interest and established the diamond as a preferred jewel. (This is despite the fact that much of De Beers product was drawn from South Africa where for many years, of course, there was oppression of workers and racial tension.)

- Bayer launched in 1996 a new direct-to-consumer advertising campaign for the first time for any of its products, and chose for this its drug Adalat which lowers blood pressure. The campaign emphasises the drug's 'value for money' benefits rather than its medical attributes. This in itself also represents a stark departure from Bayer's usual approach which is to sell and market the performance effectiveness of its drugs. Bayer's aim is to develop additional strength and advantage in the market by establishing a consumer pull and demand, getting patients to start asking their doctors for Adalat specifically. Bayer additionally earmarked £10 million for a public-awareness campaign to raise the profile of the Bayer name and brand reputation in the US.[8]

- ICI is an example of an industrial manufacturer trying to join this club of more progressive-thinking industrial companies, but it's still some way short of best-practice.

  ICI's Acrylics division manufactures the sheet used in making baths, spas and other sanitary ware and in 1996 announced it would spend £2.5m on a worldwide advertising and marketing campaign (still a tiny sum on a worldwide basis, but a start).

  'We want to be the Intel of acrylics' announced ICI's global acrylics business manager. (Contrast Intel's worldwide advertising spend of c. $500m!)

  The aim is to court the consumer thereby offering the manufacturer which incorporates its material an extra competitive edge. ICI plans to use magazine adverts and promote its Lucite and Perspex acrylic brand names.[9]

It would seem clear, however, that ICI's capabilities and skills in this area are still less developed than its rival Du Pont who has many years of experience of building and exploiting its E advantages. For example, Du Pont will only allow customers whom it has vetted and approved to sell products displaying its brand names. 'We only consider distributing our product where the distributor can provide the image consistent with the quality of the Du Pont products'

But ICI is still learning in this area and has not yet linked the use of its trademarks with any quality thresholds: 'we are not in any way able to say that by the use of this mark, ICI has reviewed and approved the assembly manufacturer's processes'.

Whether at best-practice or still at the learning stage there is undoubtedly enormous potential down this path. So why don't more organisations look to become skilled in the E arena? Many have been around for a number of years and may well have hidden or unexploited brand values. What are the roadblocks that inhibit an organisation from moving down the E development path? What do strategy makers have to do if they want to put the E opportunity firmly on the agenda and build an effective capability and programme to exploit it?

There are in fact quite a few roadblocks to be overcome:

- 'E' is commonly seen as something tactical for the marketing department rather than a mainstream opportunity.
- It can take a long time to realise the benefits.
- The investment may need to be substantial.
- The payback is uncertain.
- The organisation may lack the experience to do it effectively.
- The communication channels for exploiting 'E' are increasingly fragmenting.

'E' is left to Marketing rather than integrated as mainstream

Except in the sort of winning companies we have profiled so far in this chapter, 'E' development, such as it is, is not usually seen as a mainstream initiative and activity for the company. It rarely reaches the agendas of the senior officers or board of the company, and it's often pursued as an isolated functional activity for Marketing instead of something engaging a number of functions. As a result, it's typically seen as marketing tactics as opposed to something which could become the major driving force for the success of the **whole** company and be developed as a most competitive and effective form of strategy.

Contrast Procter & Gamble and ICI. At P&G, 'E' sits centre-stage. Brand development and advertising is approved by the senior country manager, often the European region senior VP, and sometimes the CEO. Those responsible for developing it may be called marketeers but they are commonly regarded as the high-fliers, the most able and the brightest. They are the guardians, the nurturers, the champions of the brands and other competitive E values. The senior officers of the company have typically risen up the ladder with the same ingrained philosophy, and the whole organisation pivots around the brands and continues to build them.

At ICI, we see a completely different picture. Few business units have a department fully resourced for this area. It's often been wrapped into the sales function. Where there is some form of Marketing it is typically seen as a functional 'silo', doing its own thing and coming up with the occasional piece of product promotion literature. Unlike Du Pont, branding appears to hardly enter their vocabulary.

But to succeed in this form of advantage, an understanding and awareness of the E opportunity must penetrate the entire organisation. It potentially misses an enormous competitive opportunity to leave E delegated down to a functional-only role, and treated as short-term tactics and the 'expensive foible of the marketing director'. If the market and customer immersion show that E can be a pivotal distinguishing factor between rival products or services, then to realise its fullest potential as a driving force in the business it must be completely integrated into the company's total operating goals and long-term strategy development.

At Glaxo, a recent innovation that we have referred to previously has seen the establishing of a central Strategy and Marketing Unit to ensure among other things that E type opportunities are not overlooked but are put centre-stage. Its prime task is to pull together the long-term market value proposition for its products, co-ordinate the inputs of all other departments, and especially exploit all potential forms of market place advantage – including branding development and differentiation. As Glaxo sees lasting product performance opportunities erode, this department's role is becoming increasingly critical in moving and adapting Glaxo's strategy to reflect the key levers that motivate customers in the late 1990s. The additional value achieved through Zantac branding has certainly demonstrated one route for that.

We can quickly run a test to explore how effectively integrated is a company's E thinking and development. Is it consolidated into the mainstream business decision-making or is it rather delegated or 'relegated' to a functional tactical siding? The test is shown in Table 12.1.

As with our other question tests, each question should be scored with a very strong yes receiving a 10, and a very strong no a zero. An average score is 5.

Table 12.1 Capabilities in exploiting 'E' as a source of competitive advantage

1. Is there any department within the business specifically responsible for the development and co-ordination of E type capabilities? _____

2. Does that department have a significant resource and budget? _____

3. Does the company's published literature, especially its annual reports, typically give any high prominence to the E values and strengths of its products? _____

4. If Budgets are under pressure, are E development funds among the last to be cut? _____

5. Does the leadership of the company have a background in market-led planning and marketing or E type approaches? _____

6. Of the core competencies in the organisation, would E development, or more traditionally marketing, rank as one of the major areas? _____

7. Does the E development or marketing group play a major role in the writing up of the overall business strategy and identification of its long-term plans? _____

8. Would customers rate the companies E development skills as leading edge? _____

9. Would new recruits who saw their strengths in this skill area join the company? _____

10. Is there an active and forcing debate at the company at senior level on how E could be better exploited to become a major differentiator for the company with its customers? _____

Procter & Gamble would score 90 plus in this test. Du Pont would also score highly, whereas an ICI-type still learning the ropes would quite likely score at or below the threshold level of 50.

How would your organisation rate?

It can take a long time

Many of the brands that are dominant today were of course not built overnight.

- Disney started an animated film company in 1920 but it took 17 years till his first real hit – *Snow White*. That first success started to establish associations with consumers that were especially powerful in the Depression years. Disney's image became all about hope, about good triumphing over evil and about magic.

    These characteristics became very precious and the Disney empire has taken pains to work within this identity. They have deliberately nurtured these emotional values slowly and consistently till the Disney name now naturally provides immediate market place recognition and advantages to any product it puts out. People will now see one of its films or visit one of its theme parks principally because of the particular and well-defined emotional values it conjures up.
- Shirley MacLaine said of her stardom, 'after 18 years of hard work I'm an overnight sensation'.
- The origins of Nike first came about in the early 1960s when Phil Knight and Bill Bowerman first started to sell some new designs to shoe companies. It took a breakthrough in 1975 when Bowerman invented the new 'waffle' shoe design for running shoes for Nike to establish itself. Then, consistent improvement and continuous new products were finally rewarded when their marketing and design efforts in 1985 led to the Air Jordan shoe design for Nike which then helped the company truly emerge as a powerhouse.
- Look at King's supermarkets in New Jersey with double the net margins of most of its competitors. What is the basis of its success? What Kings has done better than its rivals is establish a particular affinity and strength of 'emotional relationship' with the consumers in its neighbourhood. It is something that has been painstakingly invested in and built up over many years. It has developed values of dependability, reliability and trust. And consumers don't give that trust easily and quickly. King's consumers prefer its stores to their rivals particularly for those reasons, not because the products on the shelf are especially different.

    It's taken time, in fact it hasn't taken huge sums of money, but it has taken a clear commitment and persistence to move down that path.

It takes time to build E success. Many new products will quickly fail but some will stick, some will endure competitively and become the winners we all talk about. For sure if they have a clear technical performance advantage doing a job better than all others, customers will quickly switch to them and stay while that advantage exists and is not displaced. Service advantages too can be clear cut, obvious and immediately compelling. But E does not always act quickly. Trust builds up over a number of years. Recognition of a brand or a relationship does not happen overnight. What E development especially requires is patience, persistence and consistency. All the virtues in fact that underpin the committed companies we have spoken of – all part of the critical commitment to customers and the market place that is the essential underpinning of any effective form of lasting competitive advantage.

It takes the vision of John Reed at Citicorp, the persistence and self-belief at P&G, or the continous investment and singlemindedness at Coca-Cola to keep promoting and pushing down this path, sometimes against the odds, but with the confidence born of a complete understanding of what can motivate the customer.

Let's look at a couple of new companies trying to join the elite E club and attempting to build up the recognition among their customers that will enable them to stay there.

Case Study

Daewoo

Daewoo, the Korean car manufacturer, is trying to accelerate the E development process by spending vast sums of money on advertising and trying to put its potential customers through a crash course in awareness, trust and desire for its products. In 1995 in the UK, for example, Daewoo spent almost twice that of its nearest rivals in brand development.[10] But while this will have some success, even with very high levels of activity consumers are unlikely to give their trust that quickly. It's taken Ford the best part of the twentieth century to establish its position. Will Daewoo have the same persistence and commitment?

─────────────────────── **Case Study** ───────────────────────

Direct Line

Direct Line insurance had been established in the UK in the mid-1980s offering cheaper insurance by cutting out middle agents, brokers and distributors. For several years it grew slowly taking a small share of personal lines motor insurance and being watched by its rivals more for academic interest than treated as a serious threat. Direct Line began to realise that its potential customers weren't sufficiently persuaded by cheap insurance, they also wanted reassurance that if they needed to claim, the company would still be there, be fully-funded, be responsive – they needed to be able to trust in the company. Direct Line's response was to move to a high-level and continuous public awareness campaign, initially exploiting its links with the Royal Bank of Scotland and then focusing on building-up that consumer trust and recognition in it as a company. By 1995, Direct Line's price + brand proposition had taken it to market leadership in its sector. Its challenge now is to stay there as its rivals have finally woken up to this and are beginning to build their own price + brand propositions in direct competition.

The investment may be substantial

- Coca-Cola spent £30m in UK on TV alone in 1995 advertising its brand and building it UK sales to nearly £½bn.[11]
- Procter & Gamble spent £38m in UK on TV through 1995 just on its soap powder business of c. £400m.
- The top 20 UK brands saw spending of £200m plus on TV through one year.

These investments are not one-offs. They are at this high level consistently and persistently. It is a spending level at up to 10 per cent of revenues among the leaders. These companies are 'breaking the noise barrier' and achieving dominant market share of voice.

Building E can require these high levels of spending, especially in very competitive markets like packaged consumer goods where as far as the customer is concerned there are many similar 'me-too' products. But as spending budgets tighten through a company's financial year, funds for promoting these differentiating emotional values are often seen as discretionary and get reduced. After all, you can't as easily cut the factory or the distribution or the administration within one month.

For those strategy makers who do see opportunities with E, then this 'E funding is discretionary' prejudice is likely to be a major roadblock to achieving success. Building up a customer's trust and recognition is a delicate exercise. The reassurance and appreciation that continuous advertising for example can bring cannot be switched on and off like a tap. That is why the Coca-Colas and P&Gs of this world see E as a continuous, and not a discretionary, commitment.

Payback is uncertain

'Half of all advertising and promotion spend is a waste of money, the trouble is you never know which half'. While investment in a new factory at least results in a substantial physical asset for the company, even if the returns are uncertain, with advertising there is of course nothing immediately tangible that comes through except perhaps a 30-second television advert. For many organisations the 'softness' of emotional investment monies is simply regarded as too uncertain and risky.

Of course an organisation could start measuring its emotional values with its customers and consumers and see how they move and develop over time. But even with this it is sometimes hard to separate-out how much of any improvement is due to specific E investment as opposed to all the other things the company does in the market place. This is especially so when E values are not yet fully developed, or have not reached their critical mass as a major influencer.

For these reasons, many organisations just turn away from developing E. As one CEO of a global pharmaceuticals company said recently:

> 'It's expensive, we don't really understand this type of investment and I don't think we have the skills anyway to make a success of it. We might be able to do something more but I can't convince the rest of the Board. It's easier to invest in what we know.'

Again while these sorts of prejudices prevail at senior level in any organisation, it is impossible for a company to make any meaningful strides in exploiting any E potential that might exist. If there is an opportunity to differentiate and achieve advantage down this path, then it has to be pursued wholeheartedly and with commitment, not prejudice.

The organisation may lack the experience

There's another vicious circle here and many companies are caught up in it. They may have an E opportunity, but because they are not skilled in this area they don't understand it, so they either turn away or do it half-heartedly and fail to capture the benefits (see Figure 12.2).

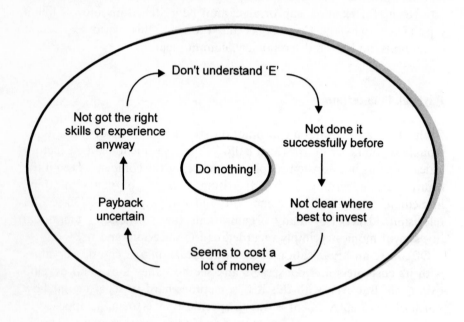

Figure 12.2 Lack of experience leads to a vicious circle

Financial institutions went through exactly this vicious circle process during the past decade. Struggling to differentiate themselves, many decided to explore how brand values could help. As a result they recruited in ex-Procter & Gamble brand managers as supposedly the experts to lead the charge. A few years and millions of pounds of spending later, disappointed and frustrated 'marketing' recruits were learning one after another that their battle to educate and transform a treacly internal culture into a market and E aware organisation was failing. Few of the senior executives took it seriously, it was an 'expensive indulgence by one function', not enough believed E values would make the difference, and so the effort was compromised and inevitably the potential not fully realised.

Now industrial manufacturers like ICI are waking up to opportunities in this area, but will they break through a culture and competency base that has historically ignored this potential? Can the advocates of E in ICI get it centre-stage with the right resources and skills to properly exploit it, in the manner of Du Pont? Only when it is truly acknowledged at senior level as at least as powerful a form of potential competitive advantage as its product technology heritage might E breakthrough.

The communication channels are fragmenting

While the target customer base often tends to stay largely the same, the means for communicating to them are now becoming ever more diverse. This is especially challenging for companies targeting mass volume audiences such as the consumer goods companies, retail banks, service groups and so on who historically could have confidently focused their energies on television advertising or a few targeted magazines.

Now, with the proliferation of media, the ability to focus and pick a few communication channels only is severely reduced. Electronic shopping, for example, especially via the Internet is growing, retailers and manufacturers are all experimenting with web sites, some are now offering free delivery within 24 hours. By 2005 some forecasts are looking at consumers buying 15 per cent of all their supermarket needs through electronic means.[12]

To succeed nowadays with E, especially on a mass consumer basis, more than ever requires high levels of experience and skills to master these channel complexities. It also needs the commitment to invest in these new channels at a level and pace that can keep it ahead of the pack.

Building such experience and developing such commitment effectively needs the removal of all the roadblocks we have been discussing and which are commonly found in many organisations. It also needs the recognition and conviction among senior management that E is not just a marketing indulgence but something that can drive the success of the company. Unless and until this market and customer awareness and understanding of E permeates the thinking and planning of the company, then any initiatives will likely fail. The necessary skills, patience with investment and organisational structure need to be in place to facilitate and support making it a lasting advantage.

*   *   *

If strategy makers manage to fight their way through the various roadblocks, then there is no doubt that getting E right can make an enormous difference. The Coca-Colas and Procter & Gambles have unequivocably demonstrated that. And we can briefly remind ourselves of this value creation potential, what it's worth to earnings and shareholder value, and emphasise again that the gain is so substantial that no company, industrial or other, can afford nowadays not to be actively pursuing and exploiting it.

In the UK, accounting rules allow companies to recognise E value creation and fully translate the developed value of brands onto the balance sheet. The aim is to acknowledge the intangible asset value, otherwise treated as goodwill and written off. While there remains some uncertainty as to the rules for this intangible asset valuation, not all companies have taken advantage of this accounting facility. Those that have done so have principally restricted it to acquired brands where there would otherwise be the goodwill write-off, rather than also trying to value brands organically built and developed.

Where the brand is valued it typically represents a very substantial part of a company's fixed asset base. Reckitt & Colman valued its trademarks at £1.27bn in 1995. This was larger than its shareholder funds at the time and some 75 per cent of its fixed assets (Table 12.2).

Table 12.2 Fixed assets – intangible assets, Reckitt & Colman

	1995 Trademarks £m	1994 Trademarks £m
Net book amounts		
At beginning of financial year	1295.6	681.6
Acquired during the year	–	636.0
Written off during the year	(2.5)	(4.6)
Disposals during the year	(47.7)	(1.7)
Exchange adjustments	27.8	(15.7)
At end of financial year	1273.2	1295.6

Note: The amount originally stated for brands represents the fair value at the date of acquisition of brands acquired since 1985. A brand is only recognised where it is supported by a registered trademark, is established in the market place and holds significant brand share.

Source: Annual Report, Reckitt & Colman.

Table 12.3 Fixed assets – intangible assets, Grand Metropolitan

	Brands *£m*
Cost	
At 30 September 1994	2782
Exchange adjustments	(9)
New subsidiaries	1067
At 30 September 1995	3840

Note: The brands are stated at fair value on acquisition, denominated in the currencies of their principal markets. An annual review is carried out by the directors to consider whether any brand has suffered permanent diminution in value. Although the current aggregate value significantly exceeds the book value, no increase is made to the original value. The principal brands included above are Smirnoff, Pillsbury, Green Giant, Burger King, Häagen-Dazs and, acquired during the year, Old El Paso and Progresso.

Source: Annual Report, Grand Metropolitan (currently in merger talks with Guinness).

Grand Metropolitan has a similar situation (Table 12.3). Its brands are treated as intangible assets to the value of £3.8bn in 1995. Again, this was larger than its shareholder funds and a significant proportion of its fixed assets.

Should we be concerned at companies strengthening their balance sheet in this way? Is it some improper artifice designed to inflate the net worth of the company? Should US accounting rules prevail where such intangible asset valuations are not allowed and goodwill must be written off? Or should we rather see this as business gradually adjusting to the realities of the late twentieth century. In fact is it not simply the accounting profession recognising the power of E and its modern day value and relevance to commerce? Are accountants in fact for once more prescient than some of their supposedly more commercial corporate manager colleagues? Is not the current debate about the legitimacy of this intangible asset valuation simply a reflection of business's own uncertainty with E, unsure whether it should remain simply the province of a marketing function or embraced more wholeheartedly and taken centre-stage as a main form of strategy and advantage and value in the company?

Are brands, designs and trademarks nowadays at least as valuable, if not more so to a company, than its plant and equipment? As we move into a world of outsourcing and toward the virtual company that British Airways and one or two others have intimated, what will underpin the balance sheet value? It's less likely to be the traditional fixed assets and far more likely to be the more intangible ones. Might not brands, designs and trademarks become the twenty-first century version of the fixed asset base, and be a truer representation of the net worth of the business? Does such a value base in fact not represent a better guide to investors as it's far more indicative of the company's future potential and its growth prospects?

Ralph Lauren, still a private company, has no embarassment about the value of its brand name. It's become a machine that coins in money. Not only is it established in men's and women's clothing, but it has spawned no fewer than 26 licenses where other companies pay to use the name to the tune of 6 per cent or more of the branded sales they make.[13]

For example $535 million of 'home collection' sales in 1995 were made up of licensed product sales spread around 9 companies:

- Paint   – Sherwin Williams
- China   – Pentland
- Wallpaper, Fabrics   – Folia
- Blankets, Bedding   – Pillowtex
- Furniture   – Henreddon
- Rugs   – Shyam Ahuja
- Table linens   – Audrey
- Bathroom rugs   – Newmark
- Towels   – West Point Stevens

In total, the licenses generate a huge percentage of revenues and make up most of the profits.

Even though US Accounting rules still prevent this kind of intangible asset valuation, some commentators are already calculating and quantifying their view as to what US brand assets might be worth on the balance sheet. A recent study by Interbrand and *Financial World* in 1996 identified the 'most valuable brands'.[14] The top ten were as shown in Table 12.4.

The calculations were made in the same basic way as at Grand Metropolitan and Reckitt & Colman – by identifying the earnings attributable to the brand and calculating a brand strength multiple.

Some of these brand values are truly massive, and even if they are not incorporated into the balance sheet they are a very powerful indication as to the value of the company. Coca-Cola's fixed asset base at $4.4bn now bears little relationship, in contrast to the way it was originally intended, to the underlying value of the company. As Goizueta has commented:

Table 12.4 Ten most valuable brands

Most valuable brand	Value (\$m)
Marlboro	44 614
Coca-Cola	43 427
McDonald's	18 920
IBM	18 491
Disney	15 358
Kodak	13 267
Kelloggs	11 409
Budweiser	11 026
Intel	10 499
Gillette	10 292

'If all our assets and buildings burned down we'd have no trouble rebuilding based on the strength of our trademarks alone.'[15]

As recognition of E values and value generally grows, so more companies are beginning to reappraise any existing brands and trademarks and check for hidden and unexploited E opportunities. There has been a surge of interest in the mid-1990s in rediscovering old brands that had been allowed to decline over the years but that still have a popular consumer franchise.[16] Brands such as Brylcream, Foster Grant, Eskimo Pie, Double Diamond beer and Mornay soaps have all been rejuvenated. In nearly every case sales were down to very low levels, there was absolutely no investment going in but there was still a core and loyal group of customers and many others who could immediately recognise the brand values that had often long ago been created. As one of these brand rejuvenators has commented: 'The cost of launching new brands is escalating, they can cost tens of millions of pounds to establish and it's far from certain a new brand will succeed, therefore it makes perfect sense to relaunch something already tried and tested.'

As a result of this sort of reinvigoration, a number of tried and tested but languishing brands have seen sales and profits turn and start to increase, sometimes as in the case of SmithKline Beecham's Brylcream and Lucozade quite dramatically re-establishing shareholder value.

Quite clearly, then, E development must be taken very seriously. If it can add so much value, if it is becoming in more and more industry situations a most powerful potential lever and influence on customer purchasing, then it needs necessarily to be shifted centre-stage and given the same attention and development time as perhaps the more traditional sources of competitive advantage.

The third dimension of emotion

We should not leave any discussion of E without looking more deeply into the third dimension of the market commitment model and illustrating the more specific suggested sources of E advantage.

As with the other prime forms of strategy, these third-level sources are drawn from an extensive amount of empirical observation and study. They represent the principal types of E advantage that have been identified. Once again I add the rider that if there are industry situations which are not adequately captured here then that will be the exception. And in any event, any strategy making in this area should certainly review and explore these specific sources of advantage described here as a first step.

Emotional values can come in different forms. Many of our examples in this chapter have been about the recognition and appreciation of established brands and their powerful influence on customer purchasing. We have also seen examples such as Nike, Swatch and Chanel where advantage can be achieved through design and style. These are the most common forms of E, but it also comes through in other ways – in being recognised for being innovative or in playing to a customer's 'political' feelings and motivations.

The four sources of advantage and opportunity specified are:

- **Recognition** – acknowledgment and appreciation of an established brand or reputation or relationship or other mark of distinction.
- **Design** – achieving a style or shape or structure, a look or a feel that is regarded as aesthetically pleasing.
- **Innovative** – a track record, a reputation particularly for coming up with new ideas, offering a fresh approach, a new way of doing things. But not a short-term fad that comes and goes overnight.
- **'Politics'** – both patriotism (e.g. 'buy British') and favouritism (e.g. exploiting government connections).

We can illustrate each of these with more examples.

Recognition

- Most commonly about the brand; for example Coca-Cola, Intel or Tide.
- Also about relationships and respect successfully established and maintained over time, for example Ernst & Young's connections with its audit clients, a bank's relationships with its customers.

- Or some other mark of immediately recognisable distinction; for example the CNN logo, the ICI 'roundel'.

Design

- Most obviously about cars; for example Ferrari, but also items like the Nike 'swoosh', *Concorde* or the Coke contour bottle.
- A certain style like Laura Ashley fabrics, IKEA furniture, Patrick Cox shoes.
- Equally important in industrial manufacturing; for example JCB's 'one-armed compact loader' – a design-led excavation loading machine.

Innovative

- P&G's continuous repackaging of Crest toothpaste, new flavours, packaging, variants, dispensers, accessories, etc.
- Sony, JVC, Sharp help differentiate themselves by continuously coming up with new product ideas and features. They create a comfort and feeling of confidence that in buying them you're somehow also buying into the leading-edge, irrespective of any specific performance advantages on any one particular product at any point in time.
- Marks & Spencer ready meals – regular new product ideas that create constant interest and trial.
- State Street's historic reputation for innovative solutions, a reputation that attracts custom by itself.

'Politics'

- 72 per cent of British people in 1996 said they would 'prefer to buy British', given a choice between 'three otherwise similar-performing and priced products'.[17]
- Unique products such as 'Clipper Teas' feature the 'Fair-trade' mark guaranteeing to consumers the manufacturer has not exploited Third World poverty, but has provided workers with fair pay and decent conditions.
- 'Germans have been brought up with the idea that German products are by far the best and should be the only ones purchased.'[18]
- Royal Sun Alliance, the British insurer, after intensive government lobbying is the first overseas insurance group to be granted a license by the Chinese government. Only five such licenses will be handed out.

'Politics', as we can see from the specific examples, can be played aggressively and deliberately. And playing it well could become increasingly important as companies expand overseas and search round the globe for new markets and new sources of business growth. Among the less-developed countries, success may critically depend on a company's skills and resources in this area. It is no longer enough to send a person out to, say, Chile with a sample bag and a briefcase. Contracts of any significance are typically awarded not only where strong relationships have been built up, but also where a company is clearly committed to doing business well in that country. Meeting local customer expectations and within the law playing to the local rules, exploiting inter-government contacts, investing and establishing a significant infrastructure and local operation – all these political initiatives can make a difference to winning business.

And surprisingly, at the personal level, individual consumers in many countries still take pride in buying locally, in being patriotic, and some suppliers seek to take advantage of this. Marks & Spencer used to proudly and very publicly proclaim how 90 per cent of its goods were sourced in the UK and many remember the 'buy British' campaigns. More recently, China has started a 'buy Chinese' campaign – though here this might be more in the face of customer preference rather than in response to it, as the government tries to control foreign brands like Pepsi and Lux soap from eclipsing their Chinese counterparts.

As for being 'innovative' the intention here is to distinguish between technical product innovation, for example that which provides the customer with some noticeable product Performance improvement, versus a more general customer appreciation of a company's historic track record and capability to be innovative.

Where an innovation has resulted in a distinct Performance advantage, then as far as the customer is concerned it is the specific Performance improvement that will drive the purchase decision. It's not the innovation *per se*. On the other hand a company's current product offerings may be seen as no better than competitors', but because it is typically perceived as at the leading-edge and has a history of coming up with a number of effective new ideas and approaches (or if we were, say, in the food industry, new flavours or variants) that can be a decisive influence by itself. There are situations where simply a track record of being innovative can be worth something and keep a customer loyal.

We can see this especially in the service industry in accountancy, consultancy and financial-services firms. It may be that the basic audit service or re-engineering product or M&A advice is no better than others. But customers often 'feel good' continuing to buy and sticking with the same provider because they know there will be a future stream of new ideas, techniques and approaches. By being associated with the most innovative provider customers feel they will be best-placed to stay at the forefront of their industry, be in touch with the latest thinking, and more easily access and take advantage of this. It's the reputation for innovation in this case, rather than the innovation itself, which makes the difference.

So customers will want to buy from 3M because there is an expectation that that company's reputation for innovation will come up with benefits, if not immediately then certainly in the future. For example, 3M was a pioneer in microreplication technology (covering surfaces with millions of precisely made minuscule structures), and it was only 3M's customers who were initially invited to participate in the early research and trial new applications. In fact 3M has many such technology centres dedicated to developing emerging new technologies, and companies want to be customers of 3M so they can somehow be associated with that leading thinking and expertise, get in on the ground-floor of any development and learn to exploit breakthroughs such as microreplication as quickly as possible for their own advantage.

Being innovative, then, can establish a feel-good factor of comfort and reassurance, of being associated with the best and buying from the most committed. And as the search for competitive differentiation grows ever more pressured and intense as we reach the millennium, so it is more likely that a customer will want to do whatever it can to tap into the latest ideas and will probably be more heavily influenced by any provider committed to delivering that.

*   *   *

Thinking about market advantage through E is to bring up to date the range of options a company has to win in the market place. In the next decade more and more companies will turn to this E factor to take advantage of many products' and services' inherent customer franchise and find new more contemporary ways to differentiate themselves.

As we have described, at present it's not easy for strategy makers to get E opportunities centre-stage. There are roadblocks in terms of structure, experience, culture and risk assessment which get in the way and will continue to delay many companies in truly getting to grips with this area of opportunity. But where a company does grasp the nettle in this area, whether it's a classical brand-builder like Coca-Cola, or a more traditional industrial manufacturer like Bayer or Du Pont, or an 'upstart' like Daewoo, the potential value to revenue, earnings and the balance sheet can, as we have seen, be extraordinary.

13   A Toolkit

The major components of the Market Commitment model have now been illustrated and explained. We have seen the power of commitment. We have demonstrated the value of deep-rooted immersion in markets and with customers to be truly in touch with future market opportunities. We have examined the prime forms of competitive advantage and strategy that can drive lasting success. We have driven down to the specific sources of advantage that can underpin the strategic options.

We now have established a complete model for strategy making. At the second-dimension level the four prime strategies – performance, service, price and emotion – represent a comprehensive set of options. Strategy must be founded along one or more of these axes. They provide a contemporary set of choices rooted in the market realities of the late 1990s. They are up-to-date and avoid the inadequacies of older strategy frameworks. They provide a fresh opportunity to reinvigorate strategy thinking and help propel it back up the agenda.

We have also aimed to be specific. We have described a third dimension which lays out what empirical observation and research suggest are the principal underlying forms of strategic advantage. Pushing out to this level of detail is a response to 'customer demand'; it's an attempt to specify as comprehensively as possible for strategy makers what are the main sources of opportunity in each strategy area. It's designed to highlight the need to be as specific as possible in formulating strategy. In today's environment, talking about service or performance quality is just not enough. There's a need to identify the specific factors influencing customer decision-making as rigorously as possible – to get down to those tangible things that customers most demonstrably recognise and to expressly direct the organisation and workforce in where to prioritise its energies and resources. There may be industry situations where the specific opportunity at the third-dimension level is not one specified by the model, but the sources that are indicated should always be the first place to look and the first stages of any specific strategy formulation.

Now that we have built our model, the next question is how should we best use it? How can we take advantage of the ideas here and apply them in the most practical and effective way through the company? How can we ensure that the model becomes a 'living tool' that can guide strategy

211

making both in its origination and subsequent fine-tuning and evolution? What can be done with it to engage the organisation and get the company thinking along these strategic lines on as wide a basis as possible? How can we encourage managers to gauge and measure their success by reference to their effectiveness in identifying and implementing these ideas?

We can develop a toolkit. We can now describe how to use this model as an ongoing device to measure and monitor strategy effectiveness. We can describe a simple system that an organisation can use and even some basic proforma illustrations. We have seen how Procter & Gamble and Unilever, for example, in effect searched around the model for new sources of advantage in their soap powder wars. We also showed how they could practically measure their competitive advantages and disadvantages with their customers to identify actions and opportunities. It is that basic illustration in using the model that we can now build on. The aim is to show through a simple set of measurements and investigations a means for substantially improving strategy making and market effectiveness skills.

The toolkit has 10 steps:

1. Market and customer immersion
2. Identifying advantages
3. Segmentation
4. Competitiveness
5. Sustainability
6. Trends
7. Organisation gaps
8. Looking to the future
9. Stakes in the ground
10. Exploitation

Each of these steps can be described in turn. They are relatively straightforward and it should be possible for a strategy maker to easily explain them and engage business teams in the thinking and analysis that is required. It is also worth emphasising that the Commitment and Immersion tests described in earlier chapters should be reviewed and preferably carried out as preparatory work. The commitment test provides the backcloth and context – 'how ready are we' – for the strategy making. The immersion check spells out the degree of market understanding required to work most effectively through the 10 steps. They can't be treated superficially. Insight and benefits only come if they are addressed in a quantifiable manner with rigorous input from customers and the market place.

1. Market and customer immersion

What's important to our customers, what drives their purchasing and persuades them to stay loyal to one supplier or switch to another? We have placed emphasis on the need to deeply understand markets and customer thinking, to be so totally immersed with them that we are totally in-tune with their needs and can indeed anticipate their future requirements.

This requires a substantial amount of in-depth investigation and research and the information will come through in a number of forms. What will be critical will be to distill that information once it is sufficiently robust into insight and understanding of potential and specific sources of competitive advantage.

Table 13.1 therefore simply lays out as step 1 in the toolkit the form to capture that. As we will see later it is likely that customer needs will segment, and that dynamic must of course also be reflected in any competitive advantage analysis with customers.

Table 13.1 What do customers value most?*

Sources of competitive advantage		Customer ranking (Score each one out of 10)
Performance:	Functionality	
	Reliability	
	Speed	
	Convenience	
Service Hustle:	Comprehensive	
	Available	
	Personalized	
	Symbiotic	
Price:	Low	
	Value	
	Premium	
	Shared	
Emotion:	Recognition	
	Design	
	Innovative	
	'Political'	

Note: * What's so important to them that it will change their long term purchasing habits if a supplier could truly excel at it.

2. Identifying advantages

In some ways this is the most important step – identifying what competitive advantage one company has over another and what is the size of that competitive advantage gap ('CAG'). Here lies the fundamental basis for strategy development and it's impossible to put too much effort and investment into understanding and resolving this area.

How do we perform versus our competitors in our customers' eyes, how do they rate what we do versus the best practices of our rivals, are we ahead of the game and is that gap significant, has the gap been growing or narrowing over time, is the 'gap-trend' in the right direction? Having a complete understanding of our CAGs – of our competitive advantage gaps – is vital. Armed with this knowledge and insight there is an immediate set of actions to defend and strengthen the gap or even more urgently address the disadvantages.

The size of the CAG is the size of how much better your customers rate you than your rivals. It's the source of market share development, increased customer loyalty, price leadership and other actions which expoit being rated the best in the market. It's the basis for the strategy that will drive success. Allied with the necessary future commitment we have the key ingredients here for effective strategy formulation.

Customers' rating of the company's competitiveness, its CAGs, can be scored out of 10, with 10 being the best score and 0 the worst. It provides a simple and immediate measure of a company's strategic competitiveness (see Figure 13.1).

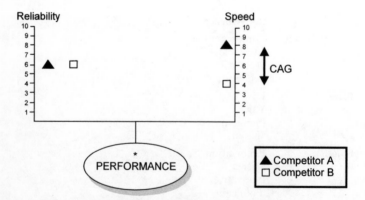

Figure 13.1 Customer rating of competitive advantage

Note: *This could be British Airways Concorde, for example.

Table 13.2 sets out a more complete picture of a company's overall competitive position. It encourages each specific source of competitive advantage and opportunity to be investigated and scored, to think through **all** the possible range of opportunities and not just focus on existing ones.

Table 13.2   How does company 'ABC' compare with its rivals?

Sources of competitive advantage		What customers rank as top 5	Customer's scoring (out of 10) of:			
			Rival 1	Rival 2	Rival 3	ABC
Performance:	Functionality Reliability Speed Convenience					
Service Hustle:	Comprehensive Available Personalised Symbiotic					
Price:	Low Value Premium Shared					
Emotion:	Recognition Design Innovative 'Political'					

By way of illustration, an engineering and manufacturing company that was a recent client found that customers ranked Performance Reliability number-1, with Service Availability and then Low Price following on. With specific reference to reliability, the client's CAG score was a little ahead of two of its rivals, but customers saw little significant difference between them and had come to acept over the years a certain standard of supply. However, it became clear that this performance area could be a major source of opportunity. Deeper CAG analysis told the company that customers had over the years suffered from unsatisfactory reliability from all suppliers and had got used to that, reducing expectations. But if one supplier was really able to make a significant difference in this area it would transform its position and definitely put it at a clear advantage. If our client company could truly deliver iding and consistent reliability, that would be highly prized. It was y slightly better than the others in this area and in fact was in the process of completely restructuring its manufacturing processes to improve right-first-time reliability. Motorola's 6-sigma race immediately came to mind as a benchmark and illustration of what the company could aim to do. Such a goal was deemed very stretching but not infeasible. It was possible to start targeting the specific advantage opportunity and setting the strategy priority.

3. Segmentation

Customers of course are not a homogeneous bunch. They differ in their needs and requirements in almost every industry situation. Through the past two decades, especially, they have become more demanding, more discriminating and sophisticated, and more demonstrative in what they value and what they do not. Each customer knows very particularly what they individually want, and a supplier is now often faced with divergent and sometimes conflicting needs and expectations.

Within the same industry, take pharmaceuticals for example, there can be very different emphases in price or service or E brand and relationship values depending on the size, sophistication and location of the customer. In motor vehicles, to take another illustration, there has been a proliferation of segments into luxury, compact, sports, pick-up, 4-wheel, hatchback, convertible, family and others. *Automotive Yearbook* defined over 30 segments in its last screen of the market. In each segment there are a set of customers with a clear set of needs and expectations. As British Airways have commented: 'last year we flew 32 million people, each expects to be treated as an individual, each has different reasons for choosing us and different expectations!'

Acknowledging and identifying the customer segmentation is a vital part of effective strategy making. It's an early step that must be taken to understand which customers a company can best achieve advantage with. And if they represent a sufficiently sizeable, profitable and attractive business base, then it is on these customer types that the company can best focus. Instead of trying to be all things to all people, the company can develop the most compelling proposition for the target audience.

From the point of view of our toolkit and building up a most competitively advantaged strategy we can capture this segmentation need in Tables 13.3 and 13.4.

Table 13.3   What do customers value most, by segment?

Sources of competitive advantage		*Customer ranking by segment*			
		Segment X	Segment Y	Segment Z	etc.
Performance:	Functionality Reliability Speed Convenience				
Service Hustle:	Comprehensive Available Personalised Symbiotic				
Price:	Low Value Premium Shared				
Emotion:	Recognition Design Innovative 'Political'				

Table 13.4   How does company ABC score in each?

Defined segments	*Company ABC's CAGs*	
	Is there a competitive advantage?	*What is the specific source?*
A		
B		
C		
D		
etc.		

4. Summarise the competitive situation

At this stage in building up the strategy it's worth simply ensuring that the understanding and sources of opportunities that are being identified are summarised and widely understood. From the market evaluation and customer segmentation, what are the principal and most compelling forms of advantage that the customer rates, what is the size of any CAG

Table 13.5   The competitive situation summarised

Company A's advantages	Size of CAG	Significance of CAG
1		
2		
3		
Company A's disadvantages	*Size of disadvantage*	*Significance*
1		
2		
3		

that's been identified and is it a meaningful and significant influence on customer purchasing, are there any disadvantages, do they matter, and what are we going to do about them? These may be summarised as in Table 13.5.

5. Sustainability

It's also important to check how sustainable are any advantages identified. Can they be relied on, can they form the basis for ongoing competitiveness, do we have enough confidence from our understanding of the market place and our target customers to invest significant resources, efforts and funds into building on these advantages and driving our organisation in this direction? Table 13.6 illustrates this area.

Table 13.6   Sustainability of advantages

Advantages	Threats					
	New competitors	New technologies	New customers	Changing customer needs	Other threats	Time till threat impacts
1						
2						
3						
etc.						

6. Trends

CAG is a simple measure but it's not static. It's not only a snapshot of how the company is performing competitively with its customers at one point in time. It can be more dynamic than that and can be easily extended to monitor performance over a number of years. What we need to know is not just what advantage we have today but even more critically: is it growing or is it slipping? Are we doing enough to maintain the gap or is some competitor doing something that is eroding our advantage?

Monitoring the CAG in this way can provide an immediate indicator as to how well the company is doing in the market, whether it's doing enough, and point up very dramatically the areas where it needs to do more to sustain any advantage and stay ahead (see Table 13.7).

Table 13.7   What's the CAG trend?

Advantages	CAG			Trend
	This year	*Last year*	*This year vs 3-yr average*	*Growing/Slipping?*
1 2 3				

7. Organisation gaps

We are deliberately being market-focused and driving the emphasis on customer and market place advantage and success. However, we must insert in the toolkit a step to check on the organisation gaps. They are expressed here in highly summarised form, but the market insight will itself raise a number of searching questions about a company's capabilities to deliver what the customer is demanding. It will also test whether a company can **deliver** those customer requirements better than any other potential rivals.

The organisation gaps can be summarised by reference to a small number of criteria which can act as a simple checklist, though recognising there is much beneath each of the overall questions listed in Table 13.8.

Table 13.8   A checklist on organisation gaps

Skills:	Have we got the right skills to deliver excellently what the customer requires?
Systems:	Do they facilitate what we need to achieve?
Structure:	Is the organisation working harmoniously and effectively across functional and other boundaries towards the same goal?
Operations:	Are we doing enough to be as cost-efficient as we need to be?
	Are we most efficient in delivering what the customer values?
Resources:	Is there enough resource to do the job on or ahead of time?
	Do we need to buy in additional resources, e.g. through alliances or acquisition?
Investment:	Can we afford to do what is required by ourselves?

This organisation checklist assumes that the strategy that has been defined and is being developed is one that provides advantage and sustainable opportunity and can be credible and motivating to the workforce. Unless that backcloth is in place, discussion about organisation gaps is of course premature.

8. Looking to the future

Just as we need to monitor the current CAG trends, we also need to look to the future. We need to start building the understanding and awareness of what sources of advantage will drive customer purchasing in 5 years time. Competitive positions will change. There will be new technologies, different competitors emerging and changing customers, too, as they consolidate or other distribution channels open up. Leading suppliers will attempt to change the rules of the game, investing in and exploiting new forms of advantage or touching the pulse of latest consumer desires with some new product. The disposable diaper, the Walkman, Netscape internet browser, McDonalds QVSC, Champney's 're-engineering' – these were all initiatives which changed the competitive ground rules, formalised a new set of customer expectations, and opened up a new era of differently-based competitive advantage.

Companies need to be searching for their own wins, their own new initiatives, so it is they who will be setting the future ground-rules not a rival. To do this we have talked at length about the need for immersion in the market and the goal of establishing a Triple-I approach – immersion, intuition and innovation – to constantly screen the market place to create the environment and the best chance of staying ahead.

We can include in our toolkit a form to encourage this thinking, but it cannot capture in a few words the effort and energy and market digging that must go on to truly be able to understand the likely future market needs and opportunities (see Table 13.9).

Table 13.9 What new advantages will there be in 5 years' time?

Sources of advantage		Top 5 customer ranking		Who is driving the change?		
		Current	Predicted 5-years' time	Customer	Competitor	Us
Performance:	Functionality Reliability Speed Convenience					
Service Hustle:	Comprehensive Available Personalized Symbiotic					
Price:	Low Value Premium Shared					
Emotion:	Recognition Design Innovative 'Political'					

9. Stakes in the ground

The strategy maker is urged to go still further and not just evaluate the future market potential but also put some stakes in the ground. Given its market understanding, where does the company want to be, what does it want to achieve in the future, what are its long-term goals? The emphasis here is on setting targets which can drive the whole orientation and motivation of the organisaton over a defined time period. It's the horizon-setting that we saw with Sam Walton, Henry Ford, President Kennedy and others. It's having the boldness to interpret the market understanding and state: here is what it will mean for us, these are our ambitions, this is what we are going to strive for and the position we are trying to carve out for ourselves in the market, this is what we will invest in and pursue knowing there will be unexpected events on the journey but which we believe in.

Table 13.10 is a simple reference point for this and another vital part of the toolkit. The form itself, however, once again cannot capture the planning and leadership required to arrive at a goal which the company has searched out, analysed, validated in so far as is possible, and is in a position to communicate persuasively and credibly to the workforce. We shall talk more about this in Chapter 15.

Table 13.10   Staking-out the future

Target customer segment	CAGs		Timeframe
	*Prime form (Level 2)**	*Underlying sources (Level 3)**	
1			
2			
3			

e.g. Motorola: 'Performance – 6-sigma reliability – within 5 years'
Compaq: 'Service – most available + comprensive – by end of century'

Note: * of Market Commitment model.

10.   Exploitation

The final step in the toolkit is to check how effectively the CAGs that have been identified are being exploited. If a company works hard to establish some recognised advantage with customers it should not be hesitant in exploiting it. Surprisingly often I come across organisations where, for example, there is superior technology and product performance, which customers demonstrably value, and yet the product is being priced tentatively, sales planning is incremental instead of going for growth and there is limited effort in translating this acknowledged superiority into building lifetime customer relationships or lasting and prevailing E brand values.

The exploitation options are considerable, and examples include:

- **Revenue**: increased sales
  increased market share
- **Pricing**: up
  down to build even further volume gain
  reduced discounts to customers
- **Investment**: increased promotion to grow sales
  invest to strengthen the specific source of advantage
- **Costs**: reduced promotion costs
  tougher debtor days
  bigger margins from own suppliers
- **Customers**: new basis for loyalty-building

Table 13.11 searches out these exploitation opportunities. Are they being rigorously thought through and actioned?

Table 13.11 Exploitation opportunities

CAGs	Exploitation actions (see above list)	Estimated value addition* $m
1		
2		
3		

Notes: *could be NPV (net present value) or EVA (economic value added) or simply $m increase in profits.

*   *   *

So we have the 10-step toolkit for identifying and measuring CAGs in the market place. A simple set of forms which can act as a checklist to ensure the proper market and customer investigation is carried out. It can also act as a guide to assist strategy makers in getting involvement and input from busy line managers and getting individual business teams to start searching more deeply for their lasting sources of market advantage.

The emphasis here is on measurement. The CAG is a measure of advantage, and so much of a company's success lies in how well it measures and how closely it continuously monitors its own performance versus its competitors. (For more on this see the sections on information and measurement in Chapters 14 and 15.) There is no substitute or short cuts in ever more competitive markets for this approach.

Winning companies are tireless in their search for advantage and for ways to sustain and improve their competitive position. They search restlessly around the market place examining the prime forms of strategy and the underlying sources. In effect they play around the market commitment model. They repeat the ten steps of the toolkit all the time, researching their markets deeply, measuring advantages, watching for new events that might threaten their position and constantly looking to the future, amending their plans, reaffirming their stakes in the ground and aiming to be first in with some new product or approach that can push them further ahead with their customers and strengthen their hand.

We saw how Procter & Gamble and Unilever played around the model in their soap wars. Others are searching out and identifying new opportunities around the model in the same way. Let's consider a few further examples of companies doing this. We can look particularly at those who had built up successful performance-based strategies and have been investigating additional or different options as their historic performance advantages erode.

———— Case Study ————

IBM

IBM appears to be on the comeback trail. Toward the end of 1996 its shares hit a nine-year high, and it's now being regarded as a growth stock by Wall Street. What lies behind the recovery? IBM under Gerstner has gone back to basics. It's been reviewing what are the forms of advantage which will have most leverage with its customers over the next 10 years of business competition. It's been spending time reviewing what are the key factors driving the purchase decision. It's been talking to customers, learning their needs and figuring how to satisfy them. As one commentator, the head of consultancy Change Lab put it: 'what IBM is doing sounds simple but show me companies who are really good at it. It's easy to say but in practice hard to do'.

Said Gerstner: 'I came here with a view that you start the day with customers, you start thinking about a company around its customers and you organise around them'. The strategy used to be to push the product technology and build product Performance advantages. But now Gerstner feels IBM's biggest opportunity and the thrust now of its new strategy, building on its technology platform, is in Service: 'I want to take IBM back to its roots'. It has started by transforming its salesforce into a global network of experts and it is setting benchmarks for the amount of time its senior executives spend out with customers – 'just listening'. It plans to provide a one-stop shop that can provide a solution and offer a 'comprehensive Service solution'. It's IBM's agenda for at least the next 5 years, and the organisation appears to be rallying around the new Service strategy wanting to become the best at it.[1]

Case Study

Amazon.com

Jeff Bezos left his Wall Street job in 1994 determined to set up a business venture to exploit consumer interest in browsing the Internet and purchasing electronically. He felt there was an opportunity to sell books online and he searched around for how he could make his new book-selling service more compelling to customers than a Barnes & Noble retail store. What could be his source of advantage? Why would customers buy from his online service? Sure he could deliver convenience by providing his electronic purchasing service but was that enough? His research showed that what customers especially valued, particularly those using the Internet, was a comprehensive selection. They wanted a service that could provide everything they might want, however obscure the title. So Bezos set out to offer the most comprehensive service selection of any bookseller – 'our goal is that if it's in print, it's in stock'. The business, Amazon.com, is booming. Orders have been increasing around 30 per cent each month and revenues after less than 2 years were forecast to reach $10m.[2]

Case Study

Blue Circle

Blue Circle has also been searching for a response to its market challenges in effect by working around the market commitment model looking for new strategies to boost its competitive position. In some of its product areas, for example bathrooms, its products are seen as largely similar to its rivals and its customers' natural response to product commodity is to start buying on price alone.

While Blue Circle has worked hard to improve product functionality and reliability through investing in new technologies it
recognised it could not rest on this.

As a result it's been exploiting other options. 'We're probably the
best known brand in the industry' has been a rallying call to review
how that can be better exploited. In addition 'We've got the best
relationship' with certain customer segments like architect specifiers
has led to more emphasis on managing that customer-base and
understanding and meeting their needs with a stronger service
proposition. For example, personalised computer links have been
established with leading customers. The aim is to help them access
and understand Blue Circle products better and to enable Blue
Circle to help its customers. While there is a way to go in achieving
true leadership in some of these newer more personalised service
areas, there is a growing recognition of their long term strategic
importance.[3]

Case Study

A. T. Kearney

A. T. Kearney is a leading international consultancy and its merger
with EDS has triggered a major review of its own strategy and how
it plans to position itself as different and better with its target
customers. It had historically focused on its products, aiming to
perform the core consulting jobs better through its re-engineering
and restructuring capabilities. But it has seen its historic leadership
in this field erode as new entrants like Gemini and CSC Index
entered its market place providing to customers what appeared to
be a similar, if not better "packaged", product performance
offering. A. T. Kearney wanted to respond and searched around
for additional sources of advantage. It needed to keep its product
excellence but identified both E and Service as additional strategic
options. It is targeting to build lifetime relationships on the back of
good work with its clients and strengthening its brand recognition.
It is also aiming, somewhat like IBM, to provide a comprehensive
service capability: 'our challenge is to capture the leadership
advantage in our industry in this evolving environment by
presenting a superior service to meet all our clients' needs'.[4]

There are other examples of this restless search for new advantage that we have referred to in previous chapters and of, in effect, using the Market Commitment model as a framework for identifying new opportunities. We discussed John Reed's plans at Citicorp to 'create the Coca-Cola of the banking world', recognising the lack of any differentiation in other prime areas of Performance, Service or Price. We reviewed actions by Bayer and Fujitsu to explore new E strategies. We have seen what Direct Line has achieved by deliberately moving away from commodity product performance and offering deliberately low price. All these organisations are breaking the mould. They know success can only come by having clear, specific and customer-recognisable advantage, and they want to explore all the possible strategies. They are searching for something that can be developed so that it is **measurably** better than anything a rival can offer. They also know that success comes not only in identifying specifically which strategy is most leveraged in the market, but also in pursuing it with a Microsoft-like vigour and determination that will beat others in achieving and realising the goal.

The 10-step toolkit is a guide for an organisation moving down this path. It will be valuable if it can be used to stimulate strategic planning and development throughout the organisation. A simple set of forms or checks can be employed to challenge market knowledge and encourage business teams to review rigorously where and how they are different and what they can do to become lastingly differentiated. If it can engage managers at all levels to start asking the necessary searching questions, then it can be an additional catalyst to give strategy making the spotlight and attention it needs.

*   *   *

Addendum

We mentioned at the end of Chapter 5 when first introducing the Market Commitment model that there may be initial uncertainty for some companies as to how the model should be applied to them. This can sometimes come about simply because a company uses different words and language to describe its strategic intent. It may understand strategy in precisely the same way we are advocating in the model, be rooted in markets and customers and be driving to find competitive advantage, but just describe that differently.

Let's consider some of the main examples that come up and add some further perspective on how the model can be applied.

1. **Global growth** – For example AgCo (the US manufacturer of agricultural equipment) describe their strategy as 'global growth'. But they go on to describe their intention to provide a Service to customers everywhere in the world, to have the most distribution and the best 'Availability'. They want to be where their customers need them and to 'provide the most extensive dealer network across the globe'. They already operate in 140 countries and have over 7000 dealers. In the context and language of the Market Commitment model their "global growth strategy" is clearly to expand and strengthen their 'Service Availability'.

2. **Product range** – A common strategy is to provide the 'widest range' of products in an industry area. Home Depot, for example, draws substantial competitive advantage by offering everything its target customers might want: 'some 40 000 to 50 000 different kinds of building materials, home improvement supplies and lawn and garden products'. In fact Home Depot is clearly developing a most 'Comprehensive Service' proposition, with its very wide range as the principal driver.

3. **Technology** – Bayer describe their strategy as 'research based targeting technological leadership in core activities'. This is certainly a drive for superior product Performance. Bayer want to get their products to perform 'functionally better' than any others: 'precedence is given in our plans to new drugs or improved medications and advances in product performance . . . for example Makrolon our flagship resin performs better than alternatives in automotive headlamp lenses'.

4. **Features** – A division of Chloride the electronics group that makes security and alarm equipment prides itself on introducing new features to make its product more distinctive. In fact, the underlying intention with the new features is very much about improving the product Performance with the customer. Their goal is to either make the product easier and more convenient to use or to make it quicker to set up the equipment. Their aim is to make their products 'Perform' more competitively with their customers in this specific way. It's not the features themselves that are the strategy. It's the intended underlying benefits they bring to the customer that matter.

5. **Relationships** – Especially among financial services institutions the business is often described as being based on successful relationships with clients and customers. What is meant by this? The implications are that their is no particular difference in the basic product offering in the customer's eyes; pricing targets and approaches are similar, the same range of add-on services are likely to be available. The difference when we investigate is something more intangible, more 'Emotional'. Clients are retained because they 'feel good' about dealing with a particular provider. Over the years their trust and respect has been built up. There is 'Recognition'. This is a relationship based on strong E values and supported by a threshold competitiveness, if not necessarily any greater strengths on the other axes of strategy and advantage.

For some companies, then, there may be initial uncertainty in interpreting and using the market commitment model. But where it is a question of words or language, that can be quickly overcome as familiarity with the market commitment model grows and recognition of its conceptual thinking and contemporary relevance develops.

14 Building a More Effective Strategy Development Process

We've now got the model but how do we get there? We've learnt what are the key elements for an effective strategy but how do we get the organisation set up to develop it? What's the process? What needs to go on within the company, who must take responsibility, who must contribute? How do we build the internal machine that will develop and systematically fine-tune the strategy to keep it at its most competitive?

It is essential to construct a strategy development process that works, that will lead to output that excites and mobilises, stretches but enthuses. An effective process will help make things happen. If the process is weak we will end up watching others make it happen or be left as one of the pack wondering what did happen and how we lost out.

We all start off wanting to build or be part of a company that does go out there and 'make it happen'. No one wants to be left at the starting post or wondering how some rival stole so much market share so quickly. The whole process of strategy development is all about building so much understanding as to the best opportunities in the market that the organisation sees what needs to be done and is able and committed to getting there quickly and ahead of its rivals. So it's vital that the process is leveraged, that it does research the key issues, challenge the market boundaries, measure the right things, develop the best ideas and get people fired up. There's got to be an effective process – institutionalised in the company – for identifying, implementing and monitoring strategy

This chapter is about putting in place the right strategy development process, the 'machine that can make things happen'. But our starting point is a dismal one. Many companies that are researched and studied in fact have a poor development process in place. This often leads to strategies which are not much more than a set of targets for the next 12 months, accompanied by some woolly statements about future goals.

In Kalchas research referred to in previous chapters we found:[1]

- Nearly two-thirds of Corporate Planning VPs dissatisfied with the strategy development process in their companies.
- Over half agreeing that their strategy process was too much an exercise in 'filling out the numbers' rather than any rigorous review of the future.
- 34 per cent strongly agreed that the corporate centre had 'given up' on strategy development, in that the strategy for the company was now simply a collection of individual business plans.

Before we look at what the right process should be, we can draw encouragement from some recent shifts in market and management thinking. Getting the strategy process right is moving up the agenda. As the millennium draws nearer, as markets in the West become more buoyant, as business starts thinking about growth more than cost cutting or re-engineering, so strategy is becoming more of a priority and so too companies are reviewing more particularly their processes for developing it.

As *Business Week* commented in the fall of 1996: 'strategy planning is making a comeback . . . at one company after another strategy is again a major focus'.[2] As companies hit the strategy comeback trail, so it also appears some are recognising that the old processes were inadequate and didn't develop strategies which could become the driving force for the company. The *Business Week* research went on to point out that 'some companies are even recreating strategic planning groups . . . but they're back with a difference'.

What are the lessions of experience and what are the key requirements for the most leveraged process? We can set up three guiding criteria:

- The process must be separate from the annual budgeting cycle.
- The proper information must be available.
- A cross-section of people in the company must be involved.

Let us look at each of these in turn and then go on to examine the specific organisational structure and responsibilities that need to fit around the process that's identified.

Separate from annual budgeting

In most companies the process for developing strategy is lumped in with the annual budgeting cycle. It's rarely a distinct process in its own right

'We're budgeting for next year so we might as well do our strategy.'

'It's an opportunity to update the next twelve-months/three-year forecast.'

'It's one of the few times we can get everyone together to talk about the business.'

When tacked on to the annual budgeting review, the strategy process invariably takes on the characteristics of that budgeting exercise. The focus is on the next 12 months, forecasts are by extrapolation of the numbers, there are forms to be filled in, deadlines for agreeing next year's spending, the priority is to get the process done 'so we can get back to the real job of running the business'.

The annual budgeting review is also generally seen as a chore. 'The one time in the year senior management really interfere.' As a result, a somewhat negative and resentful view builds up toward the work burden of the annual budget round and that also carries over into the strategy-development part.

In fact the current combined – strategy plus budget – process is destructive. The need to get the numbers agreed leaves no time for any meaningful debate about future strategy. Worse still, because the process requires some conclusion on strategy to be drawn, strategic statements of a kind do nevertheless get written and this can easily beguile busy management teams into feeling that they do have something there, that somehow the strategy has been done, that even though it's not maybe the best it's OK and 'anyway next month's sales look a bit off and that's more worrying and important than anything else'.

'Strategy away-days' can be equally misleading. They are typically once-a-year meetings where management teams will gather for a series of presentations from different business heads on the results of their annual budgeting and planning review. To provide a greater sense of purpose and importance, such a meeting is often styled a 'strategy review', the documentation may even contain words about strategy. But beneath the packaging I have found time and again that there is mostly executional detail relating to the next 12 months. (In fact such away-days might be more effective if strategy was actually dropped from the agenda and discussion focused more deliberately on 'how are we going to make at least the next 12 months happen'.)

So businesses move forward with a process that notionally does address strategy, but in practice produces something inadequate. Not surprisingly, then, the strategy statement that might appear on page 1 or 2 of the budget document is often a fairly vague expression of future intent. And because insufficient time has been made available, it is frequently 'wordsmithed' to find phrases which easily embrace everyone, can be readily agreed with, but provide limited focus or direction:

'Our central strategy is to provide world class products and services and to develop our networks at home and overseas.'

'Our strategy is to focus on providing our telecommunications services to multinational customers, their partners, major nationals and other customers in Europe, North America and the Asia-Pacific region.'

We have a three-part strategy – acquisitions, accelerated global expansion and new products and processes.'

These three strategy statements, among too many other possible examples, all come from top 100 companies in the UK or the USA.

The current process then that is commonly found in most organisations is seriously flawed – not enough time, tacked onto the budget, focused on the short term and treated generally as a chore. Not surprisingly it typically produces strategies that are weak and ineffective. Companies that behave in this way are ultimately writing the script for their eventual demise. The lucky ones will get away with it – for a while – and may be sustained by some opportunistic initiative or by the even weaker strategy processes of other rivals. But many will see success being overtaken by gradual decline.

Where there is a more effectively established strategy process it undoubtedly provides a force within the organisation, driving to look outwards, stay competitive and build up advantage with customers. It's an enabler. It provides the framework for effective competition, it sets direction and priorities which guide the energies and development of the business. It's vital, yet few can claim best practice. Most move along with the incremental budget-related approach which is simply sub-optimal.

So when we ask why do so many companies find it hard to sustain success, or why do some draw plaudits for a number of years and then sadly decline, we may have an important part of the answer right here. We've discussed some of these dinosaurs – slow to react and on the verge of extinction. Perhaps instead we should characterise them as ostriches with their heads stuck in the sand – seemingly unaware of the inadequacies of their strategies and their creeping uncompetitiveness. Why did Apple, General Motors, IBM, Pepsi and so many others fail to see the weakening of their original competitive position? Why do Coca-Cola, Glaxo and Hewlett Packard continue to stay ahead?

A key step forward is the recognition among the more successful companies that strategy development is potentially so crucial that it must be established as a discrete process in its own right. The information required, the evaluation and interpretation that needs to be done, the challenge and debate of new ideas and approaches, all require a specific set of skills dedicated to the task with sufficient time found as a priority by management teams. And we have found that winning companies like Glaxo, Guinness and Coca-Cola and others do have a high-profile and discrete strategy development team and process which continuously prompts and provokes future business thinking and is the guardian of effective strategy development for the company.

For those who continue to deny the role and power of strategy as a driving force in their business, a process recommendation to separate and embody strategy development will no doubt be ignored. Time is precious and people will naturally prioritise around what they believe is important. But for those who do see the potential an effective strategy can provide, then this process separation and distinction is the critical first step to 'making things happen'.

The proper information must be available

Imagine you have been invited to attend a properly constituted review of the company's strategic direction, what information should you expect?

The market commitment model can be our guide. Across all three dimensions it urges deep-rooted understanding, it encourages forward thinking, it specifies measurement and monitoring. Overall it suggests a process which is disciplined and rigorous. Therefore the information we should expect should start by bearing that hallmark.

We want information particularly about commitment and advantage. For this we should be looking for hard facts and quantification borne out of dedicated research. A collection of anecdotes and qualitatively-based judgement is insufficient. If the information has been properly collected, then of course the findings and conclusions will be more convincing and a management team can feel more confident that it's turned over every stone and it's not missing something.

This requires a specific and properly skilled resource, individuals with the experience of looking at strategy questions and addressing them, people who can work quickly in these areas and get hold of information others find difficult. Whether it's a project team made up of representatives from different constituencies across the company, or whether it's a dedicated functional team or a specialised firm of external advisors we shall look at later.

But as a *Business Week* editorial recently pointed out, in respect of getting the proper information: 'it's amazing how many companies don't . . . complacent or simply unaware, thousands of businesses make critical decisions based on incomplete information. Best guesses are that only 10 per cent of all companies in the US systematically gather competitive [and market] intelligence'.[3]

This is a startling research finding. It provides another reason why it's crucial to have a really effective strategy development process and good information gathering as an integral part of that. A few companies do stand out as good examples, with a deliberate and specific data gathering process and a dedicated specialist resource for doing it:

'We invest in this because I want an edge everyplace I go.'
(Quaker State Corp Chairman)

'With the quickening pace of technological change, the past isn't as relevant, we have to play the game with better information and understanding about the future.' (Lockheed Martin CEO)

'Our antenna is much more attuned to our competitive environment.'
(Charles Schwab, Senior VP Strategic Planning)

'We now have established a specific market and competitive intelligence gathering function.' (Monsanto Chairman)

What information should be gathered, what detail is required? We can set out (1) the key questions that need to be asked, (2) the research and analysis that should take place, and (3) – once the strategy has been established, a set of key ratios and benchmarks that can be examined to monitor future performance. The aim in this part of the chapter is to provide a basic checklist of what should be investigated and analysed. The intention is to get the more searching and rigorous thinking started; to focus on the core issues likely to confront most strategy makers in working with their organisations to build and develop strategy more effectively. The full information list and detail, however, can only really be developed in the context of a particular company's situation and its individual set of issues and opportunities.

Key questions to be asked

The key questions to address around commitment and advantage are listed in Table 14.1.

Table 14.1 Questions to be asked on commitment, immersion and advantage

Commitment:	• Is there a long-term view of the future five years and more ahead
	• Are there quantifiable goals and milestones (will we know when we've got there?)
	• Are we showing an organisation-wide determination to stick with it?
	• Are we sufficiently focused?
	• Are we stretching ourselves but still 'just about' being realistic?
Market immersion:	• Does the research available show we have an obviously deep-rooted immersion and understanding of markets and customers?
	• Is there an intuitive feel, as well as analytical, for what the future holds?
	• Are new product/service/strategy ideas coming through which are truly borne from this immersion and intuition?
Advantage:	• Are we measuring the CAGs?
	• Are we monitoring the trends?
	• Are we exploiting the gaps?
	• Do we know competitors' future intentions?
	• Have we understood the disadvantages?
	• Have we plans to address them?
	• Are we exploring new forms of advantage?

Research and analysis

The basic research and analysis we must carry out to address these commitment and advantage issues must of course come from customers and the marketplace. It should also be contrasted with both competitors and own employee perspectives as shown in Figure 14.1.

Has the company got good information and answers in all these areas? Can it back its conclusions with rigour and fact? Are the senior executives convincing in their understanding and evaluation of the various options and opportunities? Are they clearly immersed enough in their market place with a thorough understanding of their possible sources of advantage and with an evident commitment to back the chosen path and truly drive it through?

There are further questions not specifically included here about the profitability of various ideas and opportunities. Of course the very

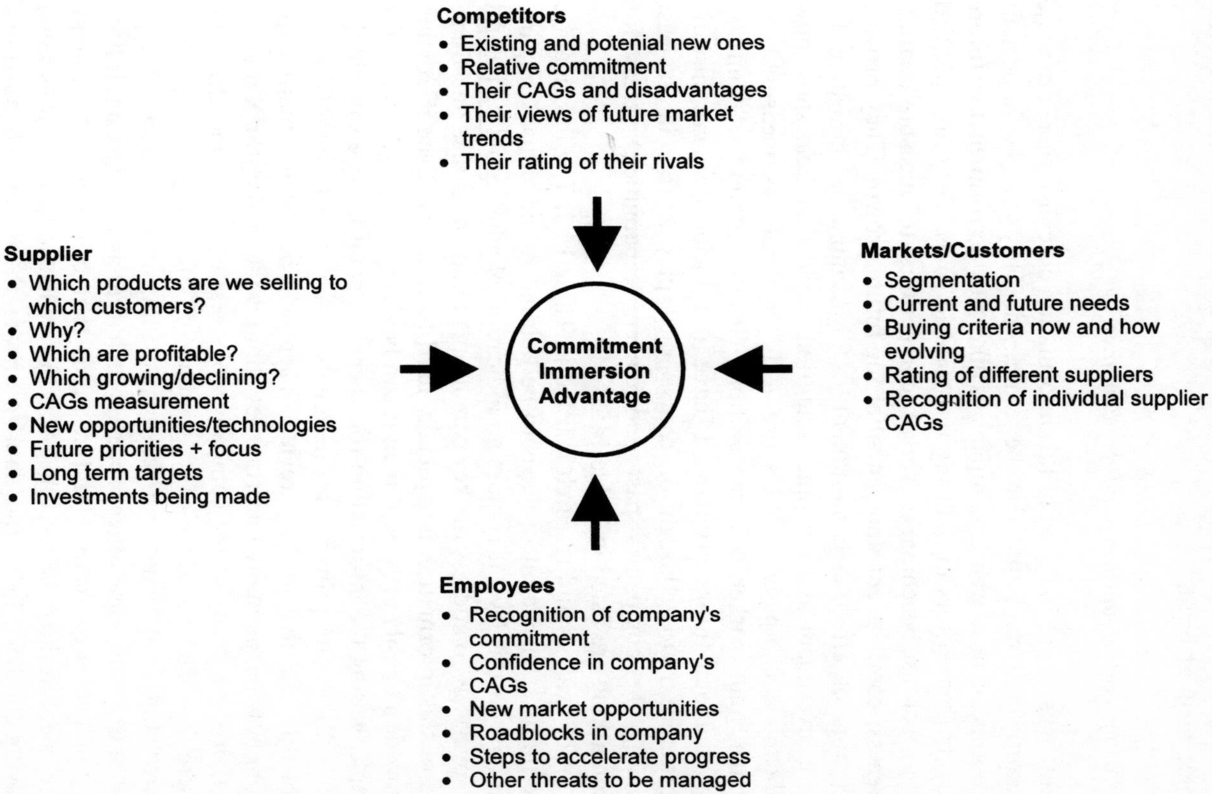

Competitors
- Existing and potenial new ones
- Relative commitment
- Their CAGs and disadvantages
- Their views of future market trends
- Their rating of their rivals

Markets/Customers
- Segmentation
- Current and future needs
- Buying criteria now and how evolving
- Rating of different suppliers
- Recognition of individual supplier CAGs

Commitment Immersion Advantage

Supplier
- Which products are we selling to which customers?
- Why?
- Which are profitable?
- Which growing/declining?
- CAGs measurement
- New opportunities/technologies
- Future priorities + focus
- Long term targets
- Investments being made

Employees
- Recognition of company's commitment
- Confidence in company's CAGs
- New market opportunities
- Roadblocks in company
- Steps to accelerate progress
- Other threats to be managed

Figure 14.1 Areas for research and analysis

necessary profit and risk trade-off must be made, but the intention is not to stifle the market immersion–intuition–innovation process. Let the profit trade-off come in **after** the various opportunities are identified, not strangle them at birth.

Monitoring performance through benchmarks

Benchmarks – as a final part of this information checklist, there are some key ratios and data that can be examined. They can be important indications of how well a company is likely to perform in the future versus its competitors in realising its strategic goals. They are specified here to act as benchmarks versus competitors to measure market awareness, commitment and potential for future growth. They provide indications of effective commitment – for example as measured by relative investment and customer retention – and they help show how significant a company's CAGs are – for example as measured by customer and marketplace recognition. (In the context of thinking forward about future strategy, I have not included many historic performance ratios, though of course they play a role in at least indicating the company's past and current capabilities.) Areas for benchmarking are listed in Table 14.2.

A lot of analysis and research is listed in Table 14.2. The information gathering is extensive but it needs to be tailored to individual company situations. At this level it is more an indication of what could be helpful as an overview to address the key commitment and advantage questions. None of this information is especially hard to come by. Even if existing systems don't easily provide it then it can be done by a project team, for example, getting the information together as a point-in-time snapshot.

But without the proper information base it is clearly impossible to conduct an effective strategic review. There will be just too many gaps and unknowns, too many uncertainties about what competitor X may be doing, or the security of the company's business with customer Y.

There is clearly a significant amount of information and insight required and so it is just not feasible to lump in or confuse strategy development with some other processes such as annual budgeting. It does need the dedicated process and resource that can approach strategy development in the most leveraged way. There has to be enormous value in having the hard facts and data to answer the issues and questions raised through the market commitment model, and being one of the 10 per cent that do it rigorously and systematically, not part of the 90 per cent that barely scratch the surface.

Table 14.2 Areas for benchmarking

Commitment:

Investment

- growth in capital investment
- capex growth versus sales growth
- size of dedicated team

New Products

- R&D as % of sales
- Growth in R&D
- trend in number of patents filed
- number of new products launched each year
- change in percentage turnover coming from new products in past 5 years
- target in next 5 years

Immersion:

Investment

- number of days spent with customers
- number of pieces of research completed
- time/resource spent collaborating with customers on new products
- 'Share of voice'

Customer Relationships

- trend in number of new customers won
- customers lost
- customers retained
- trend in customer complaints/complements
- correlate revenues with length of customer relationships
- growth in advertising promotions

Advantage

CAGs

- competitive advantage gaps
- competitive disadvantages
- rating of company in market-wide surveys
- industry association awards

Involve a cross-section of people

The third criterion for developing strategy effectively is that it cannot be an isolated process. Many people in different parts of the organisation will have information or perspective which can both inform and shape the strategic conclusions that will emerge. A small senior team acting by itself cannot possibly gather the necessary level of insight that is required. But it is available if others in the company are proactively involved.

Senior management acting by themselves are inevitably blocked by the Iceberg of Ignorance we discussed earlier. Research by The Forum Corporation among the top-500 US companies demonstrated that typically only 4 per cent of issues known to junior members of a company were also known to the most senior executives.[4] Against such a finding there should be no question as to the need to involve others as widely as is feasible across the organisation (see Figure 14.2).

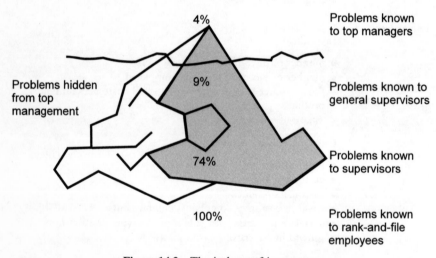

Figure 14.2   The iceberg of ignorance

In terms of cross-company involvement it is the salesforce – obviously closest to the marketplace and to customers – who are surprisingly but commonly the last group to be involved. Yet it is those nearest the coalface who will surely have the most up-to-date and market-rooted perspective. Equally, many of those who have been long-serving in the company but may not be especially senior in the hierarchy are also usually left out of the process. But they will often have developed an intuitive feel for their industry and marketplace and may well have very insightful thoughts and ideas. Attempts are sometimes made to tap into this wider cross-company market intelligence through Lotus Notes or some other Intranet system, but the data coming through is typically haphazard and its exploitation is generally poor, residing on some marketing database rather than being systematically fed in and reviewed.

Another source of challenging perspective can come from those newest to the company, whether from graduate school or recently joined from another industry or a competitor. They will have the freshest ideas and suggestions. But here too I have rarely seen any process for systematically gathering information and input from new recruits.

To be effective, the strategy planning process must embrace these different constituencies, gather these different inputs, be wide-ranging and be looking not just for information but also for challenge from different parts of the company. It is often said that all the good ideas do exist somewhere in the organisation. The goal is to develop a process that liberates these ideas and energies and channels them constructively into better strategic planning. New ways of seeing the market need to breakthrough so that new, more vital ideas and opportunities can emerge.

Encouragingly, this more enlightened approach is catching on. As companies return to strategy as we approach the millenium, there is growing recognition of the value of 'democratising' the strategy-planning process. *Business Week* research suggests 'where strategy development was once the sole province of a company's senior officers it is now being shared increasingly with teams of line and staff managers from different disciplines'.[5]

So if we do set out to involve the organisation widely in the gathering of information and ideas, in separating out the process and putting in place the proper information gathering resource, skill and system, then we are beginning to define a specific stand-alone strategy development process which can provide the right platform for getting the best possible strategy in place.

As this process starts taking shape we can more firmly delineate the organisational structure that should fit around it, and in this there are three further factors to consider:

- Who should do what – roles and responsibilities in the process.
- With what frequency.
- With what skills – the role of corporate planning.

Who should do what

Research and observation shows there are at present two predominant approaches to strategy planning which we shall call simply top-down and bottom-up. Neither of them usually work.

The top-down model vests responsibility for strategy development solely with the CEO and the corporate planning staff at the centre. Whether the information gathering is wide and involving or not, it assumes the CEO and the functional team will gather such inputs as they think fit, and then formulate a strategy to announce to others.

This approach may have some merit in the early days of a founder entrepreneur like Sam Walton or Sweet 'N Low champion Ben Eisenstadt – business leaders who are still drawing inspiration and innovation directly from their own still very relevant and personal understanding of their customers and their marketplace. But even the founder entrepreneur will struggle to stay close enough in touch as the company grows and others take over some of that market-watching, customer relationship role.

The problems with the top-down model are being increasingly recognised. General Electric and BP, for example, have significantly cut back on their previously large central corporate planning departments which used to have 200-plus staff. Their intention is to get away from a process that was too often insular – 'the view from the centre' – as well as being perceived as too functionally driven. Their goal is to move instead to project teams involving wide cross-sections of people in the company and representing the views of the marketplace. They are trying to break down the perceptions that the top-down approach results in the 'centre taking over strategy' or stifling new ideas from elsewhere in the company, removing any sense of ownership or commitment from those tasked with the implementation.

On the other hand, while the bottom-up model can be effective in drawing input and ideas from those closest to the market, it can also be inadequate as a strategy development process. It typically suffers from becoming 'politicised', and in its practical application it can result in the group CEO being left with no meaningful role in strategy at all.

The bottom-up approach becomes politicised because in practice management teams will often recommend up the line plans which are 'business as usual', which are largely incremental, and which rarely rock the boat. Whoever hears of a business head recommending their division be shut down? It's rare because it sounds like an admission of failure even if strategically that were the right move. The business head's response is naturally and inevitably to continue to look for ways to recover and grow, rather than how best to wind things down in an orderly way.

The bottom-up process also has problems in that the CEO and any central planning team often struggle to find a role for themselves in such a structure. Strategy becomes the formal responsibility and domain of the individual businesses. Indeed they are unquestionably closer to their markets than people at the centre of the organisation, so why challenge such formal responsibility, why should their bottom-up process be interfered with and on what basis could their recommendations possibly be rejected?

Where responsibility for strategy is delegated down in this way, the CEO is often left wondering what role the centre can be left to play in strategy, and he may be reduced to asking a few polite questions 'to better understand the basis' of the strategy and 'just to check' that the main issues have been addressed. There may still a specific responsibility to ensure the projected financial returns are attractive to the group, but generally in the bottom-up approach the basic formulation of the strategy is left firmly in the hands of the businesses and outside the CEO's control.

Despite these inadequacies, in practice this bottom-up approach to strategy is happening more and more. As companies globalise, individual divisions within a company become substantial businesses in their own right, and in this era of empowerment business heads increasingly and naturally seek to control the key levers of their business. This situation creates increasing tension and frustration between chief executives and their business heads.

'I feel I need to give the Division general managers the power and responsibility but where does that leave us at the Centre? Are we reduced to adding up the numbers for the statutory accounts and only intervening in the event of a crisis?'   (CEO of UK top 100 company)

A common consequence of this bottom-up approach is that the CEO is reduced to such a 'financial-control' style of management and leadership. The centre team evaluates the numbers, monitors the financial performance and intervenes only if a business is not delivering. It becomes a portfolio approach, balancing risk and return across a number of different business units. Yet such an approach to management – long-favoured by the conglomerates – is nowadays inappropriate. The ability to truly add value in such a set-up from the centre is now substantially reduced by our ever more competitive, global economy. Success today often now requires companies to think globally, not in silos, to find synergies **between** different businesses. And this is not just in costs but now even more critically with products and customers. Competing effectively is ever more about leveraging the total capabilities of the organisation rather than just leaving each unit on a standalone basis with significant potential synergies untapped. Only the 'centre' can fulfil this task. The centre's principle responsibility must be to identify these 'total-organisation' opportunities and to ensure any strategy development leverages them.

The strategy planning process cannot afford to be only a top-down or bottom-up process. It must be a combination of the two. It must contain the best elements of both and firmly set responsibility for strategy as **joint** between the group CEO and the individual business heads. Let us give it a label and call it the 'caucus' approach, picking up on the idea of people in the same group but with varying interests necessarily coming together to determine policy most effectively.

The aim is to provide a balance between the overall responsibilities of the CEO and those of the SBU (single business unit) general manager, to allow for direction and vision from the centre while encouraging strategy development closest to the market and the necessary sense of ownership and commitment among the implementers (see Figure 14.3).

The main protagonists are the CEO at the centre and the SBU heads. What role should each play, what responsibilities should each take? We can now explore and illustrate this more specifically by defining their roles and responsibilities at each stage of the strategy planning process.

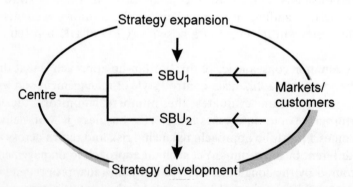

Figure 14.3   The caucus approach to strategy planning

Our process consists of seven steps. As contributors to the process we shall also for now assume a corporate planning function and that they play a role in support of the CEO. In my experience, they are a necessary and vital contributor and catalyst in the process (if effectively constituted). Their merits we shall come back to later. The caucus roles and responsiblities within the strategy planning process are shown in Table 14.3.

Table 14.3 Caucus roles and responsibilities

Strategy-planning process (main steps)	CEO	Corporate planning	SBU
Originate	X	X	
↓			
Gather + Measure		(X)	X
↓			
Recommend			X
↓			
Challenge + Review	X	(X)	X
↓			
Expand	X	(X)	
↓			
Affirm + Communicate	X		X
↓			
Implement			X

Note: (X) = secondary/support role.

Let us review each of these process steps in turn:

- **Originate**: Few CEOs would deny ultimate responsibility for strategy. As we have discussed, a number might suggest that that responsibility has been delegated to others, but nearly all acknowledge they are at minimum the mouthpiece for strategy communication. Of course many other CEOs will go a lot further and see strategy development as their defining role. Such business leaders will focus the bulk of their energies specifically on determining how their company can be the market leader of tomorrow. Chief Executives at Campbell, Microsoft, IKEA, Pilkington, Southwest Airlines, Rubbermaid, Coca-Cola and

Nestlé have all commented in various interviews how they see strategy as one of their primary if not principal responsibilities.

- **Gather** and **Measure**: At this point responsibility firmly shifts to the SBU. They are closest to the markets, they are responsible for their individual customers, they are far and away best placed to gather and analyse market intelligence. In fact a well-organised business unit should be proactively measuring its performance in the market and its competitive advantage situation without the need for any stimulus from the centre. And such ongoing data collection and measuring should become the norm.

  It's at this point where a central corporate planning department can get more particularly involved. At one level it can be a resource provider to help with data collection and analysis. At another level it can be a centre of excellence, with people who are expert in strategy formulation and data interpretation for the purposes of developing strategy. To the extent that there are any powerful new tools or techniques, it is this group that can take responsibility for best understanding them, how they can most helpfully be used in the company and communicating and educating others as to their value.

- **Recommend**: Firmly the responsibility of each business.

- **Challenge** and **Review**: This is where the shared responsibility for strategy development is most acute. While the individual business head must recommend the most forceful and stretching strategy, the chief executive must take responsibility for testing its achievability and feasibility and ensure it is stretching and testing enough. This part of the process must be shared and not suffer from the politicised, incremental problems of the old bottom-up model.

  This stage can only work well if it is explicity agreed to be a joint responsibility. The business head must acknowledge that the CEO can play a vital role in challenging and fine-tuning the strategy, and that responsibility for the success of the strategy in each business remains shared between them.

- **Expand**: It's at this point that the CEO needs to inject a corporate view and, if appropriate, a personal vision into the process.

  In principle, corporate strategy should not be simply the sum of a set of individual business strategies. It should be something significantly more than the sum of the parts. The exception to this is in the conglomerate diversified corporation where there are a number of different businesses and it is impossible to find any meaningful unifying theme or direction or source of advantage that is relevant across them all. In such diversified situations the CEO's capacity to expand further on strategy is more limited, and typically the centre reverts to a less strategic more financial style of management in the manner of 3M and Laporte (the speciality chemicals group), and in the style especially developed by BTR and Hanson (pre-demerger days).

At the other extreme where the company is focused enough that it's mainly in one business such as Home Depot, Tesco or British Airways, then we would expect to see the CEO play a much greater if not the sole leading role. In such circumstances the CEO is more able to stay in touch with the key dynamics of the single industry in which the company operates and so push out the strategic thinking even further than the recommendations of individual country or regional managers (see Figure 14.4).

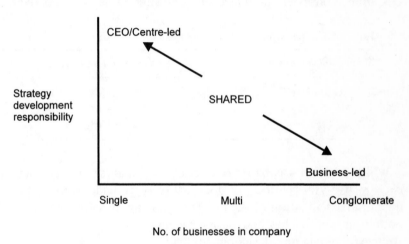

Figure 14.4   Responsiblity in strategy development

Given that the era of the diversified conglomerate is dying away and most companies are developing some form of focus and relatedness between individual businesses, then there are few situations now where the CEO should not be aiming to formally share responsibility and expand the strategy. It's at this point where the CEO's own intuition and far-sightedness as to the possibilities and potential five, ten or more years away can come into play. It's here where the big ideas can emerge of 'democratising the automobile', 'becoming the General Motors of the tobacco industry', 'beat Mercedes', 'double the number of stores and increase turnover per square foot by 60 per cent over the next 10 years', 'go for 6-sigma perfection'. This is where the

CEO stamps his mark on the company, adds to the basic strategy content of commitment and advantage, and can galvanise the organisation into a major leap foward in market position and competitiveness.

- **Affirm** and **Communicate**: As we shall discuss in the next chapter, a critical component of any implementation succes is the 'sharing and communication of the strategy' in a way that truly engages and motivates the workforce. Again this is best established as a joint responsibility.
- **Implement**: Firmly the responsibility of each business.

That a more collaborative, shared, caucus-type approach to strategy development is more leveraged is borne out in research reviewed by Goold and Campbell, on which the following Table 14.4 is based.[6]

Table 14.4 The influence of strategy planning style on return on capital

Strategy-planning style	Increase in return on capital/year
Top-down	− 4%
Bottom-up	− 6%
Shared	+ 20%

While Table 14.4 is based on a relatively small sample of companies over a five-year period, it does at least provide some additional quantitative validation of the merits of moving away from top-down or bottom-up approaches and pushing vigorously along a caucus style of strategy planning and development.

With what frequency

Strategy development cannot be left to a once-a-year review, even if separated out from annual budgeting and set up as a process in its own right. In fact it needs to be a continuous process but with some formal checkpoints.

With the pace of change ever increasing, the marketplace of the late 1990s is typically in a more fluid and volatile state than it has ever been. The need to constantly gather and analyse market data and to monitor market and customer trends is therefore ever more pressing. In this context the strategy development process must link into an **ongoing** information gathering and intelligence resource – just like companies like Monsanto, Glaxo, Kodak, Coca-Cola and others do. There must be continuous input and assessment of the competitiveness of the strategy and the plans to realise this. Not only does this monitoring help keep the organisation totally in tune with its markets and customers, but it encourages that profound immersion we have spoken of and the continuous search for new ideas and ways of competing.

As a result, strategy development need no longer be a big one-off annual event. Once the strategy has been established in the founding days, or early days of ownership, or of the new management team, then the process can move far more into monitoring and fine-tuning. Of course it's also valuable to set aside a significant amount of time say every six months to stand back and reflect on the information presented and more aggressively 'challenge and review' and seek opportunities to further expand. But these more formal checkpoints should be easy for the organisation to establish because the data should be systematised and available, its interpretation already synthesised and disseminated, the CAGs measured and the need for any strategy fine-tuning in the light of changing market conditions already identified.

With what skills – the role of corporate planning

A client recently asked: 'we want you to help us think outside of the box, to break down the barriers and rules we've set ourselves over the years, to find a different way of thinking about our business opportunities'.

Those involved in leading the strategy development process must either have themselves, or have access to, a whole range of skills from basic information gathering, through analysis, and then interpretation of what it all means. But in some ways the most vital is the ability to think laterally or differently about the market place and its opportunities and be able to see beyond the existing market boundaries and rules of the game.

Strategy consultants are one source of this expertise and experience. A highly skilled corporate planning department acting as a centre of excellence can be another. It's a developed skill in not just getting the basic market information together, but in asking questions or getting new cuts of data that throw a different perspective on a situation. It's the skill in seeing the widest range of available solutions to a particular problem – perhaps from the most radical and revolutionary to the simplest or most evolutionary – and being able to define the most leveraged. It's furthermore the skill of engaging people in this 'out-of-the-box' debate, and finding ways of opening up people's minds to new ways of thinking, perhaps by reference to what others have done or the lessons or approaches developed in other industries.

Mintzberg calls it a mix of left-brain and right-brain skills, being able to mix fact-based analysis with intuitive and creative thinking that enables the individual to think as widely as possible about a particular problem and the solution options. Of course not everyone has this skill, and if it is recognised as being important then it needs to be cultivated and developed within the company. This aptitude combined with the relevant degree of experience is probably best located amongst specialists such as corporate planners and strategy consultants who develop these particular capabilities.

This is a main reason why I am certainly a firm advocate for at minimum a continuing role for the corporate planning department. Not only are they the necessary CEO resource at several stages in the strategy planning process, but they should become a fountain of knowledge and expertise that can compliment the data gathering, analysis and interpretation tasks of people responsible in the individual business. Line and operation managers may innately have these same skills but they are less likely to be developed, as their own jobs will require a range of other capabilities more in demand.

A specialist skilled corporate planning group can therefore be a great source of value-added. Given recent history and the poor perceptions of the role of this group, however, it should certainly not be the 200-plus size of resource. But if staffed with appropriately skilled people it can provide that continuing catalyst, energy and ideas into the strategy development process.

Furthermore there is a strong argument that the head of the department should be a senior VP with a place on the senior executive committee of the company. Surely the officers of the company cannot effectively debate the business without an expert in strategic thinking around the table? This input may sometimes be provided by the CEO if he/she has had the appropriate training and experience either in corporate planning or perhaps as a strategy consultant. At other times the input may come from the senior marketing VP, if that person has a marketing skill and awareness which has moved beyond advertising and promotion and in fact encompasses the broader understanding of markets, customers and competitive advantage.

But in many situations either there is no Marketing person on the executive committee, or the CEO has perhaps a Finance background rather than one in strategy. In those circumstances it is critical that some person can act as the guardian of effective strategy. The voice must be raised that challenges among other things whether there is still the right level of commitment if investment spending is cut, or whether the focus is to be significantly undermined by a particular acquisiton opportunity, or whether a business has its priorities right in entering into a new market when its existing markets still require enormous efforts before success there is realised.

If strategy is to have the power and potential for an organisation that it can have, then it must be given the appropriate resource, skills and profile in the company. Anything less must be sub-optimal if the battle in the market is to be fought and won.

Finally, if a company truly wants to ensure its strategy planning is at its most effective, it could consider further the idea first put forward by Gordon Donaldson of Harvard for a 'strategic audit'.[7] The thinking here is not just to ensure that the strategy process is by itself asking and addressing all the right issues, but to also give a sign to investors that the company is moving forward and developing on the right track. It's a form of insurance for the investing community. There's also an argument that in the spirit of better corporate governance such an audit is actually a requirement that enables board members and non-executive directors to properly fulfill their responsibilities that the company is being well-run.

Donaldson's idea is that the audit be carried out by a professional external body who can be objective and independent. Its remit could be to address the commitment and advantage questions raised earlier in this chapter and identify performance against the benchmarks suggested. He suggests giving this task to accountants given their audit skills and because they are already engaged once a year in detailed evaluation of the company's financial position.

Whether accountants, consultants or some other group are the right body to carry out an independent audit of the company's strategy we need not resolve here, but if a company is to embrace strategy effectively it should be challenging whether an audit or some other independent review would be beneficial. It may be that it is only required for the first few years once the strategy planning process has been properly set up along the lines we've discussed here. But it could be another valuable mechanism to ensure that the company fully understands its markets and competitive position, and realises the power and potential that can come from the best possible strategy development process.

15 Making it Happen

How do we make it all happen? How do we translate the strategy development into actual bottom-line success? How do we win so well with our customers that they keep coming back for more? We've described in detail what the prime strategic options are and the strategy development process which is most effective. But we need to quickly move on from the strategy formulation to the strategy realisation, we need to turn ideas into results, we need to achieve and reach the stakes we've determined to put in the ground.

It is my observation and experience that the key lies in the people in the company. It's the people that make the difference. If they understand the strategy, see how it will indeed put them at a competitive advantage in the industry, how it's stretching but achievable, and have a commitment themselves to making it happen, then it will (see Figure 15.1).

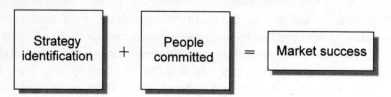

Figure 15.1 People commitment

'Corporations are learning that handsome returns come directly from a superior combination of strategic planning plus strategic execution.'[1]
(Professor Bartlett)

'More companies in all industries are finally learning that strategic advances have limits without outstanding tactics and execution.'[2]
(Warren Buffet)

It's about sharing the strategy ideas, communicating what they mean, why they're important, what are the benefits. It's about instilling that sense of passion and excitement in the goals that are set that is often seen around successful founding entrepreneurs. It's getting people to develop that sense of ownership and personal responsibility that we have seen at

WalMart, British Airways, Hewlett Packard, The Limited, Nike and Microsoft for example. It's generating an enthusiasm that finds Home Depot Associates saying: 'by giving 100 per cent to customers, I'm helping to write the success story of this rapidly expanding industry'.

If the leadership of the company has done its job well and set a strategy grounded in market and customer advantage, then the next step – enthusing the workforce – should not be that difficult. People's motivations struggle when the strategy that they are being asked to pursue doesn't make sense to them, doesn't provide a clear cut market target that is believable and achievable, doesn't strive for that specific form of competitive advantage that if achieved would clearly beat all rivals.

If it's people that help make the difference, then can we articulate more precisely how to get people onto that platform where they are eagerly driving for success; what does it take, what are the lessons learned from other winners and what are the pitfalls to avoid?

Research has suggested a number of key success factors which can drive this people-orientation. Assuming an effective strategy has been developed that is properly grounded and credible, then we can explore six factors in total that have been identified that enable people to make the difference. They are particularly about increased employee involvement and sharing in the ideas and values that drive the organisation – and in the rewards that come through when success is realised:

- **Sharing the strategy**
- **Sharing the values**
- **'Symbolic egalitarianism'**
- **Sharing the information**
- **Training**
- **Sharing the benefits**

Let's look at each of these in turn and then briefly explore the typical roadblocks winning companies have also had to overcome in order to create the environment where people actually can unleash their energies productively and practically go forward and make that difference.

Sharing the strategy

Charles Handy in his book *Age of Unreason* explored the attributes of successful leadership.[3] His analysis, corroborated by many other business commentators, shows that the most important item is that: '*a leader must shape and share a vision which gives point to the work of others*'. As we consider who are the effective business leaders of today, we can see time and again that they do communicate a compelling and believable strategy and vision of where they want the company to go and what role and responsibility their workforce has in getting the company there.

They are able to translate the strategy into something that even the most junior employee finds engaging and exciting. Toyota's formal strategy may be based on product reliability and excellence, but in its communication to the workforce it was put in the context of, 'Beat Mercedes'. Avis may have determined its strategy around service leadership, but it was communicated in a way that rallied the workforce: 'we may be No. 2 but we try harder'. McDonald's may have focused on superb performance and service, but it landed on the expression QVSC (Quality Value Service Cleanliness) as a simple mnemonic that it could charge its employees to remember, be measured against and deliver on. The ideas behind sharing the strategy in this way are shown in Figure 15.2.

To quote Anita Roddick of Bodyshop again, she has said:

'Most businesses focus all the time on profits, profits, profits. I think that is deeply boring. You have to find ways to grab peoples' imagination. You want them to feel they are doing something important.'[4]

Talking about achieving a 25 per cent return on net assets, or boosting shareholder value, or increasing MVA is unlikely to be motivating to the vast number of employees in the business. It might be well-understood by the senior management of the company who set the financial goals and are specifically rewarded on achieving them. But as Jack Welch has said:[5]

'If people are to put out the extraordinary effort required to realise corporate targets then they must all be able to identify with them and share in the ideas and goals that they represent.'

A key factor then is translating the strategy into motivating goals and describing those aims in a language and context that employees can readily buy into and accept. It must 'touch the spirit', it must be informal, it should be honest, it must come from the heart as well as the head. In other words it must sound real.

'The key to a leader's impact is his sincerity. He must believe in what he is saying. Before he can inspire he must also be swayed by the idea.'[6]

(Winston Churchill)

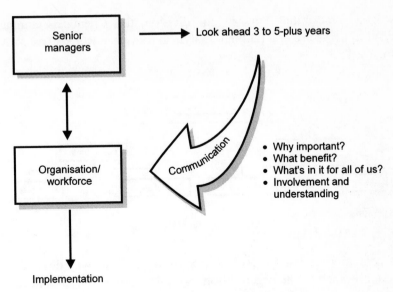

Figure 15.2 Strategy communication

When President Kennedy shared his vision to get a man on the moon by the end of the decade it struck a chord with the man in the street, it sparked a dream and united NASA into a collective effort to reach the goal. When Henry Ford talked about democratising the vehicle he too touched on something that every worker could strive towards. When Microsoft announced its comeback-strategy to dominate the internet, it immediately directed the energies of the organisation to realise a goal they all intuitively understood and wanted to succeed in.

One of the world's leading chemicals companies, ICI, has approached this challenge by striving to 'cascade responsibilities'. Their response is to try to translate their corporate goal of 25 per cent RONA (return on net assets) into: what does that mean for each employee; what is each person's contribution to that financial target? If it can be defined clearly and if it's tangible and measurable enough then at least each member of the workforce will understand how their own performance and achievements impact the total corporate result.

'Motivation depends greatly on the extent to which people understand what the company is trying to do, why it's trying to get there . . . and can track progress'.[7]

(William McKnight, former CEO of 3M)

Based on some initial work in one division, this Chemicals company decided to make use of a familiar analytical tool – the RONA tree shown in Figure 15.3.

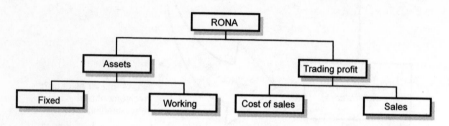

Figure 15.3 The RONA tree

Any company can use the RONA tree to drive all the way down to the root and branch of the organisation. So, for example, the sales lines can cascade down as shown in Figure 15.4.

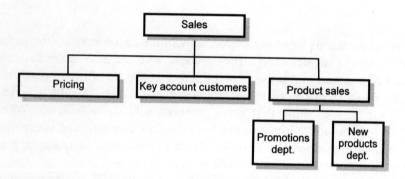

Figure 15.4 The RONA sales tree

Individual employees in the promotions or new products functions can be charged with certain goals and deliverables the achievement of which can be shown financially to contribute to that RONA target. The new products manager, for example, may be tasked with bringing in and successfully launching a target number of new products to deliver 10 per cent sales growth which, if successful, could translate to a 1 per cent addition to the trading profit and so boost the RONA.

It's a simple enough system that people can easily understand and this company has invested heavily in communication and training to ensure it has been fully understood. It's a scheme that's still in its early years and probably needs further institutionalisation but it's one way, albeit fairly mechanistic, of translating the vision into 'what does this mean for me'.

Getting people to understand the strategy, communicating the detail so they can buy into it and feel motivated by it, are so important. How can people make the difference if they don't know what specifically to make the difference in, and what standard or target they should be aiming for and measuring their personal success by? In a winning organisation, everyone **does** know what the strategy is, can articulate it in more or less the same way and in the same language, and use the strategy to prioritise and direct their own efforts and the people working for them. It can result in a simple statement of competitor advantage and future intent that is used in reports and documents. It could be a set of goals that all actions and initiatives, however low in the organisation they originate, will be tested by.

Challenge your own organisation with the '30-second test'. If any employee found themselves in the elevator with the CEO and was asked how they would describe the company's strategy, what would they say? Would they all have an answer and if they did would they say broadly the same thing? If they did answer would they say what the CEO would hope they'd say? Would they in fact describe the future strategy and direction? Would they say it with enthusiasm?

Richard Hagberg, President of a US consultancy group that specialises in understanding CEO success attributes, concludes:[8]

'Many bosses fail at two crucial tasks – communicating strategy and aligning troops behind a vision . . . they can get so wrapped up in their own ideas that they fail to communicate strategies downward.'

Hagberg's detailed research of nearly 500 CEOs across the USA shows that a majority are 'too introvert'.

But as businesses get bigger, more global and more complex, the need to create a unifying vision is even more critical. It is no use having the best thought-through and developed strategy if the messages and rationale are lost as it's communicated through the ranks and through different countries. The only possible solution path is get the best strategy formulated, translate it into a simple and exciting message and targets, and then like former Johnson & Johnson CEO Jim Burke ensure the leaders of the company 'invest a substantial amount of their own time communicating, explaining and driving it'.[9]

Sharing the values

Human beings want to pledge allegiance to something. They want to belong, feel valued and be part of something they consider important. Work by the Institute for Research on Learning set up by Xerox in Palo Alto shows that in corporations, as in life, people naturally align themselves in informal and formal groupings where there is a shared interest – a 'community of practice'.[10]

Sharing the strategy effectively is the necessary first step to create the 'community of interest', the shared goals that will bring people together and unite them around common targets. But it cannot stop there. As people come together to pursue the strategy, what values do they subscribe to, what are their ethics, their role models, what common standards do they aspire to and respect? What is it that makes people additionally feel good about what they are doing so that they are **genuinely** motivated and driven?

> 'Any organisation, in order to survive and achieve success, must have a sound set of beliefs on which it premises all its policies and actions. I believe a most important factor in corporate success is faithful adherence to those beliefs.'[11] (Thomas Watson, former CEO of IBM)

The core values Watson established could be summarised as:

- Give full consideration to the individual employee.
- Spend a lot of time making customers satisfied.
- Go the last mile to do things right.
- Seek superiority in all we undertake.

Let's consider some other examples:

- Disney developed a credo: 'Make people happy'.[12] It permeated everything the company tried to do. It was the spirit of his films – good triumphed over evil – it was the theme of the Disney amusement parks. It was deliberately encouraged as the philosophy of the people in the organisation in all their interactions with their audience and their customers.
- Sam Walton's competitive strategy was around both low prices and satisfying customer service. He wanted his organisaton to be the very best at this, and he set a number of examples that became part of the mythology and culture of the organisation. As part of the drive to lower prices he encouraged his people to be rigorous in monitoring their own costs. For example, at board meetings if his senior

executives wanted a drink he insisted they bring their own coins along and buy it themselves from the Coke machine. He also institutionalised the 'WalMart promise' which was described earlier. Every employee was encouraged to make the same wholehearted customer service commitment.[13]

People like Thomas Watson, Walt Disney and Sam Walton found a way to bring people together, and by their own actions and example set a tone and idealogy that has permeated every employee working in their companies. They achieved something unique and precious. But it was not an easy or quick win. When we review companies like WalMart we are of course considering a culture and set of beliefs developed and reinforced over many years, with internal mechanisms institutionalised to protect and nurture them.

But what can be done if there isn't a sound set of shared beliefs already established and influencing and shaping individual employees' motivation and behaviour? How to transform a group with divergent values and ideals into a more cohesive and congruent team? Can it be done nowadays when a company's leaders have to deal with the wide global spread of businesses, people and the inevitably different cultures?

Ultimately there may be no substitute for strong leadership by the senior management team, and especially the figurehead CEO. But one practical solution suggested by John Kotter is to create a sense of urgency and crisis in the organisation. If there isn't one then make one happen – 'a majority of employees must believe that considerable change is absolutely essential if they are to come together'.[14]

Paul Judge who led the very successful Premier Brands buyout from Cadbury Schweppes a decade ago illustrates this with the following story:[15]

'When we started out it was like being in a lifeboat full of water sinking fast. There was so much to do and it had to be done so quickly there was no time to sit back and talk and discuss it. We had to bail out water as fast as we could. We had to just get on , make decisions and do it – quickly.

Over the first 12 months we all had this shared sense of urgency and crisis and looking back on it we got a huge amount of stuff done. We were united by a common cause. But about a year on the crisis died down, the sense of urgency abated and it was then that things started to slow. We started spending more time in meetings, there were different views as to the way forward, that strong sense of common purpose which had been so important started to dissipate.'

Kotter concluded from his research that complacency – 'we've no need to change, to do things differently, to challenge what we do' – is the biggest enemy for today's corporations. This is especially true in established relatively mature industries such as oil or insurance. There, some of the biggest companies like Shell, Exxon and Prudential (US) appear among the slowest and sleepiest, only occasionally awakened to action and real change by some external shock.

To be a winning company and generate a sense of common purpose, Kotter urges business leaders to get to grips with this complacency and deliberately inject some shocks and crises into the system. No strategy, however good, will succeed unless the employees both understand it and **want** it to win out. There has to be a sense of common purpose **and** a shared passion and enthusiasm. If there is complacency, the first step must be to break that. Raise expectations, increase targets, shake the tree in the way the company is organised and its senior management, be intolerant of poor performance, publicly acknowledge weaknesses, acclaim and recognise employees who go the extra mile.

As one CEO put it recently: 'be honest and open in what we say and communicate, stop putting the gloss on everything. If I can create a culture where people believe what I say and I can believe them then we're building a platform to move forward'. Such a platform can be a basis for a set of values that people can relate to. And as a strong strategy emerges so they can begin to channel new found beliefs and energies towards a particular and shared purpose and direction.

Symbolic egalitarianism and information sharing

If it's the front-line employees who can make the difference (see the SAS example in Chapter 10), then why treat them as second-class citizens? Why have separate management canteens (a peculiarly European phenomenon), reserved car-parking spaces, separate floors in the building, restrictions on information flow? These things are symbols of divide-and-rule and they cut managers off from listening, interacting, sharing and communicating with the rest of the company. They are just the kind of needless barriers that get in the way of effectively sharing the values and the strategy that can unite the organisation.

How much better to have more open-plan offices as at Asda, or a 'no-closed-doors' policy as at Nike. At Solectron, a contract manufacturer that has won the Malcolm Baldridge Award, neither the chairman nor the CEO has a private office.

Why not openly share detailed financial and other information through-out the company? If the feeling is that employees cannot be trusted with that information then that is surely a sign that there is no common purpose and effective shared values and beliefs. Jack Welch at GE has a policy of open communication and explanation as to how the company is doing, what it's doing well and what it's doing badly. At Lincoln Electric, 'information is shared with all employees regarding the financial and market position of the company'.[16] At Advanced Micro Devices every employee has been specifically trained to use the company's IT network to access information about all aspects of the company's performance.

Open information sharing makes employees naturally feel more involved and more responsible for the company's performance. How much better to hear it from your department manager and be able to discuss and think through what its implications are than read about it with the rest of the world when the third-quarter results are published in the press. An openness and readiness to share and trust employees with the information has to be a major reinforcement to the strategy and values platform we have just described.

One recent and excellent illustration of 'symbolic egalitarianism' comes from an initiative Archie Norman took when CEO of Asda, the UK supermarket chain. He abolished chauffeur-driven cars – except one. He kept one, not for the senior officers of the company, but for 'the employee of the week'. Each week the employee, whoever they were, who came up with the best idea for the company to improve things, was awarded the car for the week, with the chauffeur, to take them about wherever they needed to go.[17]

This was a simple but highly symbolic act which quickly entered company mythology and helped change the way people felt about their employers. They appreciated the sharing, the 'we're all in this together', the removal of barriers. Not surprisingly it helped, with other things, to create a tremendous sense of shared purpose and mission.

Training

We can't expect people to make the difference unless of course they have all the skills required to do the job. And as the competitive environment becomes more complex and demanding, so there is a growing imperative to continue to improve the skill base and give employees from all parts of the organisation a chance to continue to learn and gain in experience and capability.

There is a constant battle in most companies today between, typically, the human resources function who are the usual sponsors of better training, versus the company's financial engineers who are concerned with reducing costs wherever an activity or investment is discretionary. It's part of the ongoing short-term vs long-term debate which continues to pressurise companies into sacrificing the long-term for the sake of short-term earnings.

However, what research has shown – conclusively – is that companies that do treat training as a priority and invest heavily in it reap benefits and dividends often far more quickly than they expect. Rather than complain about not having enough good people and not having the right skills in the company to meet the new global market challenge, advocates of increased training would argue that people do have the innate core competencies and if only they are given requisite training it will unleash a new set of energies and abilities.

Seventy-three per cent of employers in a 1993 *Wall Street Journal* survey claimed not to have a sufficiently skilled workforce. But a report by the US Government National Centre for Education concluded there was far too little investment among US corporations in training their staff: 'without significant increases in training, funding and resourcing there will be substantial skill and labour shortages in the USA over the next decade, threatening the nation's ability to compete'.

In the UK, a government-sponsored agency, Investors in People,[18] has been at the forefront in recent years in encouraging discussion and review of how effectively people in an organisation are managed, with particular reference to investment in their skill development and career enhancement. Investors in People has worked with a number of companies to encourage them to do more in this area, and has consistently generated tremendous improvement in workforce capabilities and effectiveness.

- ICL, while still independent as an IT company, committed itself to providing each employee with the equivalent of 10 days training each year and invested some £20m in training programmes and their establishment. It saw productivity respond and move up 54 per cent over 4 years. The company went on to win the European Quality Award.
- Monsanto in the UK committed to spend 3.5 per cent of the wage bill on training. It attributes a 67 per cent increase in productivity over five years and a significant reduction in absenteeism to this training investment.

- The objective of Co-Steel Sheerness is to 'develop the best-trained workforce in steelmaking worldwide'. They have established a programme where 79 per cent of employees now have a nationally recognised vocational qualification. Their drive to train and build the capabilities of the workforce has resulted in productivity up by 119 per cent, lost time accidents reduced by 97 per cent, and first-time quality hit-rate up to 99.4 per cent from 78 per cent.

And of course we've read about McDonald's 'hamburger university' which rigorously trains all its employees and recognises their achievements in Quality Service Value Cleanliness (QSVC). We've seen how Toyota will deliberately take people out of the manufacturing plant and put them in the salesforce for a period to experience first-hand customer dissatisfaction with faulty goods and customer delight with perfection, so that they can return to the production line with better experience and understanding of how important it is for them to get things right. And there is the Raychem college of further education which was the particular initiative of founder Paul Cook and which offers a substantial programme of courses open to all employees, not just related to business and management but to help improve more generally 'people's capacity for personal growth'.

These companies and others who have committed to their workforce in this way have seen the benefits that can come through from a more highly skilled and thereby moveable and more motivated workforce. It does take investment but it is certainly one of the keys in helping and getting people to make the difference.

Sharing the benefits

- The John Lewis Partnership is the largest employee-owned firm in the world. All profits are distributed as a bonus to all employees. Over two decades between 1970 and 1990 before the UK recession hit, sales grew at a compound rate of 15.2 per cent. It performed better than all its major rivals. The partnership continues to perform outstandingly well today.
- The top five performing stocks in the US between 1972 and 1992 (Southwest Airlines, WalMart, Tyson Foods, Circuit City electricals and Plenum Publishing) all appear on the 'Employee Ownership List' (a listing of 1000 companies where employees own > 4% of the stock).[19]

- 91 per cent of listed Japanese companies have employee stock ownership plans in which > 50% of the workforce are eligible and participate.
- Levi Strauss announced in 1996 that it would pay each of its 37 000 employees one year's salary as a bonus to hail the new millennium. News of the millennium bonus sparked wild celebrations at Levi Strauss, according to press reports, and predictable gloom at rivals!

> 'It's about sharing our success with our employees . . . we all want a company that our people are proud of and committed to, where all employees have an opportunity to contribute, learn, grow and advance . . . we want our people to feel respected, treated fairly, listened to and involved. Above all we want satisfaction from accomplishments and friendships, balanced personal and professional lives and have fun in our endeavours.'[20]

*   *   *

We have now described the six key success factors which appear to most motivate people to make the difference. It's crucially about getting the workforce involved – both emotionally and tangibly – in the company's endeavours. It means creating a culture where people share in the company's development, contribute ideas as well as their own energies and endeavours, and see outstanding contributions acknowledged and rewarded. It requires senior management to involve their staff in open and honest discussion about what is going on, why some things are being done and others not, what's good and what's bad, what needs fixing and what needs celebrating.

Only by opening things up in this way and by investing time in communicating can management hope to instil a commitment and desire among the workforce to want the strategy to succeed and be prepared to go the extra mile to deliver it and realise the benefits.

As we observe companies that try to move down this path, we see three particular roadblocks that need to be looked out for and managed and which typically and unnecessarily get in the way of the employee energies company leaders are trying to generate and unleash. These three roadblocks are:

- Ineffective empowerment
- Inadequate measuring systems
- Organisation structure complexity

Ineffective empowerment

A common problem slowing down people's ability to implement is too few resources to get the job done. Ironically in these times of constant change and other pressures when many tasks are becoming more complex and time-consuming, most companies have re-engineered, cost cut, downsized, delayered and outsourced so much that in some cases there do not appear to be enough people left to adequately do the job with which they are tasked. This is compounded when on top of the 'day job', employees are asked to spend time and effort on a number of additional change and improvement projects.

A frequent cry amongst employees nowadays is that there is not enough resource in the department to do everything that is expected really well, and certainly not enough to do everything they'd like additionally to do to improve things. Their work day becomes filled with fire-fighting and dealing with all the immediate demands, while longer-term thinking and planning and doing things now which will yield benefits in two or three years time just keep getting delayed or otherwise sub-optimised.

To counter this growing problem, a number of business commentators over recent years have advanced the case of separating long-term strategy tasks from day-to-day execution, splitting out the thinking and planning activities from the doing and implementing to ensure each is adequately and effectively resourced. The most manifest form of this is the recommendation that the chairman and chief executive posts are not occupied by one person but split to ensure at least one senior officer of the company is standing back from the day-to-day activities and thinking about the future.

When we consider the increasing number of change-management initiatives now added to the employee's workload, perhaps there is also an argument to make the same split at middle and junior manager level; to separate out future change initiatives from the daily management tasks and deliverables. Organisations may need to recognise that each specific change project should be treated distinctly as a project in its own right and specifically resourced and managed as such. In doing this the change challenge is more obviously recognised and the more skilled and experienced change resource can be employed and dedicated to that sort of activity. A result would be to free-up excellent managers of the current business to get on and deliver and add value to what they do, while more experienced 'change agents' focus on the future opportunities.

Such an approach could help companies reappraise the resourcing issue. It could also help create an environment where people are more effectively empowered and **enabled** to deliver both the short-term business needs as well as the longer-term strategic opportunities.

Inadequate measurement system

As Percy Barnevik, CEO of Asea Brown Boveri, has commented: 'only things that are measured actually get done'. If the workforce cannot track its progress effectively, if individual employees cannot measure their contribution to the performance of the business, then of course they cannot know if they are really doing well or enough. In particular, if there is no system to measure the company against competitors, if there is no CAG-type monitoring and review, then how can people know if their actions are sufficient to win or whether in fact there's still a lot more to do?

If the company is not performing well, then identifying good and comparable and believable measures and benchmarks of what the gaps are can be a means for creating the shock to the system, or 'engineering' the crisis that Kotter speaks of. If the company is performing well then the same measures can act as a spur and confidence booster to go further and do more 'because we're winning'. Equally, if the company's performance is effectively measured it can provide a framework for communication and sharing and involving everyone in the company, in rewarding good performance and further investigating things that are below par.

Too often research and observation show company's measurement systems as inadequate and so unable to facilitate individual performance review. This is becoming a particular problem in the globalising economy where right now multinational businesses face growing complexity in the number of different systems used, different ways of measuring data, and varied accounting systems and definitions of what's in one cost element, for example, versus another. All this leads to lack of data comparability, or so many adjustments that comparison loses credibility. So a company may be able to work out its overall RONA goals, but be very unclear at the next level of detail, say, whether the sales product development team actually did hit its trading profit target on individual new products. The available data and information that's put together just may not exist at that level, or may do so but in unreliable form. In which case, who knows if the sales team has been successful. And if they can't be monitored or measure themselves then a key part of the incentive and motivation package is evidently missing.

Fortunately the IT revolution, led especially throught the mid-1990s by SAP and more recently by Sun and Cisco, is helping companies to cut through the blockages preventing better information being accessed and improve the information that is shared so it's more detailed, more comparable and more easily measurable. If the initiatives of these leading edge information technology companies continue at the breakthrough pace we have seen in recent years, then we can hope they will provide a path for every company to make measurement and monitoring inadequacies more generally a thing of the past.

Organisation complexity

Most people today find themselves working in complex organisation matrix structures where there are functions, businesses or product groups and countries or regions. Each organisational constituency has its own department head and each often believes they are the power centre of the organisation or certainly have a right of veto over any initiative from another part of the matrix that might in some way affect them or require some contribution from them.

I have seen this matrix complexity create an organisational paralysis where most major initiatives that require cross-functional, cross-business or cross-border collaboration fail. The organisation just cannot get things done. How often have you heard these sort of comments drawn here from one multinational company VP?

'If I want to launch a new product next year in Southeast Asia I need to get the product manager from Central Marketing, the Asia region head, the country heads of Australia, Philippines, Singapore and Thailand, the group sales director, the sales managers, manufacturing support – so many people from all different parts of the organisation together and each one thinks they have the right of veto. The whole thing can fail because manufacturing for example decide they've got other production priorities next year. By the time I do get everyone together and I get something finally agreed there's usually all sorts of compromises made which sometimes make me wonder if there's anything left of the original plan that excited me. And when it's all done I'm exhausted. Now I can't go through all that every time I want to do something. All my colleagues have the same frustration so it's hardly surprising things don't get done and we've got such a poor implementation record.'

As companies increasingly recognise this organisation complexity as a major barrier to getting things done and a significant dampener on people's energies and enthusiasms, so some structural solutions are emerging. There is certainly no single model that can be heralded as the answer but there are some options which may be applicable and may help some companies to move forward more effectively.

Figure 15.5 shows the way Ford have tried to tackle the problem.

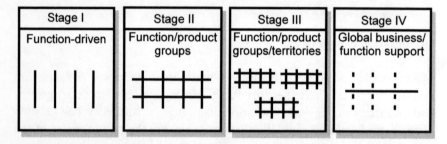

Figure 15.5   Ford's approach to managing organisational complexity

Ford have tried to cut through the matrix complexity (Stage III) by essentially doing away with it and in their most recent move (Stage IV) are driving towards single global businesses. These are established as the clear leaders of the company, with functional support increasingly seen as 'service providers' providing support, resources and skills to the extent, and when, the global business team decides it needs them.

As Alex Trotman, Chairman of Ford, has commented:

'At Ford we're proud of our traditions but we can't be complacent. We can't continue to organise in a way that slows decision-making. In today's world, development of a truly global operation is becoming essential. While developing in this way we have kept what worked, but discarded what didn't.'

Figure 15.6 illustrates how companies like Hewlett Packard, 3M, Dow, Sun Microsystems and others have found an alternative somewhat less-radical way of cutting through the organisational complexity of a multinational company.

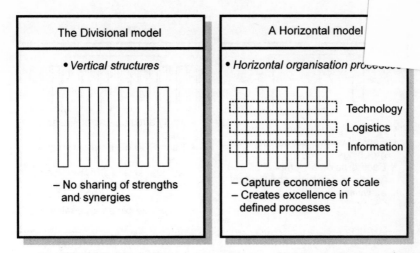

Figure 15.6 Cutting through organisational complexity

Here, these companies are retaining the structural elements of the matrix but **forcing** a 'horizontal' sharing and search for synergy across certain defined functions. The functions picked would typically have elements where there are scale benefits from putting things together, for example invoice processing in finance or the need for a 'centre of excellence' in establishing a central European product marketing team to develop marketing plans for the same product in different countries.

For many companies this is a first and easier to achieve step before the greater transformation and streamlining being sought after at Ford, and there is growing experience about how this can be made to work relatively easily and quickly.

Figure 15.7 looks at another type of solution whose arch exponent is Asea Brown Boveri.

'Think global act local' is the philosophy driving this particular organisation solution. It specifically seeks to empower local business unit heads and give them the responsibility and ability to build their business as they think fit, subject only to certain prescribed rules for sharing or collaboration on a global basis. ABB has developed this approach so that it now quite deliberately has established some 1500 separate business units. Each is run almost as an independent business but, critically, they are largely free from the matrix and other structural barriers that are slowing down decision-making and effectively disempowering people elsewhere in other companies.

Describing these roadblocks around structure, measurement systems and empowerment should be familiar to many. There has been

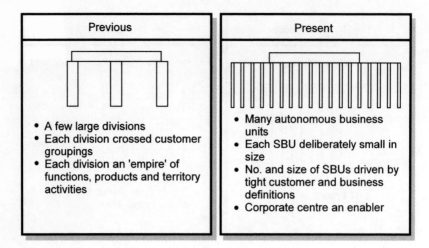

Figure 15.7 The 'autonomous' solution

considerable discussion about these sort of issues as the global economy has become a fact of life through the 1990s and as companies have begun to grapple with the implications for their business and for getting things done. There is increasing debate about how to effect change in the more complex competitive environment, how to enable people to deliver the strategy with greater speed and effect, and how to motivate people to cut through the various structural, cultural and other barriers to strive for excellence despite the inevitable pressures and problems.

Summary

This chapter has been all about finding ways to make things happen, to indicate some possible paths and solutions that may help companies realise the ambitions set in their strategies and to strive towards and achieve the winning competitive advantage they seek. Success in any field never comes easily, getting people to make the difference means battling with the wills and egos of individuals, natural concerns and fears for job security and uncertainties, and some wavering of confidence as to whether a team truly has the aptitude and energy for the battle ahead and the skills and capabilities to win. What's critical is to recognise the barriers and roadblocks and determine to break them down and cut through them in so far as it is humanly possible. What's also important is to acknowledge the success stories among the winning companies and learn from what they have done in sharing and involving, communicating to inspire a common purpose and developing a set of beliefs that can overcome the inevitable obstacles along the path in moving towards and realising lasting competitive success in the market.

Addendum

The risk with any new approach like the Market Commitment model is that it is treated superficially. Concepts like Service Hustle or price can be interpreted in a perfunctory way and it might be too readily assumed that a company is already doing all it can and all it needs to down a particular path.

Indeed that may be the case, but many years of consulting and observation have shown that more typically it is not. Perhaps one way of illustrating this is to point again to Forum Corporation's Iceberg of Ignorance which researched how much the senior management of a company knew about what was really going on in their organisation. The answer, as we've already discussed, was 4 per cent – just 4 per cent of all the issues, problems and inadequacies of an organisation are typically fully known to senior executives. And such a finding is surely no surprise especially in large multinationals spread over 50 or 60 countries, with separate business units, employing people of different ages and attitudes speaking different languages, coming from different cultures and with layers of reporting lines and procedures.

In such a situation it is clearly dangerous to assume that no matter how strong the strategy and how focused the plans, that they are being executed in an effective enough way. And if it's risky for a company to make assumptions about how effectively its own organisation is behaving, then how much more risky is it for a company to assume it's got the market and its customers fully wired and that it's truly ahead of the game and its competition on every key measure. If senior managers only know 4 per cent of the issues inside their company, what percentage of what's going on in the external market is totally familiar to them?

The exhortation here is to minimise these risks, make no assumptions and work on the basis that no matter how strong the company is it can always still **learn**. Arrogance will quickly lead to downfall. The effort to learn should be continuous and the need to keep learning more about customers and market opportunities should be deepfelt and institutionalised among the workforce. The market immersion test in Chapter 7 should be rigorously applied and regularly. The relative commitment audit in Chapter 8 should also be carried out with similar effort and desire to learn more and understand. The CAG's should be measured and monitored driven by a deep-seated anxiety that the company cannot stand still, it has to keep pushing to the boundaries and beyond what appears feasible. It has to develop a state where the deep-rooted immersion will give birth to a constant stream of innovation and new ideas that will help the company stay ahead.

None of this comes easily. A superficial view of the world should be arrested in its tracks. Complacency must be replaced by the sense of urgency and extraordinary commitment to succeed. That's what characterises the Market Commitment Model and the winning companies we have described in this book.

Notes

1 The lost art of strategy

1. *Wall Street Journal*, 4 October 1993.
2. *Ibid.*
3. Farkas, C., De Backer, P. and Allen Sheppard, *Maximum Leadership*, Orion Books, 1995.
4. *Wall Street Journal*, 21 May 1996.
5. 'America, Land of the Shaken', *Business Week*, 11 March 1996.
6. 'Ranking of Strategy', Kalchas Group, August 1996.
7. Farkas, C., De Backer, P. and Allen Sheppard, *Maximum Leadership*, *op. cit.*
8. 'Strategic Planning', *Business Week*, 2 September 1996.
9. Peter Drucker, *Management: Tasks, Responsibilities, Practices*, Harper & Row, 1974.
10. Sun Tzu, *The Art of War*, c. 500 BC.
11. Marcus Aurelius, 170 AD quoted in League's *Roman Private Law*, Macmillan, 1967.
12. 'Role of Corporate Planning', Kalchas Group, September 1995.
13. Hamel, G. and Prahalad, C. K. *Competing for the Future*, Harvard Business Press, 1994.
14. 'Growth Through Revenues vs. Cost Cutting', Kalchas Group, Summer 1995.
15. 'Downsizing', American Management Association Survey, July 1994.
16. 'Global Business Leaders See No End to Corporate Restructuring', PR Newswire, 4 April 1995.
17. 'Amputating Assets: Companies That Slash Jobs End Up With More Problems Than Profits', US News & World Report, 4 May 1992.
18. 'America, Land of the Shaken', *Business Week*, 11 March 1996.
19. 'Going for Growth', *Wall Street Journal* 5 July 1996.
20. 'Growth Through Revenues', Kalchas, 1995, *op. cit.*
21. 'Will Downsizing Still be in Vogue in 1997?' *Sunday Times Business*, 29 December 1996.
22. Gertz and Baptista, 'Grow to be Great', Free Press, 1995.
23. 'Siemens Nixdorf on a US Accent, Can This German Company be Saved?', *Fortune*, 19 August 1996; 'Killer Applications, Europe PC Makers Lose Out', *Wall Street Journal*, April 1996.

24. *Wall Street Journal*, April 1996.
25. Collins, J.C. & Porras, J.I., *Built to Last, Successful Habits of Visionary Companies*, Century Random House, 1994.

2 What is strategy?

1. 'Role of Corporate Planning', Kalchas Group, September 1995.
2. Michael Porter, *Competitive Strategy*, Free Press, 1980.
3. Kerry Napuk, *The Strategy Led Business*, McGraw-Hill, 1993.
4. Farkas, C., De Backer, P. and Allen Sheppard, *Maximum Leadership*, Orion Books, 1995.

3 The rules of the game have changed

1. 'Lucas Boss Signals Big Motor Shake Up', *Sunday Times Business*, 4 February 1996.
2. 'The Triumph of the New Economy', *Business Week*, 30 December 1996; Economist Intelligence Report, September 1996; CBI Manufacturing Survey on Competitiveness, 1996; 'Global Tremors from an Unruly Giant', *Business Week*, 4 March 1996; OECD Data 1970 to 1994.
3. 'The Age of Mergers', *Business Week*, 15 April 1996.
4. 'Riskiest Industries', *Fortune*, 1 April 1996.
5. 'The Silicon Age, It's Just Dawning', *Business Week*, 9 December 1996.
6. Jim Slater, *The Zulu Principle*, Orion Books, 1992.
7. Quoted in Richard Whiteley, *The Customer Driven Company*, Century Random House, 1991.
8. Akio Morita, *Made in Japan*, HarperCollins, 1987; Arthur D. Little; *Breakthrough*, Nick Lyons, *The Sony Vision*, Crown, 1976.
9. Michael Porter, *Competitive Strategy*, Free Press, 1980.
10. Mike Johnson, *Managing in the Next Millennium*, Management Centre Europe, 1995.
11. Steven Schnaars, *Managing Imitation Strategies*, Macmillan, 1994; Jeffrey Pfeffer, *Competitive Advantage through People*, Harvard Business Press, 1994.

4 The inadequencies of existing strategy models

1. 'Role of Corporate Planning', Kalchas Group, September 1995.
2. Bruce Henderson, 'The Logic of Business Strategy', The Boston Consulting Group, Harper & Row, 1984. Used by permission of The Boston Consulting Group, Inc.
3. Buzzell, R.D. & Gale, B.T., *The PIMS Principles*, Free Press, 1987.

4. Eurostat official Publications of the European Community, 1995; UN Statistical Office; Organisation for Economic Co-operation and Development; Bureau of Labour Statistics, Washington DC; and Liverpool Macroeconomic Research Quarterly Bulletin, June 1995.
5. Michael Porter, Professor at Harvard Business School, *Competitive Strategy*, Free Press, 1980.
6. Prahalad, C. K. and Hamel, G., *The Core Competence of the Corporation*, Harvard Business Review, May/June 1990.
7. Prahalad, C. K. and Hamel, G., *Competing for the Future*, Harvard Business School Press, 1994.
8. Goold, M., Campbell, A. and Alexander, M., *Corporate-level Strategy*, John Wiley, 1994.
9. *Ibid.*; and Goold, M. and Campbell, A., *Strategies and Styles*, Blackwell, 1987.
10. Michael Treacy and Fred Wiersema, *Discipline of Market Leaders*, Addison-Wesley, 1995.

5 Introduction to the market commitment model

1. 'Battle Hymn of the Reorg', Anonymous Microsoft employee, *MicroNews*, the in-house newsletter, as quoted in *Business Week*, 15 July 1996, 'Inside Microsoft'.
2. 'Microsoft Enters Intranet Alliance', *The Times*, 10 April 1996; 'Software Hardball', *Fortune*, 30 September 1996.
3. 'Battle of the Network Boxes', *Business Week*, 18 November 1990.
4. 'Cyberspace Showdown', *Fortune*, 7 October 1996.
5. 'Microsoft Plans to Broaden Web Use for Home Banking', *Wall Street Journal*, 18 March 1996.
6. W. Brian Arthur, 'Increasing Returns and the New World of Business', Professor of Economics at Stanford University, *Harvard Business Review*, July–August 1996.
7. 'How Honeywell Beat Litton to Dominate Navigation-Gear Field', *Wall Street Journal*, 20 September 1996.
8. 'America's Most Admired Companies', annual survey in *Fortune*, 4 March 1996.

6 Commitment: the long-term view

1. Weybright and Talley 1970; *Henry Ford, II, the Human Environment and Business*; Robert Lacey, *The Men and the Machine*, Ballantine Books, 1986.
2. 'All Over the Map', interview in *Wall Street Journal*, 30 September 1996; Farkas, C., De Backer, P. and Allen Sheppard, *Maximum Leadership*, Orion

Books, 1995; 'Yes, You *Can* Manage Long Term', *Fortune*, 21 November 1988.

3. Joe Fowler, *Prince of the Magic Kingdom and the Remaking of Disney*, Wiley, 1991; Marc Eliot, *Hollywood's Dark Prince*, Birch Lane Press, 1993.

4. Michael T. Jacobs, *Short-Term America*, Harvard Business School Press, 1991; 'Three Huge Hours in Seattle', *Business Week*, 30 December 1996; 'Boeing', *Business Week*, 20 September 1996; Paul Marsh, 'Short-Termism on Trial', London Business School, Institutional Fund Managers Association; 'Yes, You *Can* Manage Long Term', *Fortune*, 21 November 1988.

5. Cleveland, H. B. and Huertas, T. F., *Citibank 1812–1970*, Harvard University Press, 1985.

6. Professor Woolridge, 'Competitive Decline and Corporate Restructuring', *Journal of Applied Corporate Finance*, Spring 1988.

7. Collins, J. C. and Porras, J. I., *Built to Last*, Century Random House, 1994.

8. L. Galambos and J. L. Sturchio, 'Origins of an Innovative Organisation, Merck & Co 1891 to 1960', John Hopkins University, 1992; Merck, *Values and Visions: A Merck Century*, 1991.

9. 'Hewlett Packard Built by Design', AMBA Executive, September 1977; annual reports of Hewlett Packard.

10. McConnell, J. L. and Muscarella, C. J., 'Corporate Capital Expenditure Decisions and the Market Values of the Firm', *Journal of Financial Economics*, 1985.

11. 'Superior Share Price', Kalchas Group, Summer 1996.

12. Professor Woolridge, 'Competitive Decline and Corporate Restructuring', *Journal of Applied Corporate Finance*, Spring 1988.

13. 'Stock Prices Show Lots of Faith in the Future', Alcar Group and Professor Rappaport of Northwestern University's Kellogg School, reprinted in *Fortune*, 21 November 1988.

14. President John F. Kennedy, 1961.

15. Sam Walton and John Huey, *Made in America*, Doubleday, 1992; Vance Trimble, *Sam Walton*, Dutton, 1990.

16. Dean Watkins, Chairman, Watkins–Johnson Company.

17. 'The General Electric Story', Schenectady, Hall of History Foundation, 1981; Tichy, N. M. and Sherman, S., *Control Your own Destiny*, Doubleday, 1993.

18. British Airways annual reports.

19. 'Going for Growth', *Wall Street Journal*, 5 July 1996.

20. 'Amoco Seeks to Retain Polyester Crown', *Wall Street Journal*, April 1996.

21. 'Scott McNealy's Rising Sun', *Business Week*, 22 January 1996; 'Sun's Java – The Threat to Microsoft is Real', *Fortune*, 11 November 1996.

22. *Fortune Magazine* annual surveys; Robert Heller, *Superchiefs*, Mercury Books, 1992.

23. 'Value of Focus', Kalchas Group, 1995.

24. 'Daimler-Benz faces brutal cutbacks after losing £2bn', *Sunday Times Business*, 21 January 1996.
25. 'Increasing Returns and the New World of Business', W. Brian Arthur, Professor of Economics at Stanford University.
26. 'Mercedes Puts its Image on the Line', *Wall Street Journal*, April 1996.
27. 'Savile Row Seeks to Mend its Fortunes', *Wall Street Journal*, May 1996.

7 Commitment: market immersion

1. Mintzberg, H., *The Rise and Fall of Strategic Planning*, Prentice-Hall, 1994; Mintzberg, H., 'Crafting Strategy', *Harvard Business Review*, July–August, 1987.
2. 'The UK R&D Scoreboard 1996', *Financial Times*, 1996.
3. 'Keeping the Fire Lit Under the Innovators', *Fortune*, 28 March 1988; annual reports of 3M.
4. 'Successful Strategies', Kalchas Group, October 1996; *Financial Times*, 'Growing Business' articles 1992–1996.

8 The relative commitment audit

1. Richard Whiteley, *The Customer Driven Company*, Century Business, 1991.

9 Competitive advantage through performance

1. Buzzell, R. D. & Gale, B. T., *The PIMS principles*, Free Press.
2. Rommel, G., Brück, F. and others, *Quality Pays*, Macmillan, 1996; 'The Quality Imperative', McGraw Hill Business Week, Guide.
3. 'Innovation, the Best Practice', DTI/CBI (Department of Trade and Industry; Confederation of British Industry), 1993; 'Competitiveness – Forging Ahead', DTI, 1995, HMSO; 'Competitiveness – Creating the Enterprise Centre of Europe', DTI, 1996, HMSO.
4. Homenn Surion, *Die Heimlichen Gewinner* (Hidden Champions), Harvard Business School Press, 1996.
5. 'Gillette Knows How to Turn Out Hot New Products', *Fortune*, 14 October 1996; 'How Gillette Wowed Wall Street', *Business Week*, 30 September 1996.
6. Rommel, G., Brück, F. *et al.*, *Quality Pays*, op. cit.
7. *Ibid.*
8. Womack, J. P. and Jones, D. T., *Lean Thinking*, Simon & Schuster, 1996.
9. 'The R&D Scoreboard', Department of Trade and Industry (DTI), 1996, HMSO.

10. *Ibid.*
11. Booz Allen and Hamilton, *Management and Technology Survey.*
12. W. Edwards Deming, *Out of the Crisis*, Cambridge University Press, 1982.
13. Kotabe, M., *Global Sourcing Strategy*, Quorum, 1992.
14. Steven P. Schnaars, *Managing Imitation Strategies*, Free Press, 1994.
15. 'Farewell my Logo', *Fortune*, 27 May 1996.
16. Tom Cannon, *Welcome to the Revolution*, Pitman, 1996.
17. Jeffrey Williams, 'How Sustainable is Your Competitive Advantage?', *California Management Review*, 1992.
18. 'How Rapidly Does New Industrial Technology Leak Out?', *Journal of Industrial Economics*, 1985; 'How to Steal the Best Ideas Around, *Fortune*, 19 October 1992.
19. Theodore Levitt, 'Innovative Imitation', *Harvard Business Review*, September–October 1966; Theodore Levitt, 'Exploit the Product Life Cycle', *Harvard Business Review*, November–December 1965.
20. Womack and Jones, Lean Thinking', *op. cit.*
21. 'Competitiveness – How the Best UK Companies are Winning', Department of Trade and Industry; Confederation of British Industry (DTI/CBI), 1994, HMSO.
22. The potential of 'speed' as a source of competitive advantage was first recognised in a formal sense only a few years ago, in George Stalk and Thomas Hout's work on *Time-Based competition*, Free Press, 1990.

10 Competitive advantage through service hustle

1. Body Shop annual reports and interviews.
2. Sam Walton and John Huey, *Made in America*, Doubleday, 1992; Vance Trimble, *Sam Walton*, Dutton 1990; annual reports Wal-Mart.
3. Interview with Jim McCann, President of 1–800–FLOWERS, *Wall Street Journal*, February 1996.
4. Super Service, *Financial Times*, 16 June 1996.
5. Quoted in Richard Whiteley, *The Customer-Driven Company*, 1991.
6. Quoted in *Customer Centred Growth*, Richard Whiteley and Diane Hessan, Random House, 1996.
7. Jones, T. O. and Sasser, W. E., 'Why Satisfied Customers Defect', *Harvard Business Review*, November–December 1995; Reichheld, F. F. and Sasser, W. E., 'Zero Defections in Services', *Harvard Business Review*, September–October 1990.
8. *Ibid.*
9. Richard Whiteley, *The Customer-Driven Company*, *op. cit.*
10. *Customer Respect Deficits*, Bozell Worldwide, 1996.
11. *Ibid.*

12. Richard Whitely and Diane Henson, *Customer Centred Growth*, Random House, 1996.
13. 'Americans Can't Get No Satisfaction', *Fortune*, 11 December 1995.
14. Johnson, J.K. and Nonaka, I., 'Market Research the Japanese way', *Harvard Business Review*, May–June 1987.
15. 'Service Comes First', interview with USAA's Robert McDermott, *Harvard Business Review*, September–October 1991.
16. Frederick F. Reichheld, *The Loyalty Effect*, Harvard Business School Press, 1996.
17. Reichheld and Sasser, *Zero Defections in Services*, op. cit.
18. *Ibid.*
19. Jan Carlzon, *Moments of Truth*, Harper & Row, 1987.
20. 'At Nordstrom Stores, Service Comes First', *Wall Street Journal*, February 1990; annual reports of Nordstrom.
21. The Home Depot 1995 Annual Report.
22. 'Goodwill Store', *Financial Times*, Management Page, September 1996.

11 Competitive advantage through pricing

1. *Henry Ford II, the Human Environment and Business*, Weybright & Talley 1970; Anne Jardin, *The First Henry Ford*, Colonial Press, 1970.
2. '*Made in America*', Sam Walton, Doubleday, 1992; annual reports of Wal-Mart.
3. Robert W. Galvin, *The Idea of Ideas*, Motorola University Press, 1991.
4. 'Daewoo Drives into Europe', *Wall Street Journal*, October 1996 and Kalchas interview.
5. Robert Dolan, 'How Do You Know When the Price is Right', *Harvard Business Review*, September–October 1995.
6. Managers examining pricing should of course also understand the industry-wide variables of supply and demand. These set the pricing context of their markets – that is the overall direction of price pressure (up or down), and knowledge in this area allows prediction of the broad price trends.

   By definition, such macro economic factors are nothing to do with the customer's perception of how one individual product performs versus another, how it rates competitively and its relative worth versus alternatives on offer. They cannot drive choice of what is the most competitive strategy for that product.

   This does assume normal rules of competition and freedom of consumer choice. If there were a monopoly or other artificial environment, then it's not a question of strategy as defined here but rather about the product's basic elasticity. Baumol, W.J. and Blinder, A.S., *Microeconomics–Principles and Policy*, Harcourt Brace & Company, 1997, chapters 12 and 13.

7. 'Pricing – The Unexploited Tool', Kalchas Group, Spring 1996.
8. Frederick F. Reichheld, *The Loyalty Effect*, Harvard Business School Press, 1996.
9. Treacy, M. and Wiersema, F., *Discipline of Market Leaders*, Addison-Wesley, 1995.
10. 'Heat's on Value pricing', *Ad Age International*, January 1997; 'Unilever Lather', Lex Column *Financial Times*, 15 February 1996; 'P&G Price Cuts to Hit Own Label', *Marketing*, 15 February 1996.
11. 'Relationships between Retailers and Manufacturers', AGC Silverman Associates, 1996.

12 Competitive advantage through emotion

1. Annual Reports of Coca-Cola.
2. Oscar Schisgall, *Eyes on Tomorrow: The Evolution of Procter & Gamble*, Doubleday, 1981; 'The Character of Procter & Gamble' speech by John G. Smale, November 1986; annual reports of Procter & Gamble.
3. Annual reports of Rubbermaid.
4. 'Citicorp: John Reed's Second Act', *Fortune*, 29 April 1996 and annual reports of Citicorp.
5. Kalchas interviews.
6. 'Tune-up Time for Harley', *Business Week*, 8 April 1996; annual reports of Harley Davidson.
7. 'Stamp of Approval', FT Management Page, 29 February 1996 and Monsanto annual reports.
8. 'Bayer's New Ad Campaign', *Wall Street Journal*, May 1996; annual reports of Bayer.
9. 'Stamp of Approval', FT Management Page, February 1996; annual reports of ICI; Sir John Harvey-Jones, *Making it Happen*, Collins, 1988.
10. 'Biggest Brands', *Marketing*, June 1996.
11. *Ibid.*
12. Tom Cannon, *Welcome to the Revolution*, Pitman, 1996; James Martin, *Cybercorp – The New Business Revolution*, Amacom, 1996; 'Electronic Retailing', Kalchas Group, January 1996.
13. 'Who's Behind Ralph's $5bn Empire?', *Fortune*, 11 November 1996.
14. 'Brand Name Rankings', Interbrand and *Financial World*, 8 July 1996.
15. Charles Fombrun, *Reputation*, Harvard Business School Press, 1996; 'Elastic Brands', *Sunday Times*, 3 November 1996; 'The Total Package', *The Guardian*, August 1996; 'King Coke', *Sunday Times*, March 1995; annual reports of Coca-Cola.
16. 'Pumping Life Into Sagging Brands', *USA Today*, May 1995; 'Consumer Comebacks', *The Times*, February 1996.
17. *Sunday Times* Poll 1996.
18. Ibid. and 'M&S Makes Its Mark in Germany', *The Times*, July 1996.

13 A toolkit

1. Robert Heller, *The Fate of IBM*, Warner Books, 1994; Richard DeLamarter, *Big Blue*, Macmillan, 1996; 'IBM is back', *Fortune*, 11 November 1996.
2. http://www.amazon.com; 'The Next Big Thing', *Fortune*, 9 December 1996.
3. Annual Reports, of Blue Circle; Builders merchants interviews.
4. A. T. Kearney brochures; EDS annual reports.

14 Building a more effective strategy development process

1. 'Role of Corporate Planning', Kalchas Group, September 1995; 'Ranking of Strategy', Kalchas Group, August 1996.
2. 'Strategic Planning', *Business Week*, September 1996.
3. 'Competitive Intelligence Pays Off', *Business Week*, 28 October 1996.
4. Richard Whiteley, *The Customer-Driven Company*, Random House, 1991.
5. 'Strategic Planning', *Business Week*, September 1996.
6. Goold, M. and Campbell, A., 'Many Best Ways to Make Strategy', *Harvard Business Review*, November–December 1987; George Day, *Market-Driven Strategy*, Macmillan, 1990.
7. 'The Strategic Audit, a New Tool for Boards', Gordon Donaldson, Professor of Corporate Finance at Harvard Business School, *Harvard Business Review*, July–August 1995.

15 Making it happen

1. Bartlett, C. and Ghoshall, J., *Beyond Strategy to Purpose, Harvard Business Review*, November–December 1994; Bartlett, C. and Ghoshall, J., *Managing Across Boarders*, Harvard Business School Press, 1989.
2. Robert Hagstrom, *The Warren Buffet Way*, John Wiley, 1995; Bershire Hathaway annual reports and letters to shareholders.
3. Charles Handy, *Age of Unreason*, Random House, 1990.
4. Body Shop annual reports and interviews.
5. 'GE's Profits Charging Ahead', *Wall Street Journal*, January 1997; 'GE investing billions in Europe', *Fortune*, September 1996; Robert Slater, *The New GE*, Irwin, 1993.
6. William Manchester, *The Last Lion, Alone*, Little, Brown & Co. 1988; Winston Churchill, *The Gathering Storm*, Houghton Mifflin, 1948.
7. Denison, T. S., *William L. McKnight, Industrialist*, Ballantine Books, 1962.
8. 'Stirring It Up at Campbell', *Fortune*, 13 May 1996.
9. A *Company that Cares: Johnson & Johnson Credo*, Johnson & Johnson Company, 1986.

10. 'Company Values that Add Value', *Fortune*, July 1996.
11. Thomas J. Watson, *A Business and Its Beliefs*, McGraw-Hill, 1963.
12. *The Disney Studio Story*, Walt Disney, 1987; John Taylor, *Storming the Magic Kingdom*, Ballantine, 1987.
13. Sam Walton and John Huey, *Made in America*, Doubleday, 1992; Vance Trimble, *Sam Walton*, Dutton, 1990.
14. John P. Kotter, *Leading Change*, Harvard Business School Press, 1996.
15. Kalchas interview.
16. Harry Handlin, *The Company Built Upon the Golden Rule*, Haworth Press, 1992.
17. Eccles & Nohria, *Rediscovering the Essence of Management*, Harvard Business School Press, 1992; Thomas Watson Jnr., *Father & Son*, Bantam books, 1990.
18. 'Better People, Better Business', Investors in People UK, 1996.
19. Jeffrey Pfeffer, *Competitive Advantage Through People*, Harvard Business School Press, 1994.
20. 'Genius is in the Jeans', *The Times*, 14 June 1996.

List of Figures

List of Tables

Index